# NORTHERN METHODISM
# AND RECONSTRUCTION

# Northern Methodism
# and
# Reconstruction

*Ralph E. Morrow*

Michigan State University Press

1956

287.675
M883w
79097

The Lakeside Press, R. R. Donnelley & Sons Company
Chicago, Illinois, and Crawfordsville, Indiana

To Vera

*Who shared the pangs of composition.*

# Preface

SUCH EXPERT ANALYSTS of the domestic scene as Henry Clay and John C. Calhoun saw in the sectional division of American Methodism the omen of a malign fate for the nation. Equally keen observers in the age of Reconstruction believed that a truly national Methodist church would be one of the foundation stones of a restored Union. It is the design of this study to recount the manner in which the Methodists of the Northern states met the responsibilities laid on them by Reconstruction. Specifically, I have tried to do three things: first, to trace out the expansion of Northern Methodism into the South; second, to isolate the main problems arising from the Church's decision to move southward, and to explain how those problems were dealt with; third, to relate Methodist activity to the political and social background of the *post bellum* age. Others will doubtless enjoy pointing out where my performance has fallen short of my intentions. Nowhere have I attempted to erect an elaborate hypothesis by which the different phases of Methodist endeavor can be explained. To have done so would have added another volume to the redundant literature of religious controversy.

Like all historical productions, this one is essentially cooperative. The dedication acknowledges a debt that ranges from research to final proofing. To Chase C. Mooney of Indiana University, under whose direction my investigation began, I am grateful for a model of scholarship, wise counsel, and friendly encouragement. Many persons helped to unearth the raw materials of historical writing or lent enlightenment about obscure matters of fact. That individuals in neither of these categories are singled out for mention is merely a gesture to the patience of those who might take time to read this preface. The receipt of the Baruch Award for 1954 from the United Daughters of the Confederacy greatly facilitated the publication of the manu-

vii

script. Something is also due to a buried generation. My thanks go out to the Methodists of the Reconstruction period who, before their departure from the Church Militant, made written records of their scheming, working, and doing. But for these let the story speak.

# Contents

Preface . . . . . . . . . . vii

I. Of the People Called Methodists . . . 3

II. The Pattern of Expansion . . . . . 29

III. A Storm over Zion . . . . . . 63

IV. The Church and the White Folk . . . . 96

V. The Mission to the Africans . . . . . 125

VI. The Education of the Freedmen . . . . 153

VII. God's Controversy with Methodism . . . 181

VIII. The Den of Politics . . . . . . 203

IX. An Inhospitable Land . . . . . . 234

Bibliography . . . . . . . . 251

Index . . . . . . . . . . 263

# NORTHERN METHODISM
# AND RECONSTRUCTION

# I

# Of the People Called Methodists

Question: What may we reasonably believe to be
God's design in raising up the . . . Methodists?
Answer: To reform the Continent and to spread scrip-
tural Holiness over these lands.

—Proceedings of the Christmas Conference
of the Methodist Episcopal Church, 1784

*Harper's Weekly* was later than most nationally circulated periodicals to notice the centenary of American Methodism, but this
decorous paper made recompense for its tardiness by elaborate
coverage and abundant praise. It gave an entire number to com-
memorate the hundredth birthday of the Methodist Church in
the new world. To justify such a singular proceeding toward a
Christian denomination, an editorial writer asserted that "this
form of Protestantism has become the predominant ecclesiastical fact of the nation." [1] In an appraisal so generous, knowing
minds suspected the hand of Fletcher Harper, the real founder
of the *Weekly*. The youngest Harper was a notoriously good
Methodist and, to the occasional distress of the hired help, took
a very personal interest in the composition of his magazine. The
transposition of the publisher's religious bias to the page customarily reserved for the editor would be understandable in
these circumstances. But even if this assumption is uncontested,
*Harper's* estimate of the Wesleyan position in 1866 ought not
to be recklessly discounted. Where prose fails, numbers and
wealth convince and the Methodists showed well in both of
these.[2]

The seed which, tradition says, Philip Embury carried to the
western shore had in the course of its luxuriant growth shot out
numerous stems from a parent root. The most robust of any of
these was the Methodist Episcopal Church. This body, the

3

Northern residue of the great Methodist schism of 1844–46, manifested a material prosperity which seemed to fulfill the prediction of those who had said that separation from a Southern sister befouled by slavery meant new life rather than impending death. Twenty years after the Methodist temple had been rent in twain, the Northern church was greater in membership than any other Protestant sect and her property holdings put her in the front ranks of American Christendom. Some could lament with Henry Ward Beecher that "the church [was] growing dangerously rich" and all the external symbols simply proved that "the institution had supplanted the inspiration." [3] But for Beecher and other "sanctimonious carpers," a Methodist clergyman had a pious rebuke. "Our righteousness," he remarked, "hath been rewarded by the fruits of the earth." [4]

The talisman of Northern Methodism's success was an object of frequent search by publicists of the contemporary scene. Better equipped than most to speak authoritatively on this matter was Jesse T. Peck, a product of upper New York who dated his service in the itinerant ranks from the outset of the Jacksonian era. His ministerial activity had reached to both coasts and by 1872 had elevated him through various church offices to the episcopacy. It was Peck's opinion that the genius of Methodism lay in its "thoroughly alive . . . aggressive worship" which emphasized "inspiration in distinction to logic," its "system of theology," and "its grand organization." [5] And even though none of these things were *sui generis* to the Methodist Episcopal Church, wide agreement existed that the formula had contributed importantly to the stature of the Northern establishment. Feeding upon the superior resources of a section, that church had used methods owned jointly by the whole Wesleyan family to expand to imposing proportions.

Of the triune explanation advanced by Peck, no aspect was more ostentatious to saved and unsaved alike than the vibrant enthusiasm of Methodist worship. "Its worship and teaching have been directed to and developed from the feelings," commented one friendly critic. The heralds of Methodism had cannily perceived that "the minds of men are not first and chiefly logical but sensitive." Consequently, "an emotional Christianity arrests and impresses more promptly and successfully than a form in which the intellectual predominates." [6] The camp meeting was the most popular incarnation of this theory. Protracted sessions, corps of preachers who held forth in rotation, and "shouts of newly-born saints" were invaluable for quick and violent assaults on unbelief and indifference. The periodic revival, when complemented by "church services, class meetings . . . love feasts, prayer meetings, and the rest," gave to the church a formidable machinery for keeping up piety at a fever heat.

Prolonged controversy was aroused by the ethics of such evangelistic techniques. An extreme view contended that the smoke engendered by Methodist fervor was really "the breath of God blowing across the continent, refreshing and reviving . . . dying souls." A voice diametrically opposed proclaimed: "Methodist teaching seems to be framed to meet the tastes of depraved minds. . . . It labors not to bring men up to religion, but to bring religion down to depraved minds." [7] Over the effectiveness of emotionalism as a proselyting device, there were fewer differences. *The Tablet,* as cantankerous in the past century as in this one, confessed that the Methodist Church "in . . . appeals to the animal nature and sensible devotion" had "acquire[d] no little power." The ensuing observation that only "the sensitive, the ignorant, and the superstitious" had been affected was not a serious qualification.[8]

The Roman Catholic Church had long known—and Protestants quickly learned—that "excited spirits" and doctrinal unity are uneasy companions in any religious organization. The Methodist Bishop Thomas A. Morris was aware of this historical incompatibility when he thankfully wrote, "We have never had occasion to waste much time or strength in adjusting . . . our doctrinal views." [9] The "occasion" of which the venerable prelate spoke was absent mainly because his church had been relatively

unconcerned with abstruse theological questions. "The genuine
Methodist preacher . . . had but little thought of creed or cate-
chism," remarked Edwin L. Godkin.[10] Theological poverty left
broad room for the accommodation of divergent views. This
comparative indifference to recondite speculation helped
Methodism to escape the dogmatic quarrels which exhausted
and sundered other Christian denominations. While the existence in 1865 of a half-dozen groups calling themselves Methodists testified that the family was not immune to division, none
of the separations had resulted from doctrinal hostility. Each
was traceable to a contention over social policy or church polity.
The Wesleyan heirs, in "reversing the usual policy of religious
sects who [sought] to sustain their spiritual life by their orthodoxy," relegated metaphysics to an inferior role. Methodists
reconciled the intellect and the heart by the frank subordination of the first and found a bond of unity not in the fine print
of prayer books "but in that strange warming of the heart . . .
which . . . was the same to all Methodists, however variously expressed."[11]

Methodism best demonstrated its marvelous pragmatism in
its frame of government. As Methodist preachers had aggressively gone about the business of arousing and converting, the
ardor they left behind was effectively channeled to purposeful
ends. One preacher declared with a show of reason that "Methodism may be defined as organized religious enthusiasm."[12]
The Methodist system was at once flexible enough to keep
pace with an ever dynamic geographic frontier yet sufficiently
rigid to restrain an often turbulent membership. In a sense the
Methodists had succeeded in institutionalizing the gospel of
revivalism. However, differences were found in the governmental structures of the various Methodist churches and if
there was any feature of ecclesiastical economy by which the
Methodist Episcopal Church could be distinguished from its
kin, it was in the fuller development of its polity. Through in-
vention in response to a felt need or by freely borrowing from

nonreligious agencies, the Northern church by the end of the Civil War had attained a high level of organizational efficiency.

A literal reading of the *Methodist Discipline* of the middle-nineteenth century might readily leave the conviction that "the laity under the Methodist system [had] no semblance of any popular right." Many years after the membership had won canonical sanction to encroach somewhat on the clerical preserve, a Methodist fumed that "the laity of the . . . church were inferior in their . . . rights to the slaves of Rome [and] the serfs of Russia." [13] These allegations had their source in the hierarchical character of Methodist government which acknowledged the clergy's privilege to make and execute policy on almost every level of authority. In this tinge of sacerdotalism, Episcopal Methodists betrayed their Anglican origins, for Wesley's prejudices made him profoundly distrustful of popular control in either church or state. And early Methodist preachers in America, many of them English exports, could contend for their own autonomy without wholly extending it to the lower echelons. The Wesleyan church in its American evolution carried within itself the minor contradiction of a theology which placed a premium upon individual religious experience, and an organization inclined toward authoritarianism. Many thought it the "high church of evangelism."

The clergy of the Methodist Episcopal Church was graded into traveling and local ranks.[14] Members of the last, from their best-known representatives, were frequently labeled lay preachers and the sophisticated not quite accurately called them sub-pastors. Ecclesiastical law did not clearly make the distinction, but the local clergy could be conveniently divided into three grades—the class leaders, the exhorters, and the local preachers. The line separating the class leader from the ordinary communicant was blurred, for the first was armed only with the oral authorization of his pastor. To the leader was conceded the function of inquiring after the dozen or so members committed to his charge to see "how every soul of his class prospers" and "give such . . . counsel, advice, or encouragement as may be required." [15] Practically, he both exceeded and fell short of the letter of his instructions. In isolated communities he had often taken a turn at preaching, while in thickly populated areas the decline of class meetings during the nineteenth century left the leader with hardly more than a title. Above the class leader in dignity was the exhorter. Among the responsibilities of this officer were the gathering of the faithful for sessions of prayer, edification and "direct address . . . to the affections." Exhorters also did yeoman service during seasons of revival. They sometimes mounted to the preacher's stand to relieve their ordained superiors and always their entreaties to the penitents crowded into mourners' benches added several decibels to the volume of sound. So allied were the exhortation and the sermon that Methodist hierarchs recommended that aspirants for preacher's parchments first try their hand at exhorting. The local preachers comprised the aristocracy of the lay ministry and were the unsung heroes of American Methodism. Particularly, these preachers gave to individual churches a regularity of pastoral care which otherwise would have been denied. Of the lay clergy they alone were supposed to preach and after ordination were permitted to administer the sacraments. From the itinerants the local preachers were most easily differentiated because of their small part in policy making and administration. [16]

The traveling or itinerant ministry of Methodism has been glorified in the person of the circuit rider. However, from very early in Methodist history, the appellation of traveling preacher described the privileges accruing to a rank rather than a mode of performing its duties. The term mirrored an ideal of the Fathers, not a universal practice. Only an uncertain percentage of the circuit riders had been ordained traveling deacons or elders and conversely many in the itinerant connection never experienced circuit life. [17] In more populous areas of the country the circuit system, years before the Civil War, was a relic of memory. But if the horse and saddlebags did not infallibly mark the traveling clergy, it was set apart by more solid characteristics. By ecclesiastical statute or custom, the itinerants virtually alone operated the sprawling machinery of the Methodist Episcopal Church. From the right of co-optation through the acts of legislation to occupancy of the higher positions of the church, the clergy, according to the canon, enjoyed a near monopoly.[18]

For the conduct of government the clergy was assembled in conferences. In Methodist parlance the conference had a dual connotation. It meant primarily a meeting of preachers and sometimes selected laymen for deliberation on church affairs, but the conference also denoted the geographical area over which its members had jurisdiction. The Quarterly Conference was the most restricted in the scope of its authority. Composed of the traveling and local ministry, together with certain lay officials of a single station or circuit, it had immediate oversight of that charge.[19] Vastly more important in the Methodist system was the Annual Conference. The exclusive right of the itinerant preacher to participate in its proceedings made him conspicuous among Methodists. The boundaries of the Annual Conferences many churchmen wanted to make coincident with state lines, but considerations of distance, terrain and population made it impossible to follow this advice. As a constituent body, the itinerant pastors admitted candidates to the traveling connection, tried preachers for breaches of discipline, heard reports on the progress of Methodism within their jurisdiction, voted on constitutional changes, and every fourth year elected some of their brethren to attend the exalted council of the church, the General Conference.[20]

The power exerted by the General Conference was felt wherever in the world an Episcopal Methodist society existed. "We are the highest judicatory and highest legislative body in the . . . church. From our decision there is no appeal," proclaimed a member of the 1868 Conference.[21] In point of law he was very nearly correct. Sitting quadrennially, the deputies sent by the Annual Conferences excited and guided the energies of the church, the more competently because many of them were selected as delegates time after time. The principle of separation of powers found no lodgment in the working of the General Conference. Indiscriminately it blended judicial, legislative, appointive and administrative functions. A single session might see the Conference resolve itself into a court to hear cases of misconduct, legislate into being rules and regulations for the church, initiate resolutions looking toward fundamental changes in discipline or government, fix boundaries for the Annual Conferences, fill by-election positions in the Methodist hierarchical structure, and review the work of manifold agencies and officers since the previous convocation of a conference.[22] The General Conference with its plenary authority was the axle about which turned "the great iron wheel" of Methodism.

The passion for order in church government penetrated to the routine work of supervision. Assemblages which met as infrequently as Methodist conferences faced something of a problem in the day-by-day task of administration. This was solved in part by the delegation of supervisory authority to certain churchmen who mediately or directly answered to the General Conference. Locally, the preacher in charge with the help of certain laymen cared for the station or circuit. A number of charges, seldom less than a dozen, were organized into an administrative district supervised by the presiding elder. Elevated by appointment above other itinerant preachers, this satrap directed the business of the Quarterly Conference, correlated statistics for submission to higher powers, advised on the stationing of preachers, and in cases of emergency found supplies for pulpits. The presiding elders owed their positions to the bishop, whom they served collectively as a type of curia during Annual Conference meetings.[23]

The most diffuse supervision was exercised by the Methodist episcopacy. Better than other members of the traveling clergy, they had maintained a practical fidelity to the itinerant tradition. The bishops' schedule of business was outlined at their semi-annual meetings, and in the course of a year each of them accumulated a prodigious mileage.[24] Most of their peregrinations were occasioned by the duty of presiding over Annual Conferences. Here the traveling clergy most sharply felt the episcopal dominion. Besides expounding parliamentary law, they had the important right of stationing preachers. At sessions of the General Conference, members of the episcopal bench presided in rotation. However, the locus of their influence was as much outside as within the constitution of the church. By quiet persuasion, by a lobbying that was sometimes painfully evident, or by arbitrary extensions of their lawful prerogative, they could effectively hamper or inspire Methodism's action. The number of bishops had grown with the Northern church. In 1865 the count was nine, but after death and infirmity had left the Board of Bishops sparsely filled, the 1872 General Conference chose enough new general superintendents to increase the episcopal committee to twelve.[25]

Spokesmen for the Methodist Church stoutly repelled any suggestion of a correspondence between their episcopate and the historical portrait of a prelate. While admitting that the aggregate of episcopal power was considerable, they also pointed out that a Methodist bishop was amenable to the same body which elected him to his place, the General Conference. The worth of both the office and the occupant they adjudged by utility. For such dogmas as apostolic succession Methodists had no use. "To us . . . it is a matter of perfect indifference whether we can produce a catalog of bishops, in regular succession from Peter," announced a well-known churchman.[26] Since they recognized the human factor in the manufacture of bishops, Methodists did not have to be overly careful about revealing the qualifications which could change a simple preacher into a prince of the church. Usually, episcopal offices were distributed so as to mollify the tensions between various geocultural divisions of the nation. The candidate should already have made himself prominent by his work in behalf of the church. Sometimes, a powerful lay backer could smooth the way against opposition. But often several candidates met these conditions and because "there was no lack of men ready for . . . honors," the only way to avoid an *impasse* was by "electioneering, wire-pulling, log-rolling, canvassing, caucusing and all the jugglery of pot-house politicians." [27] It was not thought unseemly for a man to don episcopal robes while still panting from the exertion of political intrigue. The campaign which landed Gilbert Haven in a bishop's chair in 1872 was outlined by his New England followers more than a year before.[28]

While the lay people of Methodism were overshadowed by the itinerant clergy, the government of the church did not completely negate mass participation. The class leaders, exhorters, and even local preachers were but partly disguised laymen. Furthermore, the Discipline provided for lay trustees and stewards and assigned to them the custodianship of church property and the care of finances, respectively. The staffing and direction of the Methodist Sunday School allowed still more room for lay activity. Statistical reports reveal that the extent of lay participation in the Methodist system was anything but negligible. Of the approximately 1,300,000 members of the Methodist Episcopal Church in 1874, "a carefully estimated" 431,058 of them were trustees, stewards, class leaders, Sunday School superintendents and Sunday School teachers.[29] This proportion of lay officers to rank and file communicants compared favorably with churches which boasted more loudly of their democratic governments.

The Methodist Episcopal Church, in its advance toward maturity, found expedient the establishment of specialized bureaus for the preservation and propagation of the faith. Each of these bureaus operated under a charter conferred by a state; their boards of managers were the directors and regular administration was conducted under the supervision of one or more secretaries. The oldest of the Methodist agencies was the Missionary Society. Organized in 1819, it had done invaluable work in the home as well as the foreign field. An untold number of preachers on the American frontier were able to keep body and soul together only by the pittance given to them by this organization or its conference auxiliaries. The year 1827 saw the establishment of another bureau—the Sunday School Union of the Methodist Episcopal Church—which after a fitful life was reorganized in 1840.[30] For the circulation of publications "especially such . . . as aim . . . at the salvation of the soul" the Methodists increased the complexity of their system soon after the midpoint of the century with the foundation of the Tract Society.[31] Stimulated by war, reconstruction, and expansion, the bureaucratic structure was to grow at a faster rate in the period from 1860 to 1880.

No critique of the Methodist way can overlook its publishing interests. "Next after the preaching of the Gospel" declared the veteran editor Daniel Curry, "the religious press has . . . been the great instrumentality of Methodism . . . in America." [32] From Methodist publishing houses in New York and Cincinnati, whose managers were chosen by the General Conference, literature poured forth in profusion. Official reports, pamphlets and broadsides "for the promotion of holiness," works of theology, church history, religious fiction, Sunday School publications, and many others melted into a steady stream. The two book concerns in 1869 were listed as the publishers of 1900 different bound volumes and over 1000 unbound titles.[33] Of greatest significance to the social historian, however, are the official periodicals of the church, published by one or the other of the book concerns, and edited by a preacher who owed his election to the General Conference. This class of journals in 1865 included eight English-language weeklies,[34] the *Christian Apologist* for German-speaking Methodists, the *Ladies Repository* devoted to the monthly edification of females, and a quarterly organ, the *Methodist Review*, which was designed to answer the wails of intellectuals who alleged that "the weekly *Advocates* had not meet [sic] enough in them to keep one soul alive." [35] Supplementary to its official papers, the church reaped

benefits from several journalistic enterprises which were independently managed but uncompromisingly Methodistic in outlook. Foremost in this class were *Zion's Herald,* published at
Boston, and the *Methodist* of New York. The first had the distinction of being the oldest Methodist weekly in America and
the mouthpiece of the radical New England conferences. The
*Methodist,* founded to promote greater lay influence in church
councils, stayed alive by means of meaty subsidies from wealthy
New Yorkers, among whom was Daniel Drew.

The Methodist periodical press, which some believed to be
"the most powerful . . . in the world," was "not so occupied with
another world as to have slight concern with this one." [36] "No
class of events or topics . . . are removed . . . beyond the province
of the religious journal," maintained a Methodist editor, and his
colleagues unanimously agreed.[37] The competent Arthur Edwards spoke from a broad experience in religious journalism to
say that the religious newspaper ought to give "all Methodist
news . . . space," carry "very much religious matter not distinctively Wesleyan" and provide "secular matter so varied that
it shall not be necessary for the average reader to take any other
paper to keep abreast of the day." [38] Very often the "secular
matter" was so candidly edited that timid laymen were led to
assert that "the religious press was too belligerent" and "it
needed to be baptized with a spirit of love." However, for ruffled
readers the editorial clique had this standard reply: "It is not
ours to follow, but to make public opinion." [39]

One secular commentator, after he reviewed the wealth and
government of the Methodist Episcopal Church, was moved to
write that all "the money power and opinion power . . . concentrated in a few hands, can be worked as a tremendous machinery
for evil . . . [or] for good." [40] During the fratricidal transactions
of 1861–1865, the major architects of federal policy thought that
Methodism's might had been used only for the good. A gathering
of churchmen was delighted to hear Chief Justice Salmon P.
Chase exclaim: "I have thanked God that the Methodist Church

. . . knew only one sentiment—that of devotion to . . . our country. . . . How we have leaned upon your bishops . . . your ministers . . . and your great people." Lest it be said that Chase's Methodist affiliations jaundiced his words, the eminently un-churched Abraham Lincoln reputedly endorsed the judgment of his wartime subordinate. The "church has wielded a controlling influence in these times," Lincoln told Methodist interviewers in 1864 and went on to say that "we never would have gotten through this crusade without the steady influence of the Methodist Episcopal Church." [41] Flattering as were these solicited opinions, they were nonetheless not a jot ahead of the claims put forward by Methodists themselves. The priestly journalist who pronounced Methodism "the agency of the nation's deliverance" was in no way unique in the boldness of his statement.[42]

A bare recital of Methodist activity in the war neither confirms nor refutes the utterances of responsible clergymen and public officials. However, the compliments which rained on the denomination were induced no more by tangible contributions of men and materials than by Methodism's zealous mobilization of public opinion through the pulpit and press. As Lincoln is supposed to have said, "Her bishops . . . and pastors have a wonderful formative influence on the masses of the people" and this power was used to whip to renewed exertions a section that sometimes faltered in its purpose.[43] Out of the mouth of the church gushed exhortations for fealty and fidelity to the Union. "The cause of our country . . . we regard as the cause of God" intoned the most august assembly of the church in 1864. A deliriously patriotic Illinois clergyman called "for confiscation, subjugation, and extermination . . . for employing Negroes; mules, brickbats . . . small arms, large arms, and bayonets to kill rebels and crush rebellion." [44] Amidst the rumble of conflict the ingeniously varied slogan "Methodism is loyalty" slipped into an ostentatious place in the Methodist Discipline. "A man cannot be loyal to the Methodist Episcopal Church and at the same

time be . . . the slightest degree . . . disloyal to the government"
read a common interpretation of the current creed. Bishop Morris, the senior member of the Episcopal Committee, told the
General Conference of 1864 that treason was "a crime . . . expressly forbidden by the word of God and any man . . . guilty
of it deserve[d] to be expelled from the church of Christ." [45]

The criterion for loyalty put forward by most Methodists was
neither an absence of resistance to federal authority nor a passive adherence to its decrees. They discountenanced "faint-hearted endorsement as well as avowed opposition." In the crisis
hour there could be no middle ground. "To be neutral, or so
concealed in using words or acts as to give no public assurance
of loyalty is to be in opposition to the government," declared
a bright star in the Methodist constellation.[46] Throughout the
North, Methodist assemblies covenanted to reprobate "an attitude of miscalled neutrality" and reminded worshippers that
"loyalty [was] a religious duty as obligatory as prayer itself." [47]
To minimize the risk of church folk innocently wandering into
the labyrinth of impious opposition, ecclesiasts, in the course
of the war, spelled out the meaning of "unqualified devotion
to the government." "We hold," resolved a clerical conclave,
"that loyalty to the government is only to be understood as
loyalty to the administration of that government." [48] From this
straitened definition it was but a step to invest the administration's formula for victory with an aura of sanctity. "Every innovation . . . by the executive or Congress was adopted as . . .
a new article of religious faith," recollected an outraged layman.[49] Charles Elliot, who guided the St. Louis *Advocate*
through the war, ventilated his opinion of "some great national
measures" which he thought his compeers were bound to recognize on "moral . . . and scriptural principles." Details of the platform approved by Elliot included: Prosecution of the war "to
the entire subjugation of the rebellion," the Emancipation Proclamation, "the . . . policy . . . of arming the Negroes," "confiscation of the property of rebels," and "the conscription law." [50]

Although Elliot used fully his prerogative of indulging in editorial vagaries, in this matter he had a host of Methodist companions. Those who retained reservations about the wisdom of the federal program sometimes conjectured that the Methodist clergy had "come to believe in the infallibility of the administration" and remodelled "the church into a society for the dissemination of Republican ideas." [51]

The ardent patriotism of Methodists produced scenes reminiscent of revival meetings. A "radical . . . fanatical speech" by Illinois Governor Richard Yates teased out of his ministerial audience "loud cheering . . . clapping of hands, stamping of feet . . . pious exclamations . . . and the most boisterous demonstrations of applause." However, Bishop Matthew Simpson, the "evangelist of patriotism," ignited emotional explosions which greater orators than Yates might have envied. Treated to a Simpson exposition of Unionism, a throng of itinerant preachers "waved . . . handkerchiefs and hats . . . screamed and shouted, and saluted and stamped, and clapped and wept and laughed in wild excitement." [52] Oftentimes clergymen succeeded in infecting their congregations with a similar fervor. A backslidden churl who sat in on several sermons "full of blood, fury [and] politics" dared to relate that auditorial response partook "more of a . . . carousal than even an ordinary political meeting." [53] "Eyes suffused with tears of gratitude," fullthroated shouts, or earsplitting renditions of the Doxology in commemoration of Union military victories, favorable election results, and major items of legislation, many ecclesiasts regarded as timely fruits of Methodist orthodoxy.

Auxiliary to the earnest attempt to fuse Methodism into an impenetrable Union phalanx, the church winnowed the human chaff from its midst. "While those at the front kill rattlesnakes, we at home must kill copperheads," cried a discharged chaplain. Thomas Eddy, from his Chicago editorial seat, recommended "the social outlawry of every man and woman whose position is doubtful." A sheaf of resolutions passed by local and regional gatherings approached in rigor the declaration of an Illinois body that "members . . . who are . . . constantly speaking evil of the Chief Magistrate . . . ought to be expelled from the church." [54] Miscreants who underestimated the determination of their brethren and lingered in the Methodist fold were sometimes subjected to cavalier dismissal. An Indiana preacher "not in favor of halfway measures" interrupted the communion service "to cut off every butternut in the congregation" while a neighboring colleague concluded his Sunday expulsion service by remarking, "I don't want a copperhead in my congregation." [55] The meticulous inquiries into political attitudes even turned up instances of clerical disaffection. Along the uneasy border between slavery and freedom, Methodist Conference proceedings during the war years were disfigured by accusations and exemplary punishments ranging from censure to defrockment. The campaign to make the fact of Methodist affiliation "*prima facie* evidence of loyalty" provoked small but organized religious secessions in Ohio, Indiana, and Illinois. Among these dissenters the Southern Methodist Church later would find a hospitable reception.[56]

Methodist preachers, as they "wrote, printed, stumped, talked, prayed and voted . . . against treason," probed beneath the ebb and flow of temporal occurrences in search of a cosmic purpose in the scourge that reddened the land. Clergymen, in the light of their experience, would not admit that there was no transcendent meaning to the spectacle of Blue and Gray locked in mortal combat. While the Methodist reading of God's mind was not transparently uniform, sermons were often built about the text that the war was punitive and purgative in its design.[57] The North had been selected as the executor of a divine judgment against the "man-buying, woman-whipping, maiden-debauching, children-selling South." A New England preacher, in celebration of the fall of Charleston, sermonized on the topic "The Vial of Wrath Poured Out on the Seat of the Beast" to give his audience some staple Methodist fare about the implications of the conflict. "In the ruin that has overwhelmed it," he said, "God has written out in the eyes of all the world . . . His inevitable vengeance against sinners." [58] Concomitant with retribution the clergy saw a process of purification, and believed that the fire cleansed as it burned. The "worm in the bud of the nation's existence" could be killed only by bloodletting. War "was God's amputating knife to cut out the cancer that was destroying the life of the nation." Said one preacher, "Carnage will continue to . . . scathe the . . . face of the earth till the reign of sin shall be destroyed." [59] Through violence the distinctive cultural character of a section was to be extirpated "root and branch, stem and flower." Many Methodists needed to look no further for the rationale of the national sacrifice.

The pastorate spoke after this fashion with an eye set to the future. A "God-smitten" South was a meet and accessible object for missionary activity. Many battles were yet to be fought when a Methodist correspondent predicted that the humbling of the Confederacy would "open up a field of missionary labor . . . for the . . . M. E. Church, the like of which [had] never before been known." [60] With the ripening of Northern success, the volume of prophetic voices swelled. "Our glorious victory is . . . the signal for the initiation of a great moral regeneration," keynoted a Northern Methodist editor. A land where "mulattos swarmed like locusts, pride, luxury and idleness were general, all the commands of the Decalogue trampled . . . under foot [and]tyranny and lust reigned" lay prostrate before the federal legion.[61] There in the states of the defunct Confederacy was an incomparable proselyting opportunity. Ministers, looking upon the South, sometimes waxed rapturous at the prospects. "How glorious and wide the field before the philanthropic Christian heart!" cried Bishop Simpson. A preacher, after a prospecting tour in Tennessee, excitedly wrote back of a bonanza. "A more promising missionary field than this Southern country God . . . never opened for the church," he reported.[62] Here and there was heard the declaration that because of the peculiar advantages offered by the South, the church should give the domestic arena priority in its missionary program. A chaplain who claimed an intimate acquaintance with conditions in Florida contended that "the Southern field" presented "a far more important . . . theater of Christian and benevolent operations than all foreign nations put together." Likewise convinced that "the great work was at home" Samuel H. Nesbit, in the Pittsburgh weekly, editorially admonished his denomination to "arrest all other missionary movements" and devote its "entire surplusage of men and means . . . [to] the South." [63] The governors of Methodism never accepted the advice of Nesbit and kindred minds but they did intend that their church, by one stratagem or another, was to press southward in its efforts at the conversion of the world.

Episcopal Methodists emphatically did not consider their new role of evangelists to the South any less important to the national weal than their wartime participation. "Our mission is not fully accomplished," cautioned one clergyman; "It is no time to fold our arms and muse over the past." [64] The drudgery of physical subjugation accomplished, there remained the removal of institutional debris and above all the rebuilding of the South. "In reorganizing Southern society, and restoring civil order, moral and religious influences must be largely depended upon," [65] observed a convention of ecclesiasts. For the tedious work of reconstruction, no church regarded itself more illustriously fitted than did Northern Methodism. It was "the God-appointed church to redeem and possess the South." "There is no hope in that country but in the Methodist Episcopal Church," [66] exclaimed a missionary already seeking his salvation in Louisiana. This denominational egotism fattened on the encomiums of political figures. A Methodist jubilee in Boston listened to the Massachusetts Governor Isaac T. Bullock declare, "It is . . . the . . . duty of your church more than any other . . . to help cement . . . the Union which . . . has not been saved by war." [67]

The broad estimates of Methodism's place in reconstruction ought to stimulate the historian to ask what contemporaries expected from the expansion of the Church North into the South. Admittedly, most of the conditions which in the past have inspired the missionary motive were present in the states of the old Confederacy. The devastation of property and human and institutional life hung like a pall over the region. There was ample opportunity to vent the philanthropic impulse "to act the part of the Good Samaritan" and raise Southerners of both colors "up from their wretchedness." The frontier character of the Southland and the disorganization of religious facilities afforded a reasonable excuse for the more narrowly religious motive, "to preach the Gospel and offer salvation to all." [68] The assuagement of suffering, rehabilitation, and propagation of the faith might be validly anticipated from the Methodist venture. Yet when politicians, of whom Bullock was only representative, and many clergymen assured the Civil War generation that the Methodist Episcopal Church had a vital duty in the South, they often meant something more. The warmly pro-Unionist John M. Reid let the secret slip when he editorialized, "A united church extending from the Lakes to the Gulf will be the strongest bond of a restored nationality." [69] The Methodist Episcopal Church, as she gathered the nation into her ecclesiastical arms would pull it together politically. Thus, to a Southerner's plainly spoken question, "What is your design in coming hither?" a missionary could honestly reply, "We aim to strengthen the government." [70]

A Methodist reporter who wrote over the quaint pseudonym of "Irrey Pressibel," told how national unity would ensue from the evangelization of the South. "Every soul truly converted to Christ counts one on the side of law and order," he premised. These converts, when gathered into an "edifice dedicated to God by true old Methodism," would be a nucleus about which would coagulate "good citizens and righteous men." [71] Bishop Davis W. Clark, a dour prelate with a large hand in the southward movement of the church, publicly endorsed the idea "that the best reconstruction [was] the extension of the M. E. Church." Wherever it was planted "there the cause of . . . good government [was] planted also." Communicants were requested to continue the regurgitation of money "until the South is saved from her political . . . heresies." [72] For several years after the Civil War Northern Methodists carefully sifted the grain to find choice seed from which to plant the church in the South, and the conviction that its growth was necessary to choke out political disaffection died hard. After a decade of peace, some Northern clergymen still excused their church's presence on Southern soil with the observation that it was "needed . . . to set the example, and inculcate the lesson of fidelity to the government of the United States." [73]

The less-lettered of clergymen may not have grasped even the political implications of the Methodist mission in the South but far-ranging minds realized that national fraternity would not spring from the mere preaching of a loyal Gospel. Although mankind was yet to be afflicted by the behavioral sciences, many Methodists had the common sense to divine that political prejudices bore a relation to the social and economic milieu. The only sovereign remedy for the nation's malignancy, they believed, was "to impregnate the South with Northern ideas and civilization." The cultural imperialism which used nineteenth-century Protestantism for passing to the Orient, Oceania, and Africa sought another outlet in the American South. "Northern Methodism always carries with it . . . the highest civilization of any times," a minister boastfully chronicled.[74] George R. Crooks, a New York Methodist of conservative proclivities, sounded the hypothesis that "the theory of civilization entertained by the loyal people was made good by the might of loyal arms"; hence, "Southern society must be reconstructed according to the principles the war . . . vindicated." [75] Daniel Curry, in many journalistic battles Crook's arch enemy, concurred with him on this issue. "It is for us . . . to institute a new civilization within all the territory redeemed from rebellion," he asserted. Curry, an especially articulate apostle of the thesis of recivilization, begged his fellows to "pour . . . religious, literary, moral and educational streams over all that land" and make "the whole, broad, deep life of civilization . . . flow . . . through that arid and deadly desert." [76] Renovation, to Curry and his cohorts, had to proceed to the bowels of the Southern social order before the South would "bear any resemblance to civilization."

The assumption of cultural superiority on the part of Northern Methodism often became invidiously assertive in tone. The South and its population were judged seriously deficient in "refinement," "industry," "charity," and "general intelligence" no less than in "the common comforts, conveniences, and elegancies of life." Bishop Thomas Bowman, many years after the Methodist occupation began, returned from a Southern tour to depict the region as "crude in character and backward in development." [77] Nor did those who deplored the degraded state of Southern society circulate their opinions only among Northern residents. East Tennesseans were infuriated by the biting reproach of a Northern Methodist. "You people ought to be 'seen but not heard' on all . . . matters," ran the reprimand, "A subjugate people have no . . . right to apply their peculiar moral ideas." [78] Not even the class of the Southern population least enlightened about the merits of different cultures was spared the precepts to emulate the Northern standard. Erasmus Q. Fuller, from his Atlanta editor's office, urged the Georgia field hands to "strive after American civilization" which he called synonymous with "Yankee enterprise." [79]

If the South was to "be rejuvenated with . . . peculiarly Northern ideas," the job would be difficult in view of the "many imperfections . . . and very repulsive features in . . . Southern character." [80] Some professed the belief that the poverty of the human material in the South made the use of it impossible to revigorate that section. Curry, of the *Christian Advocate*, forever styling himself an expert on Southern affairs, alleged that the former leaders of the South were "wholly unqualified . . . in

character and circumstances" to assume leadership, the middle-
class whites lacked "self reliance and manly assertion," the
" 'poor white trash' " was barely capable of redemption, and the
Negroes were "simply crude . . . material." [81] To resolve the
dilemma, Methodist preachers called for the leaven of a
Northern element. Chaplain H. H. Moore, for a time Florida
Superintendent of Education under the Freedman's Bureau,
contended that "the people of the North and East must take this
country in hand somewhat as they did Kansas . . . and sway
its future interests." Moore's conclusion received acceptance
in respectable quarters. Thomas Eddy, with a newspaperman's
omniscience, was sure that the "problem of reconstruction would
soon be solved if preachers, teachers and . . . men and women"
would migrate South "and work for God." [82] In whatever words
Eddy's idea was dressed, it amounted to the ancient trick of
colonizing among a vanquished people. John Reid made this
clear when he exhorted members of the church to "join hand
in hand . . . for the holy work of missions" and cover the South
"with enterprising and productive Methodists." Immediately
he wanted "colonies of Methodists organized . . . for immigration . . . to Missouri, Tennessee or other open and inviting
fields." [83] In the inexpiable struggle for "one flag, one church
and one people," Methodist laymen had a place beside their
pastors in the no man's land of the South.

To the corporate personality of the church no single motive
can be ascribed for its Southern adventure. At different times
Methodist conferences, editors, bishops, and preachers gave an
astonishing variety of answers to inquisitors who wanted to
know why Methodism had moved into the Southern field. A
portion of the Northern membership, although not immediately
heard from, had an original objection to tinkering with the
South. Bishop Bowman shamefully admitted that he once was
of the persuasion that Methodism "ought not to have occupied
this Southern country." [84] Other Methodists were largely indifferent to the project, as evinced by the complaints of mis-

sionaries in the South about "those ministers who [gave] . . . neither sympathy, encouragement, common courtesy or material aid." [85] Many of both the laity and clergy had an interest that did not reach beyond unalloyed benevolence. But the cry that "reconstruction must be regeneration" caught the attention of both Methodists and non-Methodists. And the postulate upon which this declaration rested—that "the victory of the North was the triumph . . . of intelligence . . . and religion over . . . barbarism and wrong,"—muddied Methodist Episcopal activity throughout the Reconstruction period. It sometimes twisted the missionary impulse, always a pliable thing, into strange shapes and gave Southerners more reason to say: "The whole animus of the . . . movement South is of the devil." [86]

## NOTES

[1] *Harper's Weekly*, October 6, 1866.

[2] The various Methodist churches, in 1865, reported over 1,600,000 communicants. Their closest Protestant competitors, the Baptists, approached 1,300,-000. How the Methodists stacked up against the Roman Catholics was an occasion for much guessing. Most analysts estimated the Catholic membership "at between four and five million." In the aggregate value of church edifices, the census reports of 1860 put the Methodists well ahead. The nearly 20,000 Methodist churches in America were appraised at about $33,000,000. The Presbyterians and Roman Catholics were contestants for second place, each with property holdings approximating $26,000,000. Because a certain license was exercised in the compilation of denominational statistics, these totals can be regarded as having a greater comparative than absolute value. *American Annual Cyclopedia and Register of Important Events, 1865*, pp. 106, 554, 748; *The Eighth Census, 1860, Statistics of the United States. (Including Morality, Property & etc. in 1860)* (Washington, 1866), 497–500.

[3] *Christian Union*, June 12, 1872.

[4] *Northern Christian Advocate*, April 26, 1865. Hereinafter cited as *Northern Advocate*.

[5] *Methodist Review*, LI (April, 1869), 243, 245, 266.

[6] *Zion's Herald*, January 2, 1868, quoting New York *Observer*; *Methodist Review*, LI (April, 1869), 245.

[7] *Christian Inquirer*, January 25, 1866; *Western Christian Advocate*, February 5, 1868. Hereinafter cited as *Western Advocate*.

[8] Quoted in *Methodist Advocate*, March 24, 1869.

[9] Thomas A. Morris, *A Discourse of Methodist Episcopal Church Polity* (Cincinnati and New York, 1859), 19.

[10] *Nation,* February 1, 1866.

[11] *Ibid.;* Ezra M. Wood, *Methodism and the Centennial of American Independence* (New York and Cincinnati, 1876), 302.

[12] *Methodist,* November 13, 1869.

[13] *Christian Advocate,* June 28, 1866, quoting *The Boston Congregationalist;* [John A. Wright], *People and Preachers in the Methodist Episcopal Church* (Philadelphia, 1886), 6.

[14] This discussion of Methodist government, in the absence of specific reference is based upon the following: Morris, *Discourse,* Wade C. Barclay, *Early American Methodism, 1769–1844,* 2 vols. (New York, 1949), Matthew Simpson, ed., *Cyclopedia of Methodism* (Philadelphia, 1878), James M. Buckley, *Constitutional and Parliamentary History of the Methodist Episcopal Church* (New York and Cincinnati, 1912); Stephen M. Merrill, *A Digest of Methodist Law* (Cincinnati and New York, 1888); William W. Sweet, *The Methodists,* Vol. IV in *Religion on the American Frontier, 1769–1840,* 4 vols. (Chicago, 1946).

[15] *Doctrine and Discipline of the Methodist Episcopal Church, 1864,* p. 42.

[16] Merrill, *Digest,* 74–76; Sweet, *The Methodists,* 48; *Discipline of the Methodist Espicopal Church, 1864,* p. 106.

[17] Merrill, *Digest,* 82–88.

[18] In 1872, lay representation was introduced into the General Conference of Methodism. Nonetheless, clerical control was not seriously impaired because the lay delegates were numerically swamped by those of the clergy. Buckley, *Constitutional History,* 307ff.

[19] The Quarterly Conference had been supplanted in some places by the District Conference, which met once or twice a year. The District Conference, roughly equivalent in power to the Quarterly, included several stations or circuits. *Cyclopedia of Methodism,* 300ff.

[20] Merrill, *Digest,* 17.

[21] *Daily Christian Advocate,* May 16, 1868.

[22] Merrill, *Digest,* 15.

[23] Buckley, *Constitutional History,* 329ff.

[24] Although his labors were unusually heavy at the time, Bishop Edmund S. Janes calculated that he traveled 13,000 miles during 1871 in discharging official responsibilities. Henry B. Ridgaway, *The Life of Edmund S. Janes* (New York and Cincinnati, 1882), 351.

[25] *Cyclopedia of Methodism,* 109.

[26] *Central Christian Advocate,* January 24, 1866. Hereinafter cited as *Central Advocate.*

[27] Indianapolis *Journal,* June 1, 1872; [Nashville] *Christian Advocate,* August 14, 1869; January 10, 1874. Hereinafter cited as *Nashville Advocate.*

[28] George Prentice, *Life of Gilbert Haven* (Cincinnati and New York, 1885), 358.

[29] *Methodist Almanac, 1874,* p. 43.

[30] Barclay, *Early American Methodism, 1769–1844,* I, 205ff; Addie G. Wardle, *History of the Sunday School Movement in the Methodist Episcopal Church* (New York and Cincinnati, 1918), 61ff.

[31] *Methodist Almanac, 1870,* p. 11; Abel Stevens, *Supplementary History of Methodism* (New York and Cincinnati, 1889), 123ff.

[32] *Christian Advocate,* February 27, 1867.

[33] *Methodist Almanac*, 1869, p. 22.

[34] These eight periodicals distributed over the country were: *Christian Advocate*, New York; *Western Christian Advocate*, Cincinnati; *Northwestern Christian Advocate*, Chicago; *Central Christian Advocate*, St. Louis; *Northern Christian Advocate*, Auburn, N. Y. (soon removed to Syracuse); *Pittsburgh Christian Advocate*, Pittsburgh; *Pacific Christian Advocate*, Portland Ore.; *California Christian Advocate*, San Francisco.

[35] *Central Advocate*, July 11, 1866.

[36] *Harper's Weekly*, October 6, 1866; *Northwestern Christian Advocate*, November 7, 1874, quoting New York *Evening Post*. Hereinafter cited as *Northwestern Advocate*.

[37] *Northern Advocate*, November 2, 1876.

[38] *Northwestern Advocate*, January 1, 1873.

[39] *Methodism in the State of New York as Represented in State Convention, held in Syracuse, N. Y., February 22–24, 1870* (New York, San Francisco, and Cincinnati, 1870), 148; *Methodist Advocate*, January 25, 1871.

[40] *Harper's Weekly*, August 10, 1872.

[41] *Christian Advocate*, April 19, 1866; Sylvester Weeks, ed., *A Life's Retrospect. Autobiography of Granville Moody* (New York and Cincinnati, 1890), 447–48.

[42] *Western Advocate*, November 23, 1864.

[43] Weeks, ed., *Granville Moody*, 447. The standard account of Northern Methodism during the war is William W. Sweet, *The Methodist Episcopal Church and the Civil War* (Cincinnati, 1912).

[44] *Journal of the General Conference of the Methodist Episcopal Church, 1864*, p. 355; *Central Advocate*, October 26, 1864.

[45] *Minutes of the Southern Illinois Annual Conference of the Methodist Episcopal Church, 1863*, p. 37; *Central Advocate*, October 1, 1863; *Journal of the General Conference, 1864*, p. 29.

[46] Centerville *Indiana True Republican*, July 30, 1863; *Central Advocate*, August 13 and October 8, 1863.

[47] Walter L. Fleming, ed., *Documentary History of Reconstruction*, 2 vols. (Cleveland, 1907), II, 240; *Pittsburgh Christian Advocate*, April 2, 1864. Hereinafter cited as *Pittsburgh Advocate*.

[48] *Northern Advocate*, May 17, 1865.

[49] Henry C. Dean, *The Crimes of the Civil War* (Baltimore, 1868), 178.

[50] *Central Advocate*, August 13, 1863.

[51] Salem (Ill.) *Advocate*, December 24, 1863; Lancaster *Ohio Eagle*, December 31, 1863; Canton (O.) *Stark County Democrat*, April 27, 1864.

[52] Springfield *Daily Illinois State Register*, October 11, 1863; *Northwestern Advocate*, October 5, 1864.

[53] Columbus (O.) *Crisis*, June 22, 1864.

[54] *Central Advocate*, October 15, 1863; Nashville (Ill.) *Journal*, February 5, 1864; *Northwestern Advocate*, August 17, 1864.

[55] New Albany (Ind.) *Weekly Ledger*, October 7, 1863, quoting Indianapolis *Journal*; Terre Haute (Ind.) *Daily Express*, October 18, 1863.

[56] Jacob Ditzler, *Philosophy of the History of the Church from the Times of Christ to the Present* (St. Louis, 1866), 295ff; *Daily Southern Christian Advocate*, April 20, 1866; *Journal of the General Conference of the Methodist Episcopal Church, South, 1866*, p. 89.

# 28     *Northern Methodism and Reconstruction*

[57] An introduction to clerical opinion toward the war and the South is Chester F. Dunham, *The Attitude of the Northern Clergy Toward the South, 1861–1865* (Toledo, O., 1942).

[58] *Zion's Herald,* July 2, 1868; Gilbert Haven, *National Sermons: Sermons, Speeches, and Letters on Slavery and its War* (Boston, 1869), 518.

[59] James B. Shaw, *Twelve Years in America: Being Observations on the Country, The People, Institutions and Religion* (London and Chicago, 1867), 62, 103; *Christian Advocate,* March 22, 1865.

[60] *Central Advocate,* June 11, 1863.

[61] *Ladies Repository,* XXVI (January, 1866), 127; Shaw, *Twelve Years in America,* 111.

[62] *Christian Advocate,* June 22, 1865; *Western Advocate,* January 24, 1866.

[63] Quoted in Henry L. Swint, *The Northern Teacher in the South 1862–1870* (Nashville, 1941), 42; *Pittsburgh Advocate,* September 16, 1865.

[64] *Western Advocate,* May 17, 1865.

[65] *Christian Advocate,* May 11, 1865.

[66] *Methodist,* May 23, 1868; Church Extension Society of the Methodist Episcopal Church, *Fifth Annual Report* (1870), 58. Hereinafter cited as Extension Society, *Annual Report.*

[67] *Western Advocate,* June 20, 1866.

[68] Dunham, *Attitude of the Northern Clergy,* 206; *Methodist Advocate,* October 22, 1873.

[69] *Western Advocate,* May 24, 1865.

[70] *Southwestern Christian Advocate,* July 2, 1874. Hereinafter cited as *Southwestern Advocate.*

[71] *Western Advocate,* January 29, 1868.

[72] *Christian Advocate,* September 14, 1865; *Western Advocate,* April 18, 1866.

[73] Erasmus Q. Fuller, *An Appeal to the Records: A Vindication of the Methodist Episcopal Church, in its Policy and Proceedings toward the South* (New York, 1876), 419.

[74] *Pittsburgh Advocate,* August 12, 1865; *Methodist Advocate,* February 29, 1869.

[75] *Methodist,* January 5, 1867.

[76] *Christian Advocate,* May 4 and August 31, 1865.

[77] *Methodist Advocate,* February 24 and September 22, 1869; January 19, 1870; Indianapolis *Journal,* June 8, 1876.

[78] Knoxville *Daily Free Press,* November 19, 1867.

[79] *Methodist Advocate,* January 6, 1869.

[80] Quoted in Hunter D. Farish, *The Circuit Rider Dismounts: A Social History of Southern Methodism* (Richmond, 1938), 108; *Western Advocate,* January 17, 1866.

[81] *Christian Advocate,* April 6, 1865.

[82] *Northwestern Advocate,* May 3, 1865; *Ladies Repository,* XXV (July, 1865), 402.

[83] *Western Advocate,* May 31, 1865.

[84] Extension Society, *Eighth Annual Report* (1873), 77.

[85] *Western Advocate,* November 21, 1866.

[86] *Nashville Advocate,* February 13, 1869.

# II

## The Pattern of Expansion

Awake, awake, put on thy strength,
Thy beautiful array;
The day of freedom dawns at length
The Lord's appointed day

* * *

Rebuild thy walls, thy bounds enlarge
And send thy heralds forth
Say to the South 'Give up thy charge'
And 'keep not back, O North!'

—Hymnal of the Methodist Episcopal
Church, 1878 edition

THE GRANT-SHERMAN VISE, as it pressed the Confederate nation to death in the early days of 1865, caused a Methodist cleric to exult: "The old church sheltered under the good old flag, has come back to the . . . South . . . after the long exile." [1] This preacher, because he wrote under the stress of feverish times, might be forgiven for the use of a technical inaccuracy to cover a large truth. The Northern variant of Methodism never had been wholly expelled from the territory over which slavery ruled. When Southern Methodists founded a separate church in 1845, societies and individuals along the historic boundary between the sections had chosen to remain with the Northern organization. Delaware, Maryland, northern and northwestern Virginia, Kentucky, and Missouri, were unevenly sprinkled with Northern Methodists who had been grouped into conferences by 1853. From the western outposts missionaries had even carried the evangel into Arkansas and northeastern Texas before the war.[2] However, the Northern church's geographical extension in the South was always more impressive than its numerical penetration. In Delaware, Maryland, and northwestern Virginia

29

the Methodist Episcopal Church was quantitatively respectable but membership thinned to the westward. The transappalachian South in 1861 contained hardly more than 11,000 Northern Methodists and of these 7,000 were in Missouri.[3]

Whatever explained the blighted condition of the Church North in the slave states during the *ante bellum* period, one cause was the indifference felt by ecclesiastical leaders toward missionary prospects in that region. Aware of hostile public opinion with the uncertain offset of adequate civil protection, the danger of offense to the abolition faction of the church, and the inviting prospects of the West, churchmen did not burn for the conversion of the South. A by-no-means unrepresentative opinion held that "the Methodist Episcopal Church should not waste her energies by futile attempts to push . . . into . . . Kentucky, Missouri and Arkansas." Before 1860, according to this wing of the church, a "martyrdom . . . in the flames of pro-slavery hatred would be a martyrdom destitute of all honor." [4] The military conquest of the South, possibly because it diminished the chances of martyrdom, stilled this voice and replaced it with one which urged: "The South must be saved by the power of a pure gospel [and] that gospel must be given to them by us." [5]

Methodist chaplains and soldiers, sweeping South with the Union forces, and civilian officials, agents of benevolent societies, and business men who came behind them bombarded the Church North with pleas to extend the area of its ministrations into the Confederacy. Occasionally, the urgings were augmented by Southerners whose Unionism could no longer endure separation from their "loyal Methodist" brethren. By word and pen a thousand times over, Northern Methodists were told that "the people [were] extremely anxious . . . for the 'Mother Church'" or that Southern churches were "without pastors or preachers . . . and prayer and class meetings were generally suspended." This reputed dichotomy, a people crying for religious services yet unable to provide for themselves, has ever been a lure to missionaries. When the entreaties were spiced by reminders that the "sending of missionaries to the South" was "an unquestioned act of patriotism," positive action became imperative.[6] In point of time, however, the Methodist Episcopal Church began to exhibit a genuine interest in Southern expansion before promptings from that region had time to reach the ear of the North. A few weeks after the Confederacy fought and won a small engagement at Sumter, a meeting of New York Methodists recommended that "the line of our Annual Conferences . . . be extended till the banners of our Church . . . shall . . . wave in the breezes of the Mexican Gulf." The year 1861 had not passed before similar resolutions were proposed and adopted wherever Methodist clergymen convened for business.[7]

It was a happy circumstance for the Northern church that its dignitaries did not meet in General Conference until three years after the outbreak of war. By 1864, Methodist prelates had opportunity to spy out openings in the South, to interchange ideas prior to the formulation of a policy, and above all to see written on the future the precondition of their church's expansion, the defeat of the Confederacy. Although in later years complaints were to be registered that the General Conference of 1864 planned neither wisely nor fully for the South, that body cannot be accused of unmindfulness to the budding project. The subject of the South recurred again and again during the conference's monthlong proceedings. The program, evolved especially for the Southern venture, included disciplinary changes, the delegation of executive authority over the South to the bishops, and the refurbishment and expansion of the administrative structure. The Book of Discipline was revised by the conference to provide for the careful screening of any pastors who might be recruited from the Southern population.[8] In addition, members of the Episcopal Board were instructed to designate some of their number to organize Annual Conferences in the South "when in their judgment . . . the work require[d] it." [9] And cognizant that the episcopal duties attendant upon the exploitation of a new missionary area might prove onerous to only six bishops, the General Conference elected three new ones.[10]

Methodism rounded out its preliminary planning by alterations in the bureaucratic machinery of the church to permit a more efficient channeling of funds to the South. To the existing foreign and domestic departments of the Missionary Society the conference added another division, enigmatically labeled "third class of missions," and assigned to it oversight of the sectors of American territory not yet included within the geographic limits of the Methodist Episcopal Church. At the same time, the missionary program was furnished with a valuable adjunct in the Church Extension Society. By this device church leaders endeavored to solve the housing problem of congregations in financially impoverished communities through loans and donations from the parent agency. Neither of these latter reforms had exclusive application to the South but their utility for that work was apparent. The Extension Society was to furnish the physical facilities; the Board of Missions was to pay the laborers until the new Southern member could stand without props.[11]

The General Conference, although a very jealous guardian of its privileges, had many times in Methodist history been called upon to do nothing more than sanction a policy already in the process of execution. The 1864 Conference, for all its legislation regarding the South, really performed little more than this function. It simply authorized and implemented a program to which the church had previously been committed by her bishops. Several months before the ministerial delegates gathered in the Great Council of Methodism, the Episcopal Board had agreed upon and launched a quasi-systematic plan of Southern occupation, and when the General Conference met in May, 1864, the assembled clergy was told that the bishops had already "made the exploration . . . [of] the Southern territory . . . within the federal lines, and temporarily appointed a few preachers." [12] Behind this modest appraisal of the depth of Methodist Episcopal penetration into the South was a tale of ecclesiastical conquest, aided and abetted by the federal government itself.

In late November, 1863, the War Department delegated to Bishop Edward R. Ames an authority deemed to be "of great importance to the nation in its efforts to restore tranquillity . . . and peace." The War Department directive, applicable to the Military Departments of Missouri, Tennessee, and the Gulf, placed at the disposal of Ames "all houses of worship belonging to the Methodist Episcopal Church, South, in which a loyal minister . . . appointed by a loyal bishop of said church does not officiate." Vitality was given to the circular by the further instruction to military officials within the designated sector to afford Bishop Ames "all the aid, countenance and support practicable in the execution of his important mission." [13] In practice, this amounted to government subsistence and transportation for the hierarch and, whenever needed, the help of the military in the seizure of Southern Methodist churches. That Ames did not act without the approval of his prelatic partners is fairly apparent from both earlier and subsequent developments. The bishops had conferred together only a few days before the order was given to Ames by his good friend, Secretary of War Edwin M. Stanton.[14] And within a month after a part of the Confederacy had been rendered liable to Northern Methodist occupation, the three remaining bishops were invested with appropriative jurisdiction over the hitherto exempt areas of the South.[15] These decrees, while never stretched to the letter, had immense potentialities since the Southern clergy was little more loyal to the Union than its Northern equivalent was to the Confederacy. Ostensibly, the permissive authority to hold Southern Methodist Churches was based on the disinterested objectives of "preventing Southern preachers from holding their pulpits as a safe place from which to encourage treason" and curbing "the lapse into semi-barbarism" caused by disordered religious conditions.[16] However, with the right of occupancy, the Methodist Episcopal Church was presented an unexcelled opportunity to do spadework in the South.

Fortified with government credentials, each of the bishops, as far as the military situation allowed in early 1864, visited the area allotted to him and inspected the field. To give closer supervision than his labors permitted, each member of the Episcopal Board appointed for his designated territory one or more clergymen as resident agents. These agents generally had the oversight of appropriated churches, correlated the activity of Methodist chaplains and benevolent-society delegates in the area and, whenever possible, formed Northern Methodist societies. Most industrious in the confiscation of Southern Methodist edifices was Edward Ames. When this ecclesiastical chieftain swept down the Mississippi in the first days of 1864, he took guardianship of Methodist churches in Memphis, Little Rock, Pine Bluff, Vicksburg, Jackson, Natchez, and Baton Rouge. Upon arrival at his destination, Ames climaxed his work with the temporary seizure of a half-dozen Methodist churches in New Orleans.[17] At a less accelerated pace, other bishops directed the work of appropriation in the South. Insensible to any later generation's interest in their deeds, Northern Methodists never tallied up the occasions on which they used the power handed to them by the Secretary of War. Publicity was given to twenty-six cases of occupancy without any pretense that this figure was definitive.[18] Concurrent with the cannibalism practised under the Stanton directives, other Northern clergymen, armed only with local military authorization or their own pluck, took possession of more Southern Methodist meeting houses.

The War Department's civilian heads were more uniformly co-operative with Northern Methodist machinations than federal military officials in the South. Garrison commanders frequently betrayed reluctance in complying with instructions from above. Churches, they insisted, had a greater pragmatic value as hospitals, barracks, and stables than as places "to preach the Gospel and Unionism." The appropriation of McKendree Chapel in Nashville "cost hard and persevering labor" and was accomplished only after the Northern Methodist agent,

Michael J. Cramer, appealed over the heads of subordinate military officials to his brother-in-law, Ulysses S. Grant. In Chattanooga, entry was momentarily forestalled when the officer to whom application was made asserted that "there would be trouble if he removed the squad of cavalry as it was a part of Gen. Thomas' escort." [19] To the sorrow of missionaries, they sometimes learned that occupancy carried with it no guarantees. McKendree Chapel was released into Northern Methodist custody with the walls "defaced by obscene pictures," "the pews . . . destroyed" and "the floor . . . extremely filthy." When a religious emissary in Baton Rouge investigated the interior of the church turned over to him by the military he found that "it was stripped of everything" including "carpeting for the pulpit and altar." [20] However, if the fruits of the occupation program did not always equal anticipations, Northern Methodism doubtlessly derived transient advantages from its trusteeship of another's property. In several major urban communities, the Northern church enjoyed a monopoly on Methodist Christianity in the later days of the war. Every Episcopal Methodist Church in New Orleans during much of 1864 and 1865 was under the administration of the Northern branch of Wesleyans. For a briefer period the Northerners also cornered the religious market in Nashville. There, ten of the twelve Southern Methodist churches in the city and its environs had gone to speed the federal military effort. The other two were in the clutches of pro-Union Methodists.[21] Significantly, the first four Northern Methodist Conference organizations to be effected in the lower South covered roughly the same areas in which the seizure orders had been most freely invoked.

Northern Methodists, in implementing the Stanton edicts of 1863, ran headlong into a storm of opposition which had its eye on the part of slave territory within the Union lines. In a gem of understatement, Bishop Calvin Kingsley privately confessed that "there is much odium attached to our occupancy of church property." [22] A Tennessean screamed that "the Govern-

ment . . . was directly aiding the M. E. Church to establish
a religion . . . at the point of a bayonet." "Sooner than submit
to such an indignity," this speaker declared, "he would shed
his last drop of blood." That he failed to carry out the threat
does not diminish the heat of his objection. Bishop Ames, by
popular consent responsible for the confiscation proceedings,
was buffeted by ungracious characterizations. Multitudes of
Southerners undyingly remembered him as the "degenerate
ecclesiastic who dragged . . . his robes through the slums of
party politics." To a Kentuckian, the bishop was "a robber of
barnyards, a . . . cattle thief, a despoiler of graveyards, a
plunderer of churches, parsonages and kitchens." [23] But trade
in epithets was an everyday business to Northern Methodist
preachers. Of more danger to them was the organized movement which gathered momentum to combat the forcible
occupation of churches. In early April, 1864, a convention of
representative Southern Methodist preachers, mainly from Kentucky, Tennessee, and Missouri, met in Louisville to concert
plans for the abrogation or the nullification of the War Department edicts. The self-accredited delegates concocted a tripartite
policy to counteract decrees which they decried as "unjust,
unnecessary and subversive of . . . the rights of a numerous
body of Christians." Their program called for pressure on military commanders to prevent local execution of Stanton's directives, an appeal to the Northern bishops to stay the occupation
of Southern churches, and a petition to the President. As final
testimony to its earnestness, the convention, before adjourning
*sine die,* appointed a three-man committee to manage the campaign that had been outlined. [24]

The counterattack signalled by the Louisville meeting caused
alarm to ripple through the Northern church. A memorial drawn
up by missionaries in Nashville implored clerical oligarchs to
"visit . . . Washington . . . immediately" for some lobbying
to negate any effect Southern Methodist protests might have
had in that quarter. [25] In actuality, the fears of Northerners were

groundless. None of the devices suggested at Louisville had demonstrable weight in modifying either Methodist or governmental policies. Lincoln, in whom the remonstrants reposed their largest expectations, in the end proved the frailest of supports. The President was not openly sympathetic with the ecclesiastical measures adopted by the War Department. Persistent rumor even had it that he first learned of Stanton's action by reading the public press.[26] But for all his reputed innocence, Lincoln made only one significant gesture against the decrees and this came six weeks before the Southern Methodists met in Louisville. The War Department directives originally were drawn to render virtually every Methodist church in the slave states liable to Northern occupation. When Bishop Ames appeared in Missouri brandishing his delegated authority, Southern Methodists of that state sent an ambassador flying to Washington to petition for relief. Lincoln, caught between quarreling denominationalists and careful of public sentiment on the border, heatedly pressured Stanton, in February, 1864, to shrink the application of the opprobrious order "to such states as are designated . . . as being in rebellion." [27] However, beyond this rollback, Southern Methodists got little comfort from the chief executive. Through the remaining days of the war they hoped futilely for the progressive exemption of their property.

Within the federal government the most consistently loyal friends of Southern Christianity were found among the senators and representatives from the border states. It was John Hogan, Congressman-elect from Missouri and a former Methodist preacher, who was instrumental in persuading Lincoln to soften Stanton's edicts.[28] Better known but less successful than Hogan in prosecuting the Southern case was Senator Lazarus Powell of Kentucky. Whether prodded by an approaching election, his own conscience, or letters from his constituents, Powell, in March and again in July, 1864, maneuvered importantly to put a bridle on the practice of appropriating

Southern churches. He first introduced a resolution which would have required the Secretary of War to report to the Senate "all orders issued . . . authorizing any person to take possession of any church" together with information about "how many churches and how much property . . . has been taken possession of in pursuance of said orders." Powell's next move was to put a bill in the senatorial hopper which made it unlawful for "any . . . person . . . in the military service of the United States to take charge of any church . . . with a view of dismissing a minister therefrom . . . or installing a minister therein." Violation of the proposed statute was punishable by a heavy fine, imprisonment, and future disqualification from federal civil or military office. The Republicans in the Senate, however, tabled the resolution and buried the bill in the Judiciary Committee.[29] With Powell's efforts died Southern Methodist chances for federal relief. Surcease came only when steel and fire murdered the dream of Southern nationality.

Spokesmen for Northern Methodism, unbudged by the overtures to dissolve the partnership between their church and the government, unitedly lauded the Stanton decrees as acts of "enlightened statesmanship." Public admissions that the baleful effect on Southern opinion made "temporary occupation . . . a mistake" were delayed until after the war.[30] Nevertheless, the Northerners sometimes moved circumspectly in an effort to mitigate resentment. The Northern clergymen in Missouri who saw in the Stanton order incentive for more religious bushwhacking in the state requested Bishop Ames in 1864 to refrain from using his power within the jurisdiction of their conference.[31] Timothy W. Lewis, the agent personally responsible for the seizure of Charleston churches, sought to overcome Southern opposition by calling the trustees of the various Methodist properties in the city together and persuading them to request the military authority to give control over the property to Northern Methodist officials. This, he believed, avoided the appearance of military confiscation.[32] Discreet members of the episcopacy also employed caution in selecting resident agents for the work in the South. They tried to avoid, one of them said, the dispatch of men who "from lack of prudence . . . would rather increase than allay the prejudice already existing." [33]

As the Union military machine ground close to its appointed end, the evacuation and restoration of Southern Methodist churches commenced. Lincoln, some months before his death, by personal order in the case of a Memphis chapel, began to reinvest the Church South with possession of its property. In other cities, the President delegated to the local military authority the right to return property to the Church South.[34] Johnson continued his predecessor's policy and by the spring of 1866, with isolated exceptions, the control of all Southern Methodist property seized under wartime regulations had been given back to its original holders. The criterion for restitution used by public authorities was the confirmed loyalty of Southern ecclesiastical officials. Once the bishop, preacher, and trustees of a particular church had cleansed themselves of doubt about their allegiance they were restored to possession of the building.[35] Only infrequently did Northern Methodists voluntarily terminate their tenancy of Southern churches. Instead, they chose to wait for eviction by the same government that had installed them. A Northern Methodist editor summed up the attitude of his church on the abandonment of Southern Methodist property to explain this seeming aversion to evacuation. "We hold that the military power having put us in possession, it is our duty . . . to hold possession till the same power shall relieve us, or we be ousted by some other process," he wrote.[36] With a certain regularity, the interlopers from the North showed less alacrity in obeying commands to evacuate churches than they had in requesting permission to inhabit them. In Memphis, the lapse between the directive to yield up possession of the church and the date on which the order was executed was about four months. In New Orleans the interval was nearly five

months and at Nashville almost seven.[37] At the last place, continued delays finally resulted in an angry demand from Johnson
for immediate abandonment of the church house.[38] Individual
members of the Northern church even talked of resistance to
the executive decrees which looked toward restoration. John P.
Newman, the Northern representative at New Orleans, was
allegedly at first of this mind. In Nashville, the Northern trustees
of McKendree Chapel, led by William G. Brownlow, "preferred
putting [Johnson] to the necessity of ejecting them by federal
forces"; but saner counsel prevailed and the change of occupancy was accomplished quietly.[39]

The constitutionality of the Stanton orders was never tested
in federal courts either during or after the war. Methodist
writers, anxious to relieve the policy of ecclesiastical expropri-
ation from any taint of illegality, usually distinguished between
the act of seizure and that of occupation. The first, they contended, was performed by the government and permitted under
the "law of nations" or the "law of war" which decreed that "the
property of rebels is forfeited to the use of the government
against which they rebel." Since "Southern Churches, as corporations, aided the rebellion their property was liable to confiscation." The government, once in possession of the churches,
then turned them over to quasi-official agents, the representatives of Northern religious organizations who acted as custo-
dians in the public interest.[40] This jurisprudential theory, however much it may have satisfied Methodists and their friends,
left unanswered the larger question of the effect of government
seizure on legal title to the property. Public officials sometimes
admitted that Stanton's edict, reinforced by the Confiscation
Acts of 1861 and 1862, might be interpreted to give permanent
ownership to the federal government which could subsequently
dispose of the property according to its whim. To the nervous
inquiries of Southern Methodists concerning the status of their
churches, the Attorney General of the United States replied that
in his opinion "the right of title [could] be decided by the Su-

preme Court alone." Andrew Johnson was little more reassuring. When Johnson, in his capacity of military governor of Tennessee, returned a Nashville chapel to the Methodist Church South, he was careful to point out that the action was provisional. Southern Methodists were granted use of the building "until such time, as it shall be disposed of by regular proceedings in court . . . if it shall have been forfeited to the Government of the United States." [41]

From within Northern Methodism belched talk of capitalizing on this legal confusion to render permanent the dispossession of the Methodist Church South. "These churches are confiscated property," exclaimed one clerical theorist, "and they can be sold like other confiscated property." A Methodist chaplain pompously decided that the facts of "possession," "loyal rights," "equitable claims" and "military authority" ought to induce the federal government to transfer the ownership of "church property . . . to the loyal who now hold it." [42] Although they neither reflected popular feeling nor were rewarded for their endeavors, a few churchmen seemed willing to test the readiness of the national government to assist in despoiling Southern Methodism. During a White House conference between Lincoln and Northern Methodist leaders in 1864, one of the clerical participants thought it "amusing to see how Mr. Lincoln evaded a direct answer to Bishop Ames' request for an opinion relative to our rights to the . . . churches in the South." [43] Besides applications for executive help, Ames repeatedly threatened resort to court action and in 1865 challenged Southern leaders to a judicial contest over the property still held under War Department regulations. The dilatoriness in evacuating Southern churches, one correspondent unwittingly admitted, was explainable by the desire to lure "rebel Methodists" into the courts. Delay, he said, would cause the impatient Southerners "to sue for our ejectment" and thereby raise "before a court . . . the question of legal ownership of the property." [44]

By the time the nation returned to the pursuits of peace, the Methodist Episcopal Church had at least twenty accredited missionaries operating in the South and had several footholds on the yonder side of its prewar outposts. Around the mouth of the Mississippi, in central Tennessee, and from Charleston south along the coast and adjacent islands to Florida, Northern Methodist representatives had been proselyting under federal protection for a year and a half or more. In addition, other embryonic organizations of Northern Methodists were widely scattered over the South. Some had been founded by chaplains who, under the encouragement of their ecclesiastical supervisors, ranged in the vicinity of army posts to preach the correct gospel to the civilian population. A much smaller number were composed of indigenously inspired secessions from the Southern church.[45] The most glittering promise of all, however, was in East Tennessee where as early as the middle of 1864 the formation of the first Northern Methodist conference on Confederate soil waited only on the pacification of the area.

In the mountainous country of Tennessee, Southern Unionists, led by the redoubtable "Parson" Brownlow and egged on by Northern hierarchs, had been openly recruiting preachers and laymen for the Methodist Episcopal Church since early 1864.[46] In January of that year, at the insistence of Brownlow, Bishop Simpson appointed a preacher from Indiana, Calvin Holman, agent for the region and authorized him to receive members into the Northern church and organize societies. Holman's labors were quickly supplemented when four Southern Methodist pastors journeyed to Bracken County, Kentucky, in February of 1864 to be ordained by the Kentucky conference of the Church North and sent back to their native eastern Tennessee as missionaries.[47] Partly by such systematic endeavors and partly by less regular means, the stock of the Church North in the district from Knoxville to Chattanooga went steadily upward. Brownlow thought that sentiment in his bailiwick had matured sufficiently by July, 1864, to allow a conference on the future religious affiliation of East Tennesseans.[48] The call which went out through the columns of the *Whig* received a response from fifty-five delegates, hitherto in communion with the Southern Methodist Church. These representatives, almost equally divided between the laity and the clergy, assembled in Knoxville under Brownlow's watchful eye. The trend of events in the preceding months clearly foreshadowed the recommendations of the Knoxville conference. Denouncing the Church South because "she took her stand upon the treasonable and false foundation of secession" the gathering reported "in favor of returning to the Methodist Episcopal Church" and asked to be recognized "as the Holston Annual Conference." Preachers-in-charge who shared the sympathies of the conference were instructed to discuss with their parishioners a plan for transfer *in toto* to the Northern church.[49] Immediately upon recess of the meeting Brownlow and his cohorts began to implore Northern officials to organize the incipient movement into a conference. However, the unsettled condition of eastern Tennessee prompted the princes of the Church North to delay and it was not until June, 1865, that Bishop Davis W. Clark presided over the first meeting of the Holston conference of the Methodist Episcopal Church.[50]

The organizing in Tennessee, within two months after Appomattox, of a conference which included fifty itinerant preachers and 6500 laymen is license for believing that Methodist plans for the conquest of the South were well-matured before the end of armed hostilities. But valid as this inference seems, it was not shared by many Methodists of the period. During the first half of 1865, the Methodist press was a ventilator for opinions that ecclesiastical officials were guilty of nonfeasance and malfeasance in the execution of a Southern program. A magnificent opportunity was wasting away because of the failure to push ruthlessly ahead in the South. "Our church from some cause has remained too indifferent and inactive towards the South for the last two years," opined a New Englander. A middle-western Methodist condemned "the apparent neglect to enter upon the great benevolent field of the South, with all the means, zeal and power of the church." [51] In this hue and cry editors of official Methodist journals joined. Daniel Curry barked about the "strange apathy and consequent inactivity" which possessed "church authorities respecting the religious wants of the South." [52] One of the most devastating published indictments of the seeming lassitude came from the pen of an Illinois preacher, Robert Allyn, a veteran abolitionist and hater of the South. In an article, "The Fathers, Where Are They?," he laid the blame for inaction squarely at the door of the church hierarchy. Screamed Allyn: "What in the name of humanity are these official fathers doing? Where are they? Do they sleep all winter like hibernating animals? . . . What are they placed in authority for?" To Allyn and those of a similar cast of mind the "iron was hot" and "delays were fatal." [53] Northern Methodists who had been commissioned as missionaries for the Southern area were likewise bitter about the indifferent progress. "Next to nothing has been done for the colored people and . . . but . . . very little for the whites," complained one. Nelson Brakeman, an Indiana preacher who rolled up seven years of service in the South as a chaplain and mission worker, was remarkable for his persistent denunciation of the slowness with which the Church North reacted to the Southern challenge. From Baton Rouge he wrote that he had received "not a dollar . . . of the thousands set apart . . . for . . . missionary work" and was forced to struggle on with "no salary, no instruction, no supplies [and] no explanations." [54]

Church leaders waxed indignant in their denials of delay but a resumé of Methodist Episcopal activity to the fall of 1865 supports the hypothesis of a postwar lull in the prosecution of missionary work in the South. In September, 1865, eighteen Southern Methodist preachers in Kentucky, who were soon followed by a few others, transferred their allegiance to the Northern church, but this slight victory was the only evident accomplishment that the Northern church, during the first half-year of peace, could add to its resounding triumph in Holston.[55] The apparent interlude of "mysterious forbearance and hesitation" was traceable to many factors. The necessity of retooling the church for peacetime operations, the absence of a solid Union base on which to erect the Southern wing of the church, the poverty and illiteracy of the Negro material and the unsettled state of society all offered pardonable excuses for hesitation. There were some, however, who believed that the relative inaction was to be explained chiefly by official uncertainty as to the wisest course to pursue toward the South. Grave questions, particularly of relations with the Methodist Church South and the comparative desirability of proselyting Negroes or whites, tore at the minds of responsible churchmen. Dallas D. Lore of the *Northern Advocate,* while he bewailed "the want of a policy on the part of the church," had the acumen to see that the uncertainty came from doubt about "the wisdom of making overtures to the Southern church" and "the importance of incorporating the Negroes into our . . . organization." [56] Unfortunately, many Methodist captains did not foresee that momentary delay would not solve these problems, for the Northern church had to live with them far beyond the Reconstruction era.

But real as may have been the lapse of Methodist energy during the spring and summer of 1865, sure signs of reinvigoration came with the autumn. The semi-annual conference of bishops and the yearly meeting of the missionary board in October and November began to mold the amorphous mass of Methodist effort into coherent form. The territory of the exConfederacy was divided into four missionary districts, a bishop was charged with the direction of each, and appropriations were made out of a handsome surplus at the disposal of the Missionary Society.[57] These high-level decisions were followed closely by overt results which, while certainly attributable to prior labors, muffled some of the outcry about indifference. Bishop Edward Thomson visited the lower Mississippi region in December, 1865, and, at New Orleans, after "much reflection and prayer," formed a conference embracing the states of Mississippi and Louisiana. Numerically the new organization was a piddling thing, for it counted only a dozen traveling preachers and probably fifty score lay communicants; but, unlike the Holston conference, its members had not been recruited from an area conspicuous for militant pro-Unionism.[58] Less than four months later, Osman C. Baker gave canonical status to Northern Methodist societies in South Carolina, eastern Georgia, and northern Florida when he organized the South Carolina conference. Paramount credit for Episcopal Methodist success in this area should go to Timothy W. Lewis who, after his early labors in the Sea Islands and Florida, entered Charleston with the Union armies in February, 1865. When a fellow New Englander, Alonzo Webster, arrived soon after, Lewis turned over to him the superintendence of affairs about Charleston and plunged into the interior. Largely under Lewis' guidance, more than a hundred preaching places had been established in the upcountry of South Carolina before the foundation of the conference.[59] The other conference brought into life during 1866 covered the central and western portions of Tennessee. Here desultory missionary activity had first been carried on by Michael Cramer, Bishop Simpson's agent, and divers chaplains who acted in co-ordination with him. More important, however, was Bishop Clark's dispatch of a Hoosier preacher, A. A. Gee, to the section, in the late summer of 1865. Gee, by demonstrating a reasonable competence at conversion and organization, pumped some life into a project that had not been notably robust.[60]

The Methodist Episcopal Church, in the course of 1867, flung its ecclesiastical system over the remaining portions of the South. A few gospel-bearers, mainly from Louisiana, had found in eastern Texas a response sufficient to allow the formation of a conference in the first days of the new year.[61] In the lower central South, Methodist progress was slow in view of the islands of warm Union feeling in northern Georgia and Alabama. Very likely because the federal military yoke was light or absent in both of these areas until very late in the war, Northern Methodist agents did not see the way open to display their wares. Northern Methodism in both Georgia and Alabama owed its origin to dissenters who withdrew from the Southern church soon after the close of armed hostilities and for a while acted independently of any supervisory authority.[62] The incipient ecclesiastical rebellion in Georgia received some encouragement from the Holston renegades, but Northern interest waited to be aroused by the propaganda of a native Georgian, John H. Caldwell. Caldwell, a Southern Methodist preacher who enthusiastically supported the War for Southern Independence had a "profound and solemn exercise of mind" immediately afterwards which altered both his political and religious convictions. While on a four-months speechmaking tour of the Northern states in 1865 in which he scattered broadcast his new opinions with all the fervor characteristic of a newly-made convert, he took occasion to point out to prominent Northern Methodists the inviting fields of the middle South.[63] In early January, 1866, Bishop Clark met with seven Methodist Church South apostates in an attic room in Atlanta to systematize the proselyting efforts in Georgia and Alabama. James F. Chalfant of Ohio was given charge of the infant missionary district, which covered most of two states. In practice, Methodist Episcopal missionaries confined their energies north of the line running east and west through Atlanta—and when the separate Georgia and Alabama conferences were established in October, 1867, most of the converts had been made in this northern sector.[64]

Although the combined territories of Virginia and North Carolina received the accolade of an Annual Conference before Georgia and Alabama, the former for many years was much less flourishing. Bishop Levi Scott, who organized the Virginia-North Carolina conference, declared that "he had never organized one so small before" and more than a decade later a

Methodist official asserted that the area was "the weakest of our Southern work." [65] Throughout the war, the Northern church had neglected both Virginia and North Carolina. Spasmodic energy had been expended in eastern Virginia and in the Cape Fear region, but the consequences were not lasting. As late as April, 1866, only two Northern missionaries were abroad in central and south Virginia, one stationed at Portsmouth and the other at Richmond, and the members they had attracted did not much exceed a hundred. In North Carolina the Northern church "had neither minister nor member from the summit of the Blue Ridge to the Ocean." [66] Propulsion to the Methodist movement came in May, 1866, with the appointment of James S. Mitchell of New York as Superintendent of the District, and within six months those in communion with the Church North increased twentyfold. Mitchell got material aid in North Carolina from James H. Postell, a former Southern Methodist who founded a few autonomous societies and then wrote to Northern authorities requesting them to take oversight. However, the belated busyness in the upper seaboard area did not wholly compensate for previous neglect, because in 1868 the Northern church could count only about 2500 members in this section.[67]

The element of Northern clerical leadership loomed large in the formative years of the Methodist Episcopal conferences in the South. Quantitatively, preachers transferred from the North were in a majority when the Virginia-North Carolina conference was established and nearly so in the case of Mississippi-Louisiana. In the first, eight of the fourteen charter members and, in the latter, five of the first twelve recognized as affiliates had been culled from the Northern latitudes.[68] However, these two conferences were unusual. Generally, the preachers who were gleaned from the Southern population far outnumbered the imports. In Holston the ratio was forty-five to five and in Georgia it was thirty-six to five when the conferences were founded.[69] But everywhere the Northern transfers received a share of the responsible charges that bore no proportion to their numerical strength. Presiding elderships and pastorates of the largest churches, at least in the birthing days of Methodism, were clogged with Northerners. East Tennessee, where the caliber of the converts to Northern Methodism was higher than anywhere else in the middle or lower South, illustrates the subordination of native to Northern talent. When the first appointments for this area were read, three of the four presiding elders' districts were handed to immigrants and the two best stations, Knoxville and Chattanooga, had Northern preachers. This pattern, repeated endlessly, sometimes led Southerners to muse over the problem of whether "a Northern preacher was ever seen on a circuit." [70] Transfers also filled the few Northern Methodist editorial seats found in the South. The two official weeklies published by the church in the South between 1869 and 1880 both had Northern editors, and even a Southern assistant was a rarity. Methodists in the North insisted that this division of labor was temporary and would disappear when Southerners became qualified for leadership. Their plan, indelicately stated, was "to give a few well-trained men from the North the positions of leadership and let them rally around them the illiterate but warm-hearted . . . brethren." While the scheme of "using transfers to begin the work and . . . home material for the after work" had merit, the "illiterate but warm-hearted . . . brethren" sometimes grew resentful at the distribution of ecclesiastical prizes and raised indecent commotions in the church.[71]

The transfusion of strength to the Southern offspring required men but even more it demanded Methodist gold. "What we need now . . . is money . . . not eloquence," wrote James Mitchell from Richmond, "as in the field of arms so in the field of morals the largest purse must . . . triumph." A Tennessee preacher was positive that "with a blank check on the missionary treasury" the Methodist Episcopal Church could "possess the country in a very few years." [72] The conferences in the

South eternally grumbled about the parsimony of their Northern brethren, but during the chrysalis years of Methodism's expansion, the alleged fault lay not so much with ecclesiastical officials as in the unwillingness or inability of communicants to open wide their purses. No better index exists of the serious intent of Northern Methodist administrators toward the Southern field than the emptying of the treasuries of the church from 1865 through 1868 to provide what adversaries called "a corruption fund for the South." [73] The venerable Missionary Society had a surplus of nearly a half million dollars in November, 1865. Yet, before its annual meeting in 1868, the Society was forced to borrow $80,000 to fulfill promises, and the corresponding secretary, as he sadly took note of the widening gap between income and disbursements, voiced a simple truism, "The missionary contributions of our church must be . . . increased, or our missionary work must be contracted." [74] By no means all of the expenditures found their way to the South but between a quarter and a third of the two million dollars spent in the period 1866–1868 went for missionaries' salaries and the construction of buildings in that region. [75] Although their combined budget was much more modest than that of the Missionary Society, the story with both the Sunday School Union and the Tract Society was much the same. By the middle of 1867 their bookkeepers were also calculating with red ink. [76]

The load imposed by the Southern venture, heavy enough for the older bureaus of the church, proved almost fatal to the fledgling Church Extension Society. The actual financial embarrassment of this agency was caused by a shortsightedness worthy of some Methodist lay magnates of the age, but even the misadventures connected with the society were rooted in the desire to lend help in the southward expansion of the church. The Extension Society, ordained by the General Conference of 1864, spent a year in preparatory organization and did not begin operations until late in 1865, just when the church was shaking off its initial lassitude. The new agency, anxious to prove its mettle yet directed by inexperienced personnel, authorized drafts on its funds totaling two hundred thousand dollars and expected contributions to equal that amount. The latter fell a little short of anticipations, not quite reaching sixty thousand dollars. Undaunted by the disparity between outlay and income, and seemingly confident that they were immune from the ordinary laws of economics, the managers of the Church Extension Society repeated the pattern in 1866. This time local societies which desired to build churches were permitted drafts on the agency to the extent of a quarter of a million dollars. When collections for the second year hardly exceeded thirty-two thousand dollars the house of cards collapsed; the society had issued more than four hundred thousand dollars worth of paper while its cumulative cash receipts were not a quarter of that amount. Uncashed drafts were recalled, officials were forced to borrow on their personal credit, and the Missionary Society rushed aid to churches threatened with foreclosure. Not until the General Conference of 1868 thoroughly overhauled the machinery did the society commence to function efficiently.[77]

The virtual bankruptcy of the Extension Society was a serious blow to Methodist pride. Many raged at "the manifold humiliation of the church . . . to be thus shorn of all financial position." [78] Others, however, were less overcome by chagrin than by the anxiety that a failure to live up to obligations would wither the tender shoots of Methodism in the South. Bishop Janes, not given to hasty talk, confided to a colleague the fear that "we shall be damaged by the failure of the [Extension] Society to meet its drafts." [79] His concern was a valid one. Bishop Levi Scott's observation that "permanent religious prosperity was never found to exist but in connection with sanctuaries" had especial relevance to Methodism's Southern experiment. "Our movement South hinges materially on our ability to build churches," sagely opined an editorial commentator. One Methodist policy-maker flatly asserted that with adequate buildings the Northern church "could add a hundred thousand members annually . . . south of the Potomac." [80] Because the Southerners who united with the Methodist Episcopal Church "were generally poor in this world's goods . . . and . . . unable to erect churches," they depended upon the wealthier North to do the job. It was the uncommon letter from the South that did not moan of poor housing and ordinarily the laments were coupled with requests for funds.[81] The collapse of the Church Extension Society and the resultant inability to satisfy these supplications wrought incalculable damage to Northern Methodism's infant establishment. A Methodist Episcopal preacher who journeyed through Kentucky and Tennessee during 1867 viewed some mute evidence of the immediate effects. He was appalled to see "half erected churches standing a mortification to . . . friends and a laughing stock to . . . enemies." [82] Had this reporter been endowed with prophetic vision he also might have glimpsed the wraiths of never-to-be-gathered congregations.

The General Conference which met in 1868 looked upon a Southern project much advanced over that of 1864. Where four years earlier missionaries were almost as numerous as communicants, eight conferences with over ninety thousand communicants had sprung up. Large increases were also registered in the border conferences of West Virginia, Kentucky, and Missouri-Arkansas. It was the conviction of Methodism's high tribunal that "a growth so sudden, extensive and surprising" lacked "the stability, coherence, and efficiency which might be expected." [83] To remedy completely the flaws found by the General Conference required a dominion over economic, social, and political conditions which that assembly did not possess. But so far as lay within its jurisdiction, the General Conference endeavored to legislate as the situation demanded. The report on the South adopted by the assembly looked to further expansion and to the consolidation of gains already made. None of the major policies suggested to the church inaugurated new departures, rather they envisioned the elaboration or refinement of existing procedures. The lengthy legislation of 1868 is reducible to three essentials: the augmentation of financial aid to Methodists of the Southern regions, "a liberal system of transfers of suitable ministers to . . . the South," and the establishment of official weekly journals for Southern readers.[84] Of these recommendations, only one was wholly realized in the after years of Reconstruction.

The exhortation for greater financial generosity to the South came uncomfortably close to admitting the truth of a Southern Methodist sneer that "Northern Methodism has its foothold in the Southern states . . . by the outlay of money; and when the money stops the work will stop." [85] The money did not stop, but never in the Reconstruction period did appropriations rise to a sustained level much above that of 1868. Quickly there came to be popular with Northern Methodists a policy which aimed "to increase the graces rather than the number of communicants," or as one cleric put it, "to cultivate well what we have should be . . . primary, to increase our church territory secondary." [86] Either conception was a façade for the basic conviction that the church should let the South get along with less Northern money. Preachers, anxious for the extension southward, began to discern "the sentiment that the time for Southern retrenchment had come." A Virginia preacher who visited the Northeast in 1871 reported "a sentiment advocated quietly . . . to the effect that the time had come for . . . Southern conferences to think . . . of missionary retrenchment." [87] Parallel with this restiveness the Missionary Society in 1873 cut back its disbursements to the South.[88] A greater incentive to economy, however, was the financial paralysis that crept over the nation after 1873. Together with the rest of the church, the South suffered. The specialized bureaus whose operations were mainly or entirely devoted to the Southern states soon admitted that they were "embarrassed by the financial condition of the country" and that their tabulations "showed a continued decline . . . in receipts." [89]

The second ingredient in the General Conference's prescription—a request for more clerical transfers—amounted to an admission that only a small proportion of the ministerial array of the church had an interest in the South compelling enough to lead them in that direction. All that can be unequivocally said about the volume of clerical migration southward is that it fell below the expectations of church leaders. Nevertheless, the most sanguine analysts counted only three hundred transplantings from 1865 to 1873 and the rock-bottom guess was fifty.[90] Bishops, by law of the church, had the discretion of shifting preachers from conference to conference, but the prelates recognized that an unwilling preacher was worse than none. Only rarely did they transfer a clergyman without the appointee's consent. Since Northern preachers had something of an option in selecting the region of their labors, few chose to go South. Faced with the embarrassing request to change location, clergymen apologized for their refusal, in many ways. "My present church cannot dispense with my services," "a wife and eight children," "epidemics of yellow fever, ship fever, cholera and other things," "I cannot labor . . . for little things," and "I must be within reach of books," are random samples.[91]

Beneath the cleverly-voiced excuses, however, was a common objection. Bishop Thomson, whose office bore witness to his knowledge of clerical character, observed that the "things concerning which . . . ministers were unnecessarily anxious" were "appointments . . . reputations . . . support . . . [and] success" and none of these did the South hold in abundant promise.[92] "The large reinforcement of devoted Christian ministers" for which the church longed held back at the prospect of "hard work, great trials, poor pay and persecution." An Episcopal Methodist presiding elder in the South who begged his bishops for Northern trainees got only the reply "that men would not leave the comforts of home and take . . . hardships." [93] The rate of transfers increased slightly as the Northern church grew in the South, but some insisted that inferior quality nullified the augmented numbers. Native preachers complained of "the fossiliferous remains of old conferences" and fretted at the sight "of some old crony who [could] not support a congregation elsewhere." [94]

More than two years before the 1868 General Conference decreed the location of an official organ in the South, the cry of Southern converts for "a free, moral, high-toned, and truthful religious press" began to be answered by men already on the ground.[95] On December 30, 1865, John Newman, by then a veteran Southern missionary worker, commenced the independent publication of a four-page weekly paper which he called the New Orleans *Advocate*. Approximately nine months later, in another corner of the South, the Charleston *Christian Advocate* was launched as a private enterprise. The capital for the Charleston venture—even to the loan of a printing press—was furnished by the Claflin family of Boston, and the weekly was edited by Alonzo Webster, who had long training in religious journalism in the North. Neither the Charleston nor New Orleans paper was conspicuously successful; their combined circulation figure was only a thousand after two years.[96] Suffering from financial pains, both editors petitioned the General Conference of 1868 to adopt their respective weeklies, and these prayers were joined by one from the Middle South asking for the establishment of a church paper in that region. The General Conference responded to the various solicitations by authorizing the book agents, subject to certain restrictions, to publish for the South any number of papers, up to three. The publishing agents, after investigation, decided to concentrate their official energies on a single weekly at Atlanta. Publication of the paper, the *Methodist Advocate*, began in January, 1869, under the editorship of Erasmus Q. Fuller, who had been imported from Illinois especially for the purpose.

The thirteen-year life of the *Methodist Advocate* was stormy. To spur circulation, ingenious inducements were used. These included premiums for long subscription lists, cut rates, special items for Northern readers, and a promise to the freedmen that "the *Methodist Advocate* . . . will help you . . . wonderfully in learning to read." However, the different advertising devices were largely ineffectual. Never more than forty-five hundred readers paid for the paper; monetary losses averaged about five thousand dollars per annum to 1876.[97] The contentiousness of Editor Fuller was a source of more trouble. One acquaintance limned him as "that lunatic who stirs up the fires of discord." Fuller's invective, indiscriminately fired at friend and foe, so angered the East Tennesseans that the Holston conference requested his removal.[98] In 1872 Methodism's high assembly complied and replaced him with Nelson Cobleigh, a Massachusetts emigrant, but Cobleigh's death two years afterward enabled Fuller to resume editorial duties which he continued until the paper was closed out in 1881. Another difficulty stemmed from regional jealousy over the location of the *Advocate* at Atlanta. When the book agents determined not to recognize the periodicals already being published at Charleston and New Orleans, these journals were forced to cease operations. Resentment at the official decision was high and long. "It is to be regretted that the Charleston *Advocate* was ever removed from us," later lamented the South Carolina conference.[99] Both of the old publishing centers harped on the theme that a paper in the Middle South could not fill the journalistic wants of the Southeast or the Southwest. "It is unnatural and unreasonable to expect them to look to any other point in . . . the South as their center for supplying church periodicals," said one protestant.[100] Charleston and New Orleans alike saw strong feeling to resurrect the dead periodicals, and in the delta country this was eventually accomplished in 1873. Starting with the slimmest of budgets and a part-time editorial staff, the New Orleans sheet was taken over by the General Conference in 1876 under the name of the *Southwestern Christian Advocate* and after a few years became the only General Conference organ published in the South.

Seeded under the aegis of federal militarism and manured by Northern benevolence, the Methodist Episcopal Church, despite vacillations and failures, lodged itself in Southern Soil. However, a scant chronicle of Methodist physical expansion, as this one pretends to be, must yield a distorted image. Viewing mainly from the North side, it resolutely ignores the church as a Southern institution, the kind of people who were converted by the Northern gospel, and the medley of problems which confronted Methodism in the South. Described in terms purely mechanical, the expansive process takes little notice of the pressures of past and contemporary life that impinged upon the Northern Methodist establishment at every point and conditioned the church as they were conditioned by it. It is time that the picture was brought into better focus.

## NOTES

[1] *Western Advocate*, February 22, 1865.

[2] A highly biased but factually reliable account of Northern Methodist work in the South before the Civil War is Charles Elliot, *Southwestern Methodism. A History of the M. E. Church in the Southwest from 1844 to 1864* (Cincinnati, 1868).

[3] *Methodist Almanac, 1861*, p. 19.

[4] Elliot, *Southwestern Methodism*, 64, quoting *Northwestern Advocate*.

[5] *Christian Advocate*, June 6, 1867.

[6] *Pittsburgh Advocate*, August 12, 1865; Joseph Jones to Matthew Simpson, February 22, 1864, Matthew Simpson Papers (Division of Manuscripts, Library of Congress).

[7] Elliot, *Southwestern Methodism*, 318; William W. Sweet, "Methodist Church Influence in Southern Politics," *Mississippi Valley Historical Review*, I (March, 1915), 548.

[8] *Journal of the General Conference, 1864*, p. 241.

[9] *Ibid.*, p. 388.

[10] Davis W. Clark, Calvin Kingsley, and Edward Thomson were added to Matthew Simpson, Edmund S. Janes, Osman C. Baker, Edward R. Ames, Levi Scott and Thomas Morris, *Journal of the General Conference, 1864*, p. 264.

[11] *Annual Cyclopedia, 1865*, p. 551.

[12] *Journal of the General Conference, 1864*, p. 279.

[13] *War of the Rebellion: A Compilation of the Official Records of the Union and Confederate Armies*, 130 vols., (Washington 1880–1901), Ser. I, Vol. XXXIV, Pt. II, 311.

[14] *Journal of the General Conference, 1864*, p. 279; *Zion's Herald*, January 20, 1864.

[15] Edward McPherson, *The Political History of the United States of America During the Great Rebellion*, (2nd ed., Washington, 1865), 521. Ames' order was dated November 30. On December 9, 1863, Osman C. Baker received authority to occupy Southern Methodist churches in Virginia and North Carolina, and Edmund C. Janes received the supervision of those in the Department of the South. Bishop Simpson, on December 30, was named custodian of Church South property in Kentucky and Tennessee. However, the Northern Methodists were not the only culprits occupying churches belonging to a sister denomination. During the first quarter of 1864, the Northern Baptists, United Presbyterians, Old and New School Presbyterians, and United Brethren in Christ obtained governmental permission to pursue the same course in regard to their respective Southern counterparts.

[16] Fuller, *Appeal to the Records*, 381; *Western Advocate*, August 23, 1865.

[17] *Zion's Herald*, February 10, 1864; *Christian Advocate*, June 22, 1865; *Northwestern Advocate*, February 15, 1868; *Methodist Advocate*, May 4, 1870; William J. Leftwich, *Martyrdom in Missouri; A History of Religious Proscription, the Seizure of Churches, and the Persecution of Ministers of the Gospel in the State of Missouri*, 2 vols. (St. Louis, 1870), I, 255ff.

[18] In addition to Ames' twelve intrusions, the following, with the number of churches occupied indicated in parentheses, are other instances of seizure by episcopal direction: Nashville (2); Murfreesboro, Tenn. (1); Chattanooga (1); Norfolk (1); Portsmouth (1); Fernandina, Fla. (1); Jacksonville, Fla. (1); St. Augustine, Fla. (1); Beaufort, S. C. (1); Charleston (4).

[19] M. J. Cramer to Simpson, February 1, March 19, and June 20, 1864, Simpson Papers.

[20] *Western Advocate*, July 20, 1864; April 26, 1865.

[21] *Methodist Advocate*, May 4, 1870; Holland N. McTyerie, *A History of Methodism* (Nashville and Dallas, 1904), 672; W. Hobson *et al*: to Andrew Johnson, December 31, 1864, Andrew Johnson Papers, LXXIV, No. 6326 (Division of Manuscripts, Library of Congress).

[22] Calvin Kingsley to Simpson, July 24, 1864, Simpson Papers.

[23] J. William Hoover to Simpson, April 22, 1864, Simpson Papers; *Zion's Herald*, May 23, 1866; *Nashville Advocate*, September 9, 1876.

[24] *Annual Cyclopedia 1864*, p. 515; J. William Hoover to Simpson, April 22, 1864, Simpson Papers; P. M. Pinkard and S. D. Baldwin to Clinton B. Fisk, July 31, 1865, Bureau of Refugees, Freedmen, and Abandoned Lands Papers (War Records Division, National Archives). Hereinafter cited as B.R.F.A.L.

[25] J. William Hoover to Simpson, April 27, 1864, and M. J. Cramer to Simpson, April 30, 1864, Simpson Papers.

[26] New Albany (Ind.) *Weekly Ledger*, March 9, 1864, quoting St. Louis *Republican*; *Central Advocate*, March 17, 1864.

[27] McPherson, *Political History*, 522; *Official Records*, Ser. I, Vol. XXXIV, Pt. II, 453; J. C. Nicolay and John Hay, "Lincoln and the Churches," *Century Magazine*, XXXVIII (August, 1889), 566.

[28] *Official Records*, Ser. I, Vol. XXXIV, Pt. II, 453; Leftwich, *Martyrdom in Missouri*, I, 265–66.

[29] *Congressional Globe*, 38 Cong., 1 Sess., 1361, 1417, 3448.

[30] *Christian Advocate*, September 8, 1864; *Northwestern Advocate*, November 22, 1865.

[31] *Christian Advocate*, March 17, 1864.

[32] William H. Lawrence, *The Centenary Souvenir, Containing a History of the Centenary Church in Charleston* (Charleston, 1885), vii–viii; *Missionary Advocate*, XXI (June, 1865), 21.

[33] Calvin Kingsley to Simpson, July 5, 1864, Simpson Papers.

[34] *Christian Advocate*, June 22, 1865.

[35] Johnson's Order dated January 23, 1865; Johnson Papers, LXXIV, Nos. 6328–6329; *Western Advocate*, September 20, 1865.

[36] *Ibid.*, August 30, 1865.

[37] McTyerie, *History of Methodism*, 673; *Western Advocate*, September 20, 1865; Missionary Society of the Methodist Episcopal Church, *Forty-seventh Annual Report* (1865), 137. Hereinafter cited as Missionary Society, *Annual Report*.

[38] McKendree Chapel exemplified the difficulties experienced by Southern Methodists in regaining possession of their buildings. In August, 1864, legal counsel for the Church South petitioned Lincoln for restoration of the chapel. Lincoln referred the petitioners to the military governor of Tennessee, Andrew Johnson, and in late December, 1864, prayer was made to Johnson. By order dated January 23, 1865, Johnson ordered the chapel returned to the Church South. However, Northern Methodist rear-guard tactics prevented the Southern church from coming into physical possession of McKendree until August 26, 1865, more than a year after recovery proceedings had been instituted. The various maneuvers and counter maneuvers in the long contest are found in Johnson Papers, LXXIII, Nos. 6074–6075 and LXXIV, Nos. 6318–6336.

[39] A. A. Gee to Simpson, August 22, 1865, Simpson Papers; *Southern Review*, X (April, 1872), 414.

[40] Elliot, *Southwestern Methodism*, 464; *Western Advocate*, February 22, 1865.

[41] P. M. Pinkard and S. D. Baldwin to C. B. Fisk, July 31, 1865, B.R.F.A.L.: Johnson's Order, dated January 23, 1865, Johnson Papers, LXXIV, No. 6329.

[42] *Central Advocate*, March 24, 1864; *Western Advocate*, October 5, 1864.

[43] Quoted in George R. Crooks, *Life of Bishop Matthew Simpson* (New York, 1890), 397.

[44] A. A. Gee to Simpson, August 22, 1865, Simpson Papers.

[45] Sweet, *The Methodist Episcopal Church in the Civil War*, 176; Missionary Society, *Forty-Seventh Annual Report* (1865), 147–159.

[46] The founding of the Northern Church in East Tennessee is one of the few phases of Methodist activity during Reconstruction which has been attentively chronicled. A good brief study is William Hesseltine, "Methodism and Reconstruction in East Tennessee," East Tennessee Historical Society, *Publications* No. 3 (1931), 42–61. Valuable, although shot-through with denominational bias, is R. N. Price, *Holston Methodism From Its Origin to the Present Time*, 7 vols. (Nashville, 1912). E. Merton Coulter, *William G. Brownlow: Fighting Parson of the Southern Highlands* (Chapel Hill, 1937) sketches Brownlow's part. Thomas H. Pearne, *Sixty-One Years of Itinerant Christian Life in Church and State* (Cincinnati and New York, 1899), is a firsthand account by a Northern minister but frustratingly meager at critical points.

[47] Simpson to Calvin Holman, January 21, 1864, Simpson Papers; "Journal

of the Kentucky Conference of the Methodist Episcopal Church, 1864." (Typescript, in the private library of John O. Gross, Nashville, Tennessee.)

[48] Doubtless Brownlow was advised in his course by the Northern bishops. While attending the Baltimore convention of the Republican Party in 1864, he found opportunity to discuss with Bishops Simpson, Kingsley, and Clark the problem of the Southern expansion of the Church North. See Isaac P. Martin, *Methodism in Holston* (Knoxville, 1945), 81ff.

[49] Knoxville *Whig*, July 23, 1864.

[50] *Western Advocate*, June 14, 1865.

[51] *Zion's Herald*, May 31, 1865; *Northwestern Advocate*, May 31, 1865.

[52] *Christian Advocate*, May 11, 1865.

[53] *Central Advocate*, May 24, 1865.

[54] *Central Advocate*, April 26, 1865; *Christian Advocate*, April 27, 1865; *Methodist*, May 13, 1865.

[55] "Journal of Dr. Daniel Stevenson," 2 vols.(Typescript, in the private library of John O. Gross, Nashville, Tenn.)

[56] *Northern Advocate*, June 7, 1865.

[57] Missionary Society, *Forty-Seventh Annual Report* (1865), 136.

[58] *Western Advocate*, January 10, 1866.

[59] Piecemeal descriptions of Lewis's career can be found in Francis Simkins and Robert H. Woody, *South Carolina During Reconstruction* (Chapel Hill, 1932), 376ff; *Methodist Review*, LVI (January, 1874), 33; Missionary Society, *Forty-Seventh Annual Report* (1865), 155–57; Lawrence, *Centenary Souvenir*, xii.

[60] Daniel Curry, *Life Story of Rev. Davis W. Clark* (New York and Cincinnati, 1874), 230ff.

[61] *Annual Cyclopedia*, 1866, p. 489.

[62] Edmund J. Hammond, *The Methodist Episcopal Church in Georgia* (Atlanta, 1935), 114ff.

[63] John H. Caldwell, *Reminiscences of the Reconstruction of Church and State in Georgia* (Wilmington, Del., 1895), 3–7.

[64] Hammond, *Methodist Episcopal Church in Georgia*, 110–115; *Missionary Advocate*, XXII (April, 1866), 5.

[65] James Mitchell, *The Life and Times of Levi Scott, D. D.* (New York and Cincinnati, 1885), 218; Freedmen's Aid Society of the Methodist Episcopal Church, *Twelfth Annual Report* (1879), 37. Hereinafter cited as Freedmen's Aid Society, *Annual Report*.

[66] Missionary Society, *Forty-Seventh Annual Report* (1865), 158–161; *Forty-Eighth Annual Report* (1866), 143; Extension Society, *Sixth Annual Report* (1871), 50.

[67] *Ibid.*, 51; Missionary Society, *Forty-Eighth Annual Report* (1866), 144. In 1869 the subdivision of existing conferences commenced. This tediously involved process can be followed through the annual digests of conference proceedings, *Minutes of the Annual Conferences of the Methodist Episcopal Church.*

[68] Western Advocate, January 10, 1866; Missionary Society, *Forty-Eighth Annual Report* (1866), 144.

[69] *Christian Advocate*, June 15, 1865.

[70] *Western Advocate*, June 14, 1868; *Nashville Advocate*, January 24, 1869.

[71] *Northwestern Advocate*, February 19, 1868; *Proceedings of the Southern*

Methodist Convention, held at Athens, Tennessee, June 15–19, 1871 (Cincinnati, 1871), 11.

[72] James Mitchell to Simpson, July 15, 1867, Simpson Papers; *Methodist,* August 24, 1869.

[73] *Methodist,* December 4, 1875.

[74] Missionary Society, *Fiftieth Annual Report* (1868), 31–32.

[75] The statistics have been compiled from the *Annual Reports* of the Missionary Society. The sum of $2,080,000 was disbursed during the three years and of this amount about $600,000 was given to conferences covering former slave territory. This proportion, however, does not include special appropriations for church and educational buildings and the pay of teachers.

[76] *Methodist,* June 1, 1867.

[77] Bits of this unorthodox financial history can be exhumed from Extension Society, *Second Annual Report* (1867), 14–17; *Journal of the General Conference, 1880,* pp. 590–594; *Western Advocate,* July 31, 1867.

[78] *Western Advocate,* July 17, 1867.

[79] Edmund S. Janes to Simpson, February 14, 1867, Simpson Papers.

[80] *Pittsburgh Advocate,* March 24, 1866; Extension Society, *Third Annual Report* (1868), 15; *Zion's Herald,* January 22, 1874.

[81] These opinions from widely separate parts of the South are gathered from a single issue of the *Western Advocate* (August 28, 1867): "The great defect of our Southern work is lack of churches"; "Our great need . . . is Houses of Worship"; "Our great want is houses."

[82] *Western Advocate,* July 17, 1867.

[83] *Journal of the General Conference, 1868,* pp. 362–64, 562.

[84] *Ibid.,* 562–64.

[85] *Nashville Advocate,* September 3, 1870.

[86] Freedmen's Aid Society, *Tenth Annual Report* (1877), 11; [?] to Simpson, December 3, 1868, in Simpson Papers.

[87] *Methodist Advocate,* July 19 and August 3, 1871.

[88] *Methodist Review,* LVI (January, 1874), 43.

[89] Freedmen's Aid Society, *Seventh Annual Report* (1874), 23; Extension Society, *Eleventh Annual Report* (1876), 83.

[90] *Methodist Review,* LVI (January, 1874), 36; *Western Advocate,* February 6, 1872.

[91] The above have been gathered principally from the Simpson Papers.

[92] *Methodist Advocate,* November 3, 1869.

[93] *Christian Advocate,* November 22, 1866; *Central Advocate,* November 8, 1871.

[94] *Methodist Advocate,* January 12, 1870; *Zion's Herald,* February 15, 1872.

[95] *Central Advocate,* September 12, 1866.

[96] *Western Advocate,* January 10, 1866; February 24, 1869; *Zion's Herald,* September 12, 1866; *Journal of the General Conference, 1868,* p. 555.

[97] *Journal of the General Conference, 1876,* pp. 561–565.

[98] *Minutes of the Holston Annual Conference of the Methodist Episcopal Church, 1871,* pp. 34–35; *Christian Advocate,* November 11, 1875.

[99] *Minutes of the South Carolina Annual Conference of the Methodist Episcopal Church, 1875,* p. 17.

[100] *Proceedings of the Southern Methodist Conference, 1871,* p. 31. Big in this

regional controversy over Methodist journals was the specter of race. The Middle South had the bulk of whites in the Northern church, while Charleston and New Orleans were in the midst of a colored membership. The *Methodist Advocate* was constantly charged with being not only local in its interests but prejudiced in favor of white communicants.

# III

# A Storm over Zion

This quarrel between us and them stands out above
all quarrels in history, sacred or profane.

[Nashville] *Christian Advocate*
August 1, 1874

Behold, how good and how pleasant it is for brethren
to dwell in unity.

Psalm cxxxiii

"WHAT are to be our ecclesiastical relations to the Methodism
of the . . . seceded . . . states?" queried Daniel Curry in the
waning days of the war for Southern nationality.[1] The question,
never more than tentatively settled, had been brought again to
the fore of discussion by the Northern Methodist resolution for
a trial of strength in the land of the Confederacy. The North-
South separation of the great Wesleyan body had begun peacefully enough in 1844 with a pact which divided the common
property and confined the labors of each branch of Methodists
behind a line approximating that between the free and slave
states. However, the Northern clergy's antagonism to the agreement was so strong that their General Conference in 1848 re-
pudiated it and refused official recognition of the corporate
existence of the Church South. Violations and counter-violations
of the proposed covenant ensued, accompanied by bitter wrangling and lawsuits over disputed property.[2] Northern Methodist
writers before 1860 had discoursed exhaustively on the relation
of their church to "the illegitimate offspring of slavery" but their
cogitations were usually fired by a remembrance of old antagonisms rather than by a consciousness of any present need. Only
along a narrow border did Northern and Southern Methodist
congregations dwell in such proximity as necessitated a practical

definition of their relationship. The Northern decision to expand changed this condition and made imminent the prospect of Methodist rivalry over a large territory. A policy toward Southern Methodism then became an urgently utilitarian matter.

To be sure that the Methodist Episcopal Church steered a true course in regard to its Southern sister, Northern preachers used to the fullest the right of free expression. Few Methodists of the period who had any facility with a pen lost the chance to relieve themselves of their opinions. So plenteous and jangling were the ideas that the outlines of a fixed policy toward Southern Methodism did not clearly emerge until several years after the war. The Church North at first failed to aim consistently at "division and ecclesiastical devastation," as the Southern bishops contended, nor did it seek "to work side by side with the Church South in love," which was a later interpretation of the Northerners. Within Northern Methodism, individual belief and action ranged between the two extremes and obscured the development of a program that justly can be described as official. However, while the initial policy of the church defied neat categorization, the totality of Northern Methodist thought about relations with their Southern brethren took on distinguishable shades. These attitudes were respectively arrogant, vicious, magnanimous, and stern.

The first of these viewpoints on church diplomacy was succinctly phrased by George M. Steele, the president of a small Methodist college in the Genesee country. He recommended that his sect look upon Southern Methodism "not only as an unevangelical, but as an essentially vicious organization, which the true church of Christ cannot . . . recognize." The expansion southward should be made, he said, in studied ignorance of a competing group of Methodists, "without negotiation . . . any attempt at reunion, or any recognition of . . . a clearly anti-Christian body." [3] The advocates of a policy which called for the Church North "to prosecute her missionary activities . . . regardless of . . . favor or opposition from the Church South" were sometimes asked to explain how they would handle "antagonisms [which] would arise . . . in the prosecution of such a work." They usually replied in one of two ways. William G. Brownlow promised Southern Methodism that if it opposed the "organization . . . that had talents, members, energy, money, and right on its side" it would "come out of the conflict second best." [4] But more often the proponents of the policy of non-attention denied the assumption of a conflict for the reason that the Southern church was in the process of dissolution. Imbued with the conviction that Southern Methodism was umbilically attached to the Confederacy, these people predicted that "with the restoration of the authority of the government . . . the Methodist Episcopal Church, South . . . will inevitably collapse." "It is the manifest destiny of the Church South to go out with the rebellion," oracularly announced an on-the-spot reporter.[5] With the return of peace, many professed to see what they had anticipated, a "Southern church so shattered and torn by confusion and desolation" that a long life was unlikely. "The Methodist Episcopal Church South is in ruins," gloated one clergyman and even some of the episcopate were heard to agree. Bishop Clark, as he inspected the scene, said that the days of Southern Methodism's life "were numbered" and that its downfall was "only a question of time." [6] Since the Church South was "going to pieces . . . stung in the vitals by the treason it was instrumental in originating," all the opposite organization had to do was to "watch this process of disintegration [and] gather up the fragments of the crumbling church." Overtures of any sort were out of order when true Methodism might win by default.

However, other Methodists maintained that the atomization of the Church South would not be automatic or at any event it would be protracted, and they recommended that the catalyst of a Northern onslaught be added to hasten the process of decay. A conference of Northern clergymen pronounced the judgment that Southern Methodism "had been so completely leagued with

detestable sin that its . . . apostate church should be extermi-
nated." [7] This program, although its strongest endorsement
came from New England Methodists, received classic formulation in the prose of Daniel Curry of the New York *Advocate*.
"A policy of earnest and antagonistic aggression must . . . be
adopted and put into action," he said. "With this we may . . .
certainly disintegrate the rival body, and absorb whatever of it
shall be found worth preserving." The naked details of the plan
contemplated "the direct invasion of the South . . . without
any regard for the Methodist Episcopal Church, South, the disintegration of the latter whenever it can be effected . . . , and
the absorption of its fragments." [8] The battle cry of "disintegration and absorption" probably benefited Southern Methodism more than the church to which it was recommended. Not
only did it become "the . . . scorn of Northern Methodism"
but propagandists for the Church South seized upon the slogan
to rally their denomination to defense. Southern ecclesiasts
elaborating without stop on the theme that "Northern Methodism proposes to take possession of the field, to press us to the
wall, and finally to . . . exterminate us" toughened the fiber of
the membership for the rigors of religious war. Schooled in the
practical effects of Curry's catchwords, a Northern publicist
subsequently declared that "a more unfortunate suggestion
could not have been made by any . . . man in the church." [9]

It was ironical, however, that the recognized champion of
"disintegration and absorption" was entrenched in New York.
Economic ties with the South had long since bred a tolerance of
Southern ways in the metropolitan area, and Manhattan Methodism was prominently colored by its environment. A short walk
from the New York office where Curry spoke for the party intent
on "expunging the Church South," the mouthpiece of wealthy
laymen and their clerical partners stumped "for a formal and
general restoration of the unity of American Methodism." This
latter clique, which used the *Methodist* as a primary medium,
had as its most conspicuous ministerial participants George

Crooks and his editorial staff of Abel Stevens, John McClintock, Henry B. Ridgaway, and Benjamin H. Nadal. These men, the brightest intellectual lights of Northern Methodism, had the company of Daniel Whedon of the *Methodist Review*, the only official periodical to join the parade of reunionists, and possibly Bishop Janes. Sufficiently prescient to see that a malicious assault on the Church South would break open Pandora's box and compound Southern Methodism into a phalanx, this group urged the rapid introduction of "generous overtures" to bring the dissevered Wesleyan parts together. "Let us be prompt," they urged, "[or] we may soon be wrangling over questions about mutual interference, claims for church edifices, etc." [10] The plan of reunion did not merely envision the acceptance of individual Southern Methodists; it envisioned nothing short of a mutual annulment of the 1844 divorce. The intent was, said Abel Stevens, that Episcopal Methodism, through negotiation, should "again be one" with "a common organization . . . a common name . . . and a common membership." [11] Specifications of the reunion proposal were not immediately forthcoming, but its protagonists pleaded for "all . . . Methodists to look well to [the] matter" and demanded that "bishops, editors and people . . . move in that direction." As a point of departure, the moderates advised the substitution of counsels of "wisdom, benevolence, and peace" for the fulminations of "air beating, conch blowing stormers." [12]

Methodist Thomases of the age wanted to know, "What hope is there that the Methodist Episcopal Church South would accept an invitation . . . to union?" Many took it as elementary that "the haughty Southron would glory in the privilege of spurning the offer." [13] Nevertheless, the partisans of Methodist reconciliation carted up much evidence to refute the allegations of their skeptical confreres. In nearly every Southern state, one or more Northern correspondents felt that the clergy of the Church South "would favor a formal reunion . . . if the matter were fairly presented." Nor were dispatches of this kind always composed by "smooth tongued deceivers" who panted for Southern Methodism's embrace. After extended investigation the life-long abolitionist Mansfield French proclaimed "that the Church South can be brought back as a body into the old Methodist Church." [14] Especially alluring were reports that the Southern Methodist officialdom was not adverse to the re-establishment of a nationwide ecclesiastical union. A. A. Gee, superintendent of Northern missionary work about Nashville, although it seared his prejudices to admit it, said that there "was probably no doubt . . . that the leaders of the Church South would accept 'magnanimous' overtures to come back and bring with them . . . the whole Methodist Episcopal Church South." John Newman, stationed at New Orleans, may have been unreasonably sanguine but he asserted "from personal knowledge" that three of the six Southern bishops would likely support plans of union. Robert Paine was allegedly "moderate in his . . . views"; George F. Pierce was "outspoken on the restoration of fraternization," and Hubbard H. Kavanaugh believed that "the American Methodist Churches should be one again." Of the remaining Southern bishops, one was removed from the doubtful ranks by other interviewers. The aged Joshua Soule was said to have "endorsed the wish . . . of a reunion of the church." This left James O. Andrew, center of the 1844 controversy, as "uncertain" and John Early, the elder brother of the Confederate cavalry general, "probably opposed." [15] Both Andrew and Early, however, were so infirm that their influence thrown in either direction would not have been important. Even with the subtraction of the subjective factor in news-gathering the Northern advocates of reunion seemed to have ground for encouragement as they examined Southern Methodist opinion.

The Northern Methodist "trucklers to slavery" were furiously denounced by fellow churchmen of divergent ideas. A New England preacher, alarmed by the prospect of fraternizing with the Southern church, shrieked "that we should form with that spiritual Babylon no alliance whatever." Enemies of reconcilia-

tion warned that any official attempt to implement the suggestions of the New York coterie "would be the signal for the most
undesirable agitations" and in such an eventuality the hierarchy
should "look out for war." [16] Although definite complaints
against reunion were many, the conciliationists believed that the
foremost objection to their position was "that it did not require
Southern Methodism to humble itself in the dust and confess
its sins." And upon the claim that "confession and repentance
must precede forgiveness" rested still another hypothetical
policy of ecclesiastical diplomacy—reunion with conditions. Because Methodists in the Confederate states had "sinned against
their country, their Discipline and their God," many Northerners wanted as a prerequisite to any reconciliation "a frank
acknowledgment of the fault with sorrow for sin and hearty
promise to do right hereafter." [17] The Church South was asked
to make repentance by some ceremonious means for the crimes
of which they had been adjudged guilty. "Until they . . . re-
pent before God and the nation in sackcloth and ashes for their
offenses," said one Northern clergyman, "we believe them unfit
for communion in Christ's Church." [18] The sins for which Southern Methodists were supposed to confess contrition "in due,
solemn and official form" were generally cataloged as "acts of
apostasy," "approval of slavery," "sympathy with treason," and
"innocent blood they have caused to be shed." Then after the
purgation of guilt "the North might . . . approach them with
beating heart and open hands." [19] This formula, denuded of its
camouflage, was a mutation of the Wesleyan criteria for church
fellowship. There was applied to an entire religious organization
for heresies largely political the conception that the deserving
Christian is one who sorrows for his waywardness, begs for a
mercy that is gratuitously bestowed, pledges a better life, and
finally is adopted into the company of the redeemed. The corporate repentance theory won wide favor in Northern circles and,
in the first days of peace, came nearest to representing majority
thinking on the matter of reunion. But the doctrine was popular

not merely because it accorded with the Methodist understanding of justice but because it effectually closed the door to any serious negotiations for reunion. Such embittered crusaders against Southern Christianity as Brownlow and Gilbert Haven could declare themselves inclined toward a merger of the churches "on the right platform," smugly knowing that the proffered terms of "contrition, confession, and repentance" would be rejected by indignant Southerners.[20]

As the respective ideas on procedure toward the Southern church jostled each other in quest of official approval, future relations between the Methodisms were partly decided by the supposedly vanquished portion. During the spring and early summer of 1865 the bishops of the South had maintained silence on the status of their ecclesiastical organism and reports of their ideas were nearly all secondhand. These reports coupled with other tokens were confusing enough to justify about every expectation in the North. For the first time since the outbreak of the war the world had a chance to listen to something akin to an official voice when the Southern bishops met in late August, 1865, at Columbus, Georgia. The tone of the address which emanated from the conference was unequivocal. It urged the separate maintenance of Southern Methodist institutions and enumerated many reasons why "no good result" could be anticipated "from even entertaining the subject of reunion." [21] While Northern commentators saw in the episcopal declaration "a decree of extinction" and "the death warrant of Southern Methodism," the message shocked vigor into the body that some had pronounced already dead. Succeeding months saw the Southern hulk slowly righting itself; and in May, 1866, the Church South's first General Conference in eight years gathered. The administrative and disciplinary reforms of the conference and the election of younger bishops girded the church for further action. Northern Methodists who caught the direct force of the ensuing vitality soon whined that "the M. E. Church South [was] the . . . most vigorous and aggressive of all churches in the South." [22]

The failure of Northern Methodists to annihilate, absorb, or unite with the opposing faction left competition as a result. The fray which found "brethren . . . snapping and snarling, quarreling and brawling, envying and backbiting, reproaching and deriding, tearing and devouring one another" did not result in onesided victories for the North. In the border areas, particularly northern Virginia, the Church South scored important advances. The bulk of Wesleyans in upper Virginia had clung to the Northern church after the schism of 1844, but with the reservation that antislavery tests never be incorporated into the Methodist creed. When the General Conference of 1860 tampered with the disciplinary chapter relating to slaveholding, many Virginians cancelled their allegiance to Northern Methodism and founded an autonomous organization. In 1865 this rump voted to move into the Southern fold. The Church South also crossed the Ohio to root itself in Illinois where pro-Southern sentiment and the introduction "of unwholesome themes" into the pulpit during the war had conspired to make the Church North repugnant to a scattering of tender natures.[23] The maneuvers of the rival religious bodies and the accompanying transfers of membership from one denomination to another spawned a galaxy of property disputes which continued in a grosser form the controversies ignited by the Stanton directives of 1863. Not satisfied with a mere change of communion, the seceders often tried to carry the title to the church house with them. The withdrawal of a few members, or one or two church trustees, or a preacher was sometimes thought adequate to set up a claim to a house of worship. Methodism's many-sided conflict during the reconstruction period became most overt in the contention over real estate. As a Northern preacher wrote, "This property question is a source of great strife. Wherever it does not exist the . . . two churches are more friendly and fraternal." [24]

Hardly a spacious sector of Southern territory was free from the rancorous discussions about property. In the lower South, most of the differences revolved about the ownership of Negro churches, built during the *ante bellum* period. The titles to these edifices were vested in local boards of white trustees who held them for the use of Southern Methodist Negro congregations. Upon the abolition of slavery and the shift of Methodist affiliation by many blacks, the Church North endeavored to get title of the buildings transferred to itself and trusteeship given to a board of Negro members.[25] However, difficult and numerous as were the puzzles posed by freedmen's churches, much more attention was focused on the possession of property for whites in the upper South. Here the majority of cases were found in the Holston area and in the north part of Virginia, both of which had seen wholesale changes of membership. The conference of rebel Southern Methodists which met at Knoxville in July, 1864, had indicated the shape of things to come in East Tennessee when they formulated an extraordinary theory for determining the title to churches. This conclave assumed that "all who willingly engaged in . . . rebellion . . . forfeited all rights," and consequently "loyal members and ministers . . . are entitled in law to all [church] property." Fragile though both premise and conclusion were, the dissenters carried out their threat "to claim and hold the same." [26] Because many of the skirmishes in East Tennessee never passed beyond local notoriety, the aggregate of property which was thrown into dispute can only be guessed at. In 1868 a Southern Methodist testified that Northerners were still holding "illegally" over a hundred churches and "several" parsonages.[27] From this estimate, the number steadily slumped in succeeding years by voluntary evacuation, purchase, and in isolated instances by judicial decree.

While the warfare over property in eastern Tennessee was better advertised, it was not as intense or widespread as that in Virginia where the Church North maintained the status of the injured party. When the Virginia Methodists who previously had been in connection with the Northern organization resolved to go to the South, they sought to retain the ownership of over two hundred meetinghouses.[28] This action set in motion a chain of large-scale legal intrigues which, though the Northern Methodists seemed to have an advantage, left the status of the disputed property so clouded that neither side felt secure in its tenancy. In January, 1866, some months after the Virginia seceders voted themselves into the Church South, Bishop Ames repeated his wartime feat of employing the power of the federal government in behalf of his denomination. Halfheartedly supported by Bishops Simpson and Janes, he secured President Johnson's consent to a War Department order which gave the use of disputed churches in the northern third of Virginia "to those ministers and members who remain with and act under the ecclesiastical jurisdiction governing said churches prior to 1861." [29] This technical language cloaked the simple judgment that the disputed property was to be occupied exclusively by persons communing with Northern Methodism for that denomination before 1861 had held sway over the area defined in the directive. What arguments prevailed upon Johnson to interfere in Virginia constitute a first-rate mystery. Ames, who had been industrious in seeking governmental intervention, had sunk into despair before seeing his project crowned with success. Only a few weeks before the order was issued, Ames wrote that Johnson seemed "shut up to the necessity of granting what we . . . ask." Perhaps the President arrived at the realization, as did some of the Northern episcopate, that a refusal would present the Methodists with "a good case to take before the country which [was] worth more than ten-fold the value of the property involved." [30]

The decree obtained by Ames, however, had a loophole through which Southern Methodists slipped to stymie the Northerners momentarily. It denied the construction of "deciding any question of title between conflicting claimants" and merely regulated the occupation of property in contention "until the title shall be adjudicated." Southern Methodists gained an *a priori* advantage in the event of any adjudication when the

Virginia Legislature in 1867 enacted a statute providing that "conclusive . . . title to and control of . . . [church] property" should in each contest be decided "by a vote of the majority of . . . communicants." [31] Since most Methodist societies involved in fratricidal war over their meeting places contained a majority of Southern sympathizers, the act promised to confer material benefits upon the Church South. But the Northern denomination had a remaining trump card which it played at the Virginia Constitutional Convention of 1868. Through the assiduous lobbying of Northern preachers [32] a clause was inserted into the new state constitution which declared that "the parties set forth in the original deeds of conveyance" were "the rightful owners of ecclesiastical property and any act or acts of the Legislature in opposition . . . [were] null and void." [33] Inasmuch as the deeds originally had been executed in favor of the Northern church, this constitutional mandate effectively erased Southern Methodism's previous gain. Unhappily, it also raised questions of law to complicate an already perplexing situation. Ere the State Court of Appeals in 1875 upheld the validity of the constitutional clause relating to church property, Virginia Methodists spent much strength in untangling the legal snarls which had arisen from the shuttling of real estate by executive decree, legislation, and constitutional provision. It was deplorable "to go to law with brethren" but juridical procedures were "necessary to aid . . . in securing . . . property." [34]

As high-level argumentation continued, Methodist preachers and laymen in the South learned from their routine experience the meaning of warm religious antagonism. Scoured clean of his illusions by the hostilities, a clerical warrior expostulated that he had "never seen more evidence of . . . deepseated hatred, of a lack of . . . charity, and of . . . thoroughly unchristian prejudice." [35] Neutrals who observed this denominational competition could detect overtones of comedy. The Virginia scene offered especial fare for quipsters. A Connecticut preacher, busy at the conversion of the state, vowed that he knew of an instance where a Northerner was confronted in the pulpit by a minister of the Southern connection "who took the hymn book out of his hand and went on and preached the sermon." Another complained that his expositions on theology were bothered by the simultaneous discourses of a Southern Methodist elsewhere in the church. A third Northern clergyman reached his Virginia appointment, dismounted, hastily thumbed through his Bible for a sermon text and walked into the meetinghouse only to find "his church nearly filled with the rankest rebels and a rebel class leader of the Methodist . . . Church South in the altar conducting an enthusiastic class meeting." [36] The change of locks on doors and the nailing down of meetinghouse windows to thwart the ingress of enemy preachers were fairly monotonous practices in Virginia. Other parts of the South furnished scenes alike in kind if not in incidence. "Results were not edifying" at an outdoor Northern Methodist meeting in the North Carolina mountains because adjacent to it was a similar Southern gathering and "when one congregation would hear preaching [the] other would sing." The struggle for the Southern soul even touched the dead. In eastern Tennessee, interment rites started under the auspices of a Northern preacher were interrupted and then completed by a parson of the Church South.[37]

If there were elements in Methodism's controversy which tickled the risibilities others conveyed a semblance of tragedy. Encouraged by the friendship between their superiors and government officials, Northern preachers sometimes called in United States troops to oust from churches "the slimy cowards . . . too corrupt for loyalty." An immigrant Virginian who found Southern Methodists barring the door against him explained his technique for gaining entry. "I wrote to General Schofield in regard to the matter . . . whereupon he sent . . . an officer to place me in possession of the churches," he said. At Winchester, Virginia, after a Southern preacher made a lusty try to insinuate himself in the pulpit he "was politely requested by soldiers to remain in his dwelling." [38] Tempers occasionally erupted into violence. Dispatches originating in both branches of Methodism frequently complained that congregations had "not been able to occupy . . . churches on account of mob violence." A Maryland report of a clash "with clubs and stones" in 1866 counted four casualties "on the rebel side" and two on the Union from such assorted causes as "a blow struck on the back of the head," "a blow . . . on the arm" and "a blow in the side." [39] To conscientious folk the saddest of all products to come from the clash of Methodisms were riven families. Religious separation filtered down through states and neighborhoods to parents and their progeny. A preacher in the copper area of eastern Tennessee noticed that "in some instances the wife and children were in one church while the husband and father were in another" and so divided were they "that there was no likelihood of their being brought together in their church relations." [40]

Strife and discord aplenty marked the behaviour of one body of Methodists toward another, but the whole of their church relations constituted a contradiction. A northside Methodist in Tennessee innocently exposed the true complexion of things when he wrote, "In some places . . . the Southern Methodist preachers fraternize with our preachers. At other places . . . they treat us as aliens and our folks . . . treat them in the same way." [41] Alongside the bad manners displayed by prelates, pastors, and people, lived instances of personal and professional friendships between members of the denominations. The evidences of harmony were not generally found in episcopal manifestoes, conference resolutions, or above all, editorial columns of religious journals. They have to be looked for under the personal items and revival notices of church newspapers and in the all-too-scarce journals of unpretentious preachers. Many by their actions deserved the censure of a dignified Episcopalian who said that "no . . . religious controversies . . . have been waged with more indifference to the courtesies of life . . . than has been exhibited by these . . . followers of Wesley"; yet others advocated and practised tolerance.[42] After a few years of peace, unmistakable evidence appeared that some of the ecclesiastical elite could also be counted among the charitable ones.

Before 1869 the churches could and did argue over the fact of reunion proposals. The Southern Church stoutly contended that it had received no sincere communications pertaining to relations between the Methodisms, an assertion that the North warmly denied. Both could offer substantiation for their positions. Neither the Northern General Conference of 1864 nor that of 1868 had expressed any positive thought on reunion with the Southern church, but ambiguous propositions had come from other quarters. Most celebrated of these was the bishops' circular of 1865. From their meeting at Erie, Pennsylvania, in June of that year, the Northern princes announced that with the removal of slavery "the great cause which led to the separation from us . . . of the M. E. Church, South has passed away . . . and the day is not far distant when there shall be but one organization which shall embrace the whole Methodist family." Details of the method of achieving this reunion went unmentioned and, significantly, the address did not invite to communion any Methodist Church as an organic whole but only "all ministers or members of whatever branch of Methodism who will unite . . . on the basis of our . . . Discipline." [43] Possibly the excruciating language of the prelatic proposal was designed to satisfy all opinions in the North, but the message and a few other amicable overtures arising from annual conferences seemed to rest on the premise that the conditions of religious peace were not to be bilaterally determined. A secular newsman observed, not inaccurately, that there was "a desire on the part of the Church North to reunite with the Church South—on its own terms." [44] However, in 1869 and again in 1870, officials of the Northern church—with reunion as their intent—made bold strokes to initiate unfettered conversations between the Methodist bodies.

Members of the Southern episcopal committee, at their St.

Louis meeting in May, 1869, had as visitors Bishops Janes and Simpson. The latter had been sent by their Northern colleagues to confer with the bishops of the South "as to the propriety, practicability, and methods of reunion." This frontal assault of Janes and Simpson was quickly repulsed by the Southerners. They replied that "we have no authority to determine anything as to the 'propriety, practicability and methods of reunion' " [45] and backed up their answer with a severe lecture on the past misdoings of the Methodist Episcopal Church. Nevertheless, the reunionists in the North professed to see some hope even in the curt refusal to entertain discussions, because the Southern bishops had merely denied any intrinsic right to commit their church. The next Northern attempt at reconciliation came before the Southern tribunal competent to act on the matter. At the 1870 Southern General Conference in Memphis, Bishop Janes and William L. Harris, himself to be a bishop two years later, put in an appearance. Although devoid of express permission to bind the denomination they represented, these delegates asked for the appointment of a Southern commission to meet one selected by the North in order that a union "on terms equally honorable to all" might be effected. The Northern emissaries were handsomely entertained and politely heard, but on the day after their departure from Memphis the General Conference endorsed the St. Louis action of the Southern bishops and declared that "the true interests of the church . . . require and demand the maintenance of . . . separate and distinct organizations." [46] Whatever the impending years might hold for the two Methodisms, they were not going to face it together.

Propositions from the North for a rewelding of Methodism immediately put Southerners on guard. The swiftness with which "feelings of love" became apparent after a period of dormancy provoked a suspicion of motives. A Southern Methodist in Tennessee expressed one popular interpretation of the action. He said that "the disintegrating and absorbing policy has been abandoned. The Church South has proved too tough for convenient mastication and our friends have concluded to swallow us whole." Observing the mounting treasury deficits of Northern Methodism, a Kentuckian surmised that the union movement signified that the North's "cause [was] upon its last legs and must erelong topple unless union [was] consummated." Another specialist in religious diplomacy suspected that the Church North wanted "no unfriendly rivalries" which might "impede the work of disintegration." [47] Even though it was a mere incident of their thought, churchmen of the North wisely recognized that they stood to gain in the South even if their proposals were rejected. In the heady sport of church politics, they believed that charity and expediency nicely dovetailed. As one of the enthusiasts of reunion commented, "If we can approach these [Southerners] after having made a magnanimous and brotherly overture of reunion to the leaders of the Church South, the rejection of it . . . will give us a moral power . . . of inestimable importance among these hosts." Erasmus Fuller saw in the decision of the Southern General Conference of 1870 a huge profit for the North. The Southern Methodists, he wrote, "defined their position before all the world . . . and . . . untied those who were waiting for the action of the General Conference to unite the whole body." Those designated could now move over to Northern Methodism "without censure." [48]

Out of the swirling debates over reunion can be glimpsed jagged differences in the enemy Methodisms. Some of these in truth went no deeper than the conceit of stubborn hardheadedness. The assertion of a Southern Methodist editor, "If there is strife and schism in the church, we do not . . . have the blame of it attaching to us," was matched by a Northern opponent who wrote, "It is the Southern not Northern religionists who are bent on . . . perpetuating disunion and strife." [49] Additional causes of divergency sprang from a remembrance of past wrongs which built up into a mighty torrent of prejudice. "We have not forgotten . . . and it is useless to talk of union while we remember," said one preacher who gazed back over the decades of conflict.[50] Churchmen, no less than ordinary mortals, were also anxious for place, and the smaller organization offered bigger chances. Reunion would inevitably bring a "sacrifice of power and position." The best argument one Southern pastor could lodge against Methodist union was the probability that "the North would have all the bishops in less than forty years." [51]

Pharisaic righteousness, the unreasoning prejudice of tradition, and lust for advancement each bore a share of the responsibility for Methodist separation, but these considerations were less fundamental than the wedges driven by environment. The sectional distinctiveness that led to mutual slaughter was mirrored in the respective churches. During a moment of unusual insight, Daniel Curry wrote: "The dividing forces of Methodism . . . like those that disrupted the nation were within . . . Two nations lay together in the womb of early American Methodism and while there 'the children struggled within her' and their separation was a prerequisite to their peace and increase." [52] Oneness in doctrine and polity could not overcome the cultural polarity of North and South. "Sectional . . . asperities hinder cordial relations more than anything denominational," candidly stated a Southern potentate.[53] Many abhorred but could not reverse the tendency of the "great Methodisms" to gravitate toward "the extremes on all questions between the North and South." In this collision of cultures Southern Methodism appeared as the custodian of a sectional heritage. Customary habits of doing and thinking, trodden under on the battlefield, were carefully nursed by it through the *post bellum* period. The statement that "Southern Methodists [were] generally antagonistic . . . to . . . the . . . progressivism of the new era" was intended as an aspersion by the deliverer, but Southerners wore it as a badge of honor. Like the civilization to which it was wedded, the Church South had a stubborn fondness for the old ways in religion. So tenaciously did Southern Methodism cleave to its own that one Confederate predicted, "The separation from the M. E. Church will continue until the Bible is repealed." [54]

To encompass all the differences, recognized and unrecognized, holding them apart from the North, Southern Methodist leaders fastened upon a principle painfully evolved by *ante bellum* statesmen—in an organic union, minority interests are ultimately defenseless in the face of greater numbers. The Southern bishops, in reply to the 1869 union invitation, complained that in the previous league the Northern wing had shown itself "oppressive and destructive of the rights of the numerical minority." [55] Words strangely reminiscent of Calhoun were employed by delegates to the Southern General Conference of 1874 to tell why they had not been able to live under a written compact with the church of the North. Their apologia read: "The Northern members who were a controlling majority claimed . . . prerogatives which seemed . . . unconstitutional and . . . although restricted in the exercise of . . . power by a constitution [they were] the judge of the restrictions, and . . . thus practically unlimited." And complete reconciliation, in the face of superior Northern numbers would again "expose the minority to harassing legislation if not oppression." [56] A relatively moderate Southern periodical spoke what must have been plain to everybody: "The policy of the reunited church would be the policy of the Northern party. Their views of ecclesiastical polity and of current policy would control the body. The Southern wing would be in a hopeless minority." [57]

The friendly gestures of 1869 and 1870 did not betoken a change of attitude within the Northern sect, that approximated unanimity. The conclusion of one publicist that "in the Methodist Episcopal Church the feeling is . . . almost wholly in favor of reunion" had enough flagrant exceptions to raise doubts about its accuracy.[58] Neither the mission of Janes and Simpson in 1869 nor that of the following year was an evident reflex of swelling opinion in favor of reconciliation. Janes and Simpson journeyed to St. Louis over the objections of a minority of the episcopal committee and in full knowledge that "the General Conference did not . . . authorize specific action" of the kind they took. The emissaries who visited the Southern General Conference in 1870 negotiated with even less canonical sanction. They carried credentials from a committee whose primary business was to explore possibilities of a merger between the African Methodist denominations and the Methodist Episcopal Church and which, in striking for reunion with the South, exceeded the spirit of its instructions.[59] Furthermore, a sizable group of bitter-enders in the North tilted vigorously "against any attempt, on the part of Northern Christians, to unite the . . . Southern religion and that of Jesus Christ." Sickened by the gushing sentimentality of the reunion faction, a hoary veteran of religious feuding snapped, "I never let my judgment run out of my eyes." [60] Men of this stripe, in the declining years of reconstruction, were to hinder resourcefully the search for common Methodist ground between North and South.

However, the offers for union did mean that the conciliationists had grasped the handles of governmental machinery and had enough rank-and-file tolerance to make their influence on church policy sensible. Nor did they lose control in 1870 when their proffer for "marriage now and courtship afterward" was exploded by the Southern Methodist refusal. A rejected but not wholly downcast suitor, the moderate faction, altered its aims and strategy. In place of impulsive insistence on union, these Northerners resolved to seek the affection of the Church South on the latter's terms. Southern Methodists had indicated a willingness to be approached in this way when their General Conference of 1870 anticipated the "day . . . when proper Christian sentiments and fraternal relations between the two great bodies of . . . Methodism shall be permanently established." [61] But the South would have no consolidation of the Methodist units; they merely wanted the formal inauguration of diplomatic relations. The immediate end now was "fraternity," and even this goal had to be pursued warily.[62] Before the beginning of harmonious intercourse lay prolonged and complex preparations.

Negotiations on the new basis commenced when the Northern

General Conference in 1872 authorized three emissaries to visit its Southern counterpart which met two years afterward at Louisville. These Northern delegates, although it was not explicitly set forth in their instructions, intimated that an appointment of a commission by the Church South to parley over grievances between the opposing organizations would meet a like response from the 1876 General Conference of the Methodist Episcopal Church. The Southerners, with appropriate hesitancy, acted upon this intelligence. They established the suggested commission and dispatched messengers to the next meeting of the great convocation of the North to inform that body that the Church South was ready for a settlement of differences and an opening of formal relations. The Northern Conference reciprocated in 1876 by the accreditation of agents to fill out "the joint board of discreet brethren intent upon Christian peace" and correspondence between the chairmen of the respective delegations fixed a meeting for the middle of August, 1876, at Cape May, New Jersey. Here the joint commission was to seek the removal "of all obstacles to formal fraternity between the two churches." [63] These "obstacles" were defined as the failure of the Northerners to recognize the Church South "as a coeval and co-ordinate family of Methodists," and a plethora of property contests.

Each church chose three clergymen and two laymen to prepare and present its case.[64] The advocates were selected to placate the nuances of opinion in the rival denominations, and "it was thought . . . by many that the composition of the joint commission made agreement impossible." Of the combined committees, two members exemplified in their previous clashes the incompatibilities of Methodism and breathed reality into the fear that the consultations would be abortive. These were Erasmus Fuller, from the North, and Edward H. Myers, the chairman of the Southern delegation. The biographies of the two men showed surface parallels. Both were products of upper New York who by circuitous routes had wended their ways to Georgia where they achieved churchwide notoriety as editors of religious papers. The likenesses, however, went no further. Fuller, from Atlanta, used the *Methodist Advocate* in bitter warfare with Myers, who edited the *Southern Christian Advocate* at Macon, Georgia. In the journalistic hostilities, extending from 1869 to 1874, Fuller reputedly became so "radical and incendiary that . . . Myers . . . refused to have any further intercourse with him in any way." [65] This conflict Myers and Fuller carried into the joint commission, for in the twelve months which preceded the conference, the first published a 200-page volume in defense of the Church South and his adversary replied with a still heavier tome. Possibly because Fuller had to hurry his rebuttal to beat the deadline imposed by Cape May, *An Appeal to the Records* lacks the literary polish and, more important, the fine dialectics of Myers' *Disruption of the Methodist Episcopal Church.*[66] After thirty years of church forensics, neither man can be blamed for the failure to say anything new, but Myers, by skillfully knitting together the threads of past arguments, riveted attention upon the foundation demand of Southern Methodism. Before any consent to "fraternity" would be given, an acknowledgment must be squeezed from the North that the Church South was "a legitimate branch of Episcopal Methodism in the United States." [67]

A stereotyped Northern version of the origin of Southern Methodism was expounded by a Virginia missionary who said that "a parcel of . . . slavery advocates seceded and organized a bogus church of their own and called it the Methodist Episcopal Church, South." [68] Hurtful though it was to pride, Southern leaders believed that such historifying concealed a truly fatal danger. When the Northern General Conference in 1848 renounced the Plan of Separation signed by the dividing factions four years before, it threw into doubt the status and the privileges of the separate Methodist Church in the South. The compact originally conferred upon the Southern wing the right to possess all existing property (and any that might thereafter be acquired) south of a line drawn by common consent. The Plan also provided for a cash payment to the Southern group for its share of the publishing interests of the church. Six years after the North refused to recognize any feature of the agreement, Southern Methodists obtained their portion of the book-concern proceeds by a United States Supreme Court decision.[69] However, Justice Samuel Nelson's rendition of the judgment was latitudinarian enough to leave excuse for debate about what had been settled beyond the immediate point at issue. Some proclaimed uncertainty over the ability of Southern Methodists to hold their property if squarely faced by the Church North in legal battle. "The greater part of the . . . property . . . of the . . . Church South could be claimed by the Methodist Episcopal Church and would probably be awarded to it by a[n] impartial court," boasted Edward Thomson a few months before his elevation to the Northern episcopate. If Methodism had been split by what Northerners called an "unauthorized, violent, and unjustifiable secession" rather than by mutual consent as the South claimed, the latter's right to real estate, at least that owned before the division, might be controverted.[70]

Southern pretensions of fear over the security of property heightened in the postwar era as Southerners listened to the mouthings of Northern Methodists. Southern religious periodicals widely reprinted a Northern clergyman's question "whether the Church South [had] a shadow of either legal or moral right to property . . . built . . . before the Church South had an existence." The choleric Fuller advised Northern preachers in the Southern field that if they were in the neighborhood of a Methodist meetinghouse but "denied the use . . . of a suitable place of worship" then "duty lay in the direction of that which is our own." [71] The Northern clergymen thought the stumbling block imposed by the 1854 federal court determination could be surmounted in either of two ways. Some believed that "the decree of Justice Nelson never touched . . . the title of . . . houses built before the Plan of Separation was adopted" but "had respect only to the general funds of . . . the book concern." [72] Other Northern Methodists recommended that the South's great defense, the courts of the nation, be turned against it. "It is of infinite moment . . . that an unjust judgment on the records . . . be forever wiped out, as it unquestionably will be," cried a Northern Methodist journalist. A missionary in the South argued that the Church North ought to regard the decree "with anger and a firm resolve to rip it up." "It would be wrong if we did not strike it down if God gives us the power," he exclaimed. Even the conciliatory *Methodist* mused that "the Supreme Court of the United States has been known to reverse its decisions, and in the present altered temper of the times might do so again." [73]

Church South leaders admitted to a sharp anxiety over the possibility of being hauled into court by Northerners. John Keener, a bishop after 1870, felt sure that Edward Ames "seriously thought of instituting a test case in the courts to check the validity of the [title of] Southern Methodists to their property." Nor did they expect a favorable outcome. Keener asserted that he had no "confidence in the courts of the country from the least to the greatest," especially with "Mr. Chase . . . associating with Bishops Simpson and Ames." William Wightman, a protégé of the beloved Capers and a member of the Southern episcopal class of 1866, was equally skittish of the judiciary. "It would not be safe to allow . . . property to go into courts," he said, "nor would it be safe in the hands of the Chief Justice." [74] This disquietude was sustained more by talk and rumor than by deeds, but Southern Methodists could point out instances in which Northerners had tried to implement their threats. In 1874 Methodist Episcopal affiliates in East Tennessee entered suit for title to two disputed churches, not so much, explained a plaintiff, "for the sake of the particular property, as to rectify the unjust and damaging decree of [Justice Nelson] through review by the present Supreme Court." [75]

With the purpose of precluding all such legal contention over realty, Southern Methodist prelates insisted that their organization be denominated a legitimately derived successor of the church as it had existed before 1844, for in this recognition of legitimacy was "the title deed to all the Southern Methodist Church property." "So long as there was no . . . authoritative acknowledgment of our legitimacy . . . security forbade fraternal relations," later explained one Southern discussant in the consultations of 1876.[76] Before the Cape May conference convened, the Southern commissioners compacted to agree to an "adjustment of difficulties and establishment of formal fraternity" only on the basis of the Church South's claim "to be a cognate and co-equal section of the original Methodist Episcopal Church of the United States . . . organized in 1784." The legal reliability of the admission to be extracted from the Northern Church was questionable but Methodists of the South thought it would constitute a promise that no forays would be made against their holdings. As Edward Myers said, "We can never feel secure against attempts to deprive us of [property] until that purpose is effectually disavowed." [77]

The conversations of the joint commission extended over a week. That harmony was achieved in view of the earlier personal collisions between delegates and "the questions . . . so interwoven with moral obligations" sounds the depths of the desire to replace the three-decade brawl with something less jarring. After the key demand of the Church South had been granted that "she was no offspring of . . . secession but entitled to a place . . . of equal legitimacy with her twin sister, the Methodist Episcopal Church," the commission members turned to a consideration of the property in dispute between the two denominations. Because each item of real estate was controlled by an autonomous board of trustees, the delegates could arbitrate only in cases which had been specifically referred to them. Of the property contests many fewer than a majority came before the Cape May arbitrators for review, and most of those that were submitted were returned to the petitioners without judgment. For the many individual controversies on which the commission did not reach a decision and the greater number never referred to them, the conference agreed upon rules to guide local officials of the two churches in determining possession.[78] With the points at issue resolved by the delegates so far as they were able, the joint commission was fulsome in praise of "the blended sweetness of fraternal harmony," hailed its work "as uniting . . . the broken cords of affectionate . . . fraternization," and asserted that "these fraternized churches have no further reason for . . . disputes or acrimonious differences." This put a high estimate on the efficaciousness of parliamentary resolutions.[79]

Within the Methodist Episcopal Church, articulate reaction to the Cape May agreement was distributed with some reference to geography. In the North, sentiment generally endorsed the settlement, except for New England and upper New York. *Zion's Herald,* the journal of the New England clergy, was noncommittal in its editorial comment, and waited three weeks to print even an abbreviated account of the proceedings at Cape May. The indifference of the Boston paper, however, was a more subtle manifestation of hostility than that demonstrated by the organ of the northern New York preachers. Save for New England, Methodists of this area were considered the most ungenerous toward the South, and they tried to deserve their reputation. The *Northern Advocate,* spokesman for the middle and northern New York regions, scourged the peace commission because of its ascription "to the origin of the Methodist Episcopal Church, South, anything like legitimacy." "Leading minds . . . will think as they have thought before respecting this dispute," it asserted.[80] The recusancy of the *Advocate's* editor, Orris H. Warren, was caused, said those who knew him, by his belief that the concession made by the North "acknowledged the right of secession, a principle disastrous alike in church and state." The itinerant clergy served by the *Northern Advocate* rallied to support the stand of their paper and to denounce the "sell out" at Cape May. With only one dissent in 113 votes, the preachers of central New York petitioned "the General Con-

ference of 1880 to emphatically disapprove the work of the commissioners." [81]

Clergy and members of the Northern church in the South,
"being on the field," claimed "to know something better than
those who merely theorized" about the accomplishments of the
fraternity council. Among the men of this section discernible
opinion seemed decidedly less favorable than in the North. "We
met the enemy and we surrendered," parodied one unfraternal
Methodist. Although some official gatherings on Southern soil
gave unreserved approval to the Cape May covenant, others
picked apart the pact by sections or else urged the church to
ceremoniously "disapprove the report of the commissioners." [82]
A part of the restiveness found in the Southern extension resulted from a misinterpretation of the decisions reached at Cape
May. Some thought that the agreement amounted to a resuscita-
tion of the 1844 Plan of Separation with its territorial limitations
on the activity of the Northern church. Southern Methodists
blandly encouraged this error. "If the action of the Joint Commission means anything," wrote one of them, "it says to Southern
Methodists in the North, unite with the M. E. Church, and says
to Northern Methodists in the South, unite with the M. E.
Church, South." [83] Members of the Northern organization in the
South did not relish the theory that their church was obliged
to abandon the area and hand over its membership to the tender
mercies of Southern Methodism. "We desire to be understood as
not endorsing fraternity with anybody that . . . questions our
perfect right to occupy these Southern states," announced the
traveling preachers of North Carolina. The Kentucky clergy
used almost the same language to correct the parts of the commission's report which has "been differently interpreted." They
wanted to go on record "as endorsing no fraternity with anybody that questions our right to . . . work in the Southern
states." [84]

Another source of dissatisfaction, however, came from a too-
clear understanding of the decisions and recommendations

emanating from Cape May. Some Northern societies had their claims to meetinghouses adjudicated adversely, and others found their shelters in jeopardy because of the rules for local arbitration adopted by the Joint Commission. In the northern part of Virginia, where the Church South was confirmed in the ownership of property valued at two hundred thousand dollars, Northern Methodists were avowed to be "somewhat disheartened, and in several places temporarily crippled by the action of the commission." [85] From other regions also, came cries of protest. One South Carolina preacher objected to "the taking of property . . . occupied by the M. E. Church . . . and placing the same in the hands of the M. E. Church, South" because it "not only destroys fraternity, but creates an ill feeling toward the mother church." In a single line of a published letter from Louisiana, the property provisions of the Cape May treaty were described as "very bad," "very unjust," and unproductive "of real fraternity." To a Tennessee Methodist, the unequitable disposal of real estate made fraternity "all on one side [and] at our expense." [86] Since the ending of disagreement over land and buildings depended ultimately upon each cell of Methodists, the rank and file expressed their distaste for high-level decisions by prolonged hesitation in complying with the wishes of the church nabobs. Into the middle eighties, if not beyond, the noise of some property quarrels was still audible.[87]

The composite response which greeted the action at Cape May corroborated a priestly axiom that "you cannot legislate men into . . . fraternity any more than you can into religion." [88] Disputation, individual and collective, continued to mar the relations of the Methodisms. "The clash of ideas continues to the present time," wrote a Northern clergyman a decade and a half after "fraternity" had been restored.[89] Nevertheless, the importance of the Joint Commission of 1876 should not be reduced to a cipher. For the first time in thirty years, accredited agents of the opposite denominations used ordered conversations rather than anathemas in an effort to resolve differences. Probably the

Peace Commission was worth less in concrete achievement than as a symbol. "If we ever unite it will be by growing into Union," concluded one clergyman, and Cape May marked a convenient point from which to measure that growth.[90] Northern conciliationists, when they found that they could not hastily force Episcopal Methodism into one mold, professed a willingness to wait because they were sure of an assist from time. "The question of reunion is . . . only a question of time," asserted one protagonist of union. George Crooks, boundlessly optimistic, told opponents of Methodist unity that "the great social and political forces of the country" were on his side. These forces, he said, had "decided that Methodists [were] to be one people." [91] For once a preacher guessed well.

## NOTES

[1] *Christian Advocate,* February 2, 1865.

[2] Superabundant and biased are the correct terms for the literature of this controversy. An introduction to the subject can be had in William W. Sweet, *Methodism in American History* (Cincinnati, 1933) and Barclay, *Early American Methodism,* II. Their respective bibliographies will start the reader along the right path for further exploration.

[3] *Zion's Herald,* July 14, 1865.

[4] Knoxville *Whig,* November 15, 1865.

[5] *Christian Advocate,* February 9, 1865; *Pittsburgh Advocate,* September 30, 1865.

[6] *Western Advocate,* February 22 and July 10, 1865. The advantage of hindsight makes it easy to smile at the optimism of Bishop Clark, but his statement should be judged in the context of the times. Many Southern Methodists were not hopeful about the future until the meeting of their General Conference in 1866.

[7] Quoted in Oliver S. Heckman, "The Penetration of Northern Churches into the South 1860–1880," (PhD Dissertation, Duke U., 1938), 185.

[8] *Christian Advocate,* May 25, 1865; April 25, 1867; *Methodist,* June 17, 1865.

[9] *Christian Advocate,* February 22, 1866; *Methodist,* July 18, 1874; *Southwestern Advocate,* November 6, 1874.

[10] *Christian Advocate,* May 25, 1865; *Methodist,* May 27 and June 17, 1865; *Methodist Review,* XLVII (October, 1865), 636.

[11] *Christian Advocate,* May 25, 1865.

[12] *Ibid.*, April 6, 1865; April 5, 1866. Paradoxical as it was, Crooks, Stevens, and their associates encouraged expansion into the South. Brought up to the likelihood that Southern Methodists would be offended by the presence of Northern missionaries, their only suggestion was that the latter's "efforts be so conducted as to favor a complete . . . restoration of the old unity of the two sections of the denomination." This was indeed a large order. *Methodist*, June 24, 1865.

[13] *Western Advocate*, June 7, 1865.

[14] *Pittsburgh Advocate*, July 1, 1865; *Zion's Herald*, July 12, 1865. Reports of this type obtruded from all Northern Methodist weeklies during the late spring and early summer of 1865.

[15] *Western Advocate*, June 28, 1865; May 23, 1866; *Zion's Herald*, July 12, 1865.

[16] *Ibid.*, May 31, 1865; *Christian Advocate*, June 8, 1865; January 25, 1866.

[17] J. H. Lennin, *TEKEL: The "Non-Political" Church Weighed in the Balance and Found Wanting, or, a Critical Review of the Methodist Episcopal Church South* (Edinburg, Ind., 1871), 14; *Northern Advocate*, January 27, 1876.

[18] *Northwestern Advocate*, May 2, 1866.

[19] *Western Advocate*, June 7, 1865; *Northwestern Advocate*, October 11, 1865; May 2 and August 29, 1866; *Christian Advocate*, June 7, 1866.

[20] Knoxville *Whig*, July 5, 1865; *Christian Advocate*, February 29, 1866.

[21] Fleming, ed., *Documentary History*, II, 233.

[22] *Methodist*, September 1, 1865; October 5, 1867; *Western Advocate*, September 6, 1865.

[23] Price, *Holston Methodism*, V, 37ff; William H. Lewis, *The History of Methodism in Missouri for a Decade of Years from 1860 to 1870* (Nashville, 1890), 64–67.

[24] *Methodist Advocate*, March 24, 1875.

[25] *Pittsburgh Advocate*, February 24, 1866; *Methodist Review*, LIII (October, 1871) 616f; "Journal of the Cape May Conference," MS, (Emory University Library, Atlanta, Georgia)

[26] Knoxville *Whig*, July 23, 1864.

[27] Knoxville *Press and Messenger*, October 29, 1868.

[28] Bishop Ames set the number at 210 churches and 32 parsonages. Ames to Simpson, January 19, 1866, Simpson Papers.

[29] E. S. Janes to Simpson, December 28, 1865; Simpson Diary, 1866; War Department, Office of the Adjutant General, Special Orders No. 24, January 18, 1866, Simpson Papers.

[30] Ames to Simpson, January 2 and January 19, 1866, Simpson Papers.

[31] A reprint of this act dated February 18, 1867, can be found in *Christian Advocate*, April 25, 1867.

[32] This is not merely an inference. A leading Northern clergyman in Virginia, Charles King, bluntly stated, "We secured the insertion of the clause in the new constitution . . . with a view of avoiding expensive law suits." *Methodist Advocate*, May 5, 1869.

[33] Francis N. Thorpe, ed., *The Federal and State Constitutions, Colonial Charters and Other Organic Laws, etc.*, 7 vols. (Washington, 1909) VII, 3847.

[34] *Minutes of the Virginia Annual Conference of the Methodist Episcopal Church, 1870*, p. 14. A convenient discussion of the legal implications of the

church property clause in the Virginia Constitution of 1870 is in Price, *Holston Methodism*, IV, 28ff.

[85] *Southwestern Advocate*, January 1, 1874.

[86] *Report of the Joint Committee on Reconstruction*, 39 Cong., 1 sess. (Washington, 1866), Pt. II, 39, 45; *Western Advocate*, May 22, 1866.

[87] Knoxville *Whig*, January 23, 1867, quoting Jonesboro (Tennessee) *Flag*; *Methodist Advocate*, October 6, 1875.

[88] *Central Advocate*, August 2, 1865; *Western Advocate*, October 4, 1865; *Methodist Advocate*, May 5, 1869.

[89] *Northwestern Advocate*, November 7, 1866; *Methodist Advocate*, April 21, 1869.

[40] *Methodist Advocate*, January 14, 1874.

[41] *Western Advocate*, October 7, 1868.

[42] *Methodist Advocate*, January 5, 1870, quoting *The Church Register*.

[43] *Formal Fraternity Proceedings of the Methodist Episcopal Church and the Methodist Episcopal Church, South* (New York and Nashville, 1876), 4.

[44] New York *Herald*, May 14, 1868.

[45] *Formal Fraternity Proceedings*, 8, 12.

[46] *Journal of the General Conference of the Methodist Episcopal Church, South, 1870*, pp. 196, 200ff.

[47] Knoxville *Whig*, November 24, 1869; *Nashville Advocate*, April 25, 1874; Lennin, *TEKEL*, 43.

[48] *Christian Advocate*, June 8, 1865; *Methodist Advocate*, August 24, 1870.

[49] *Pittsburgh Advocate*, September 30, 1865; *Nashville Advocate*, June 20, 1874.

[50] *Nashville Advocate*, May 30, 1874.

[51] *Zion's Herald*, August 23, 1865; *Methodist Advocate*, September 14, 1870, quoting *Christian Observer*.

[52] *Christian Advocate*, April 15, 1875.

[53] *Southwestern Advocate*, September 14, 1876, quoting New Orleans *Christian Advocate*.

[54] *Christian Advocate*, February 21, 1867; *Pittsburgh Advocate*, April 20, 1867; *Southwestern Advocate*, May 21, 1874.

[55] *Annual Cyclopedia, 1869*, p. 443.

[56] *Journal of the General Conference of the Methodist Episcopal Church, South, 1874*, p. 496.

[57] *Southern Review*, X (April, 1872), 386.

[58] *Methodist*, June 18, 1870.

[59] *Zion's Herald*, June 11, 1868; *Formal Fraternity Proceedings*, 14–18; *Journal of the General Conference of the Methodist Episcopal Church, South, 1870*, pp. 196–200.

[60] Charles Stearns, *The Black Man of the South and the Rebels* (New York, 1870), 377; *Methodist*, July 18, 1874.

[61] *Journal of the General Conference of the Methodist Episcopal Church, South, 1870*, p. 318.

[62] A Southern pastor wanted to know, "What is that thing called fraternity—in what does it consist, exactly? What is embraced in it?" *Nashville Advocate*, September 5, 1874. The historian is apt to be similarly puzzled. "Fraternity" indicated an official recognition of one Methodist body by another, a thing that

the Northern church had refrained from doing. Among the practical effects of "fraternity" were the exchange of greetings between conferences, co-operation in revivals, and the opening of pulpits and churches to the opposite denomination. Of course, many single instances of co-operation were present before the churches ever formally admitted the fact.

[63] For the official correspondence which preceded the Cape May conference see *Formal Fraternity Proceedings*, 20–56.

[64] The clergymen representing the South were Edward H. Myers of Savannah, Robert K. Hargrove of Nashville, Thomas Finney of St. Louis. The laymen were David Clopton of Montgomery and General Robert Vance of Asheville. Ministerial delegates for the Northern church were John Newman of Washington, D. C., Erasmus Fuller of Atlanta, Ga., and Morris D'C. Crawford of New York. The lay delegates included General Clinton B. Fisk of St. Louis and Enoch Fancher of New York. Myers headed the Southern committee and Fisk was his Northern opposite. For brief biographies of the clerical commissioners and Fancher see *Cyclopedia of Methodism*. Sketches of Fisk and Clopton are in Allen Johnson and Dumas Malone, eds., *Dictionary of American Biography*, 20 vols. and index (New York, 1927–1938). Vance is treated briefly in John P. Arthur, *Western North Carolina, A History* (Raleigh, 1914), 646ff.

[65] *Western Advocate*, September 6, 1876, quoting *Pacific Advocate*.

[66] Edward H. Myers, *Disruption of the Methodist Episcopal Church, 1844–1846 . . . Comprising a Thirty Years History of the Relations of the Two Methodisms* (Nashville and Macon, Ga., 1875).

[67] *Formal Fraternity Proceedings*, 67.

[68] Solomon L. M. Conser, *Virginia After the War. An Account of Three Years Experience in Reorganizing the Methodist Episcopal Church in Virginia at the Close of the Civil War* (Indianapolis, 1891), 25.

[69] William Smith *et al. vs.* Leroy Swormstedt *et al.*, 16 *Howard*, 288.

[70] *Christian Advocate*, February 11, 1864.

[71] *Methodist Advocate*, April 21, 1869; *Nashville Advocate*, September 4, 1869, quoting *Methodist Advocate*.

[72] *Central Advocate*, September 6, 1865; *Western Advocate*, February 22, 1865.

[73] *Ibid.*, December 6, 1865; *Christian Advocate*, October 3, 1867; *Methodist*, July 18, 1874.

[74] Knoxville *Whig*, May 30, 1866; *Northwestern Advocate*, May 30, 1866.

[75] *Methodist*, January 23 and March 20, 1875.

[76] *Nashville Advocate*, August 22, 1874; *Northern Advocate*, September 14, 1876.

[77] "Journal of the Cape May Conference"; Myers, *Disruption of the Churches*, 199.

[78] These rules recommended that: (1) Where a court had decided title the judgment should immediately be carried out; (2) in the absence of a judicial decree, either the denomination which had a majority of members in its society should be given the edifice; or (3) the contesting congregations should each appoint one arbiter. These two would select a third and the three, by majority vote, would decide ownership. In its address to the churches, the Cape May Commission also suggested that where competing societies were poor in members and wealth they might "compose their differences by uniting in the same communion." This advice was unsweetly received by the Church North in the South.

[79] The most accessible source for the work of the Cape May Conference is *Formal Fraternity Proceedings*, 66–82.

[80] *Northern Advocate*, August 31 and September 7, 1876.

[81] Ibid., October 19, 1876; *Central Advocate*, December 6, 1876.

[82] *Northern Advocate*, September 7, 1876; *Zion's Herald*, October 12, 1876; *Western Advocate*, November 15, 1876.

[83] *Zion's Herald*, September 14, 1876, quoting *Western Methodist* (Memphis).

[84] *Minutes of the North Carolina Annual Conference of the Methodist Episcopal Church, 1876*, p. 16; *Minutes of the Kentucky Annual Conference of the Methodist Episcopal Church, 1877*, p. 15.

[85] Extension Society, *Eleventh Annual Report* (1876), 31.

[86] *Methodist Advocate*, September 13, 1876; *Zion's Herald*, October 12, 1876; *Southwestern Advocate*, November 23, 1876.

[87] *Minutes of the Virginia Annual Conference*, 1884, p. 14; Lewis, *Centenary Souvenir*, XX.

[88] *Minutes of the South Carolina Annual Conference, 1875*, p. 24.

[89] Daniel Stevenson, *The Methodist Episcopal Church in the South* (Cincinnati and New York, 1892), 31.

[90] *Methodist*, June 5, 1874.

[91] *Western Advocate*, February 2, 1870; *Methodist*, June 13, 1874.

# IV

# The Church and the White Folk

Just as rapidly as American patriotism, a hearty love for
the old flag possesses the South, will the Methodist Episcopal Church spread among the white people of the South.
Wherever the eyes of white men dance to see the Star-
Spangled Banner floating in the sky, there will be as many
hearts to bid the Methodist Episcopal Church welcome.

Western Advocate
November 30, 1870

METHODISTS were filled with anticipation that hordes of Southern whites would receive them hospitably. As he looked southward "to fields ripe for the harvest" a preacher predicted that
"millions of white men there will soon learn to love our holy,
benignant, antislavery gospel." [1] The Methodist clergy, like most
of the Northern Protestants, played with the idea that the South
had been duped into war by a scheming oligarchy. The mass
persistence in rebellion was due more to ignorance than to
perverseness. Once the spoiled crust of leadership had been
whittled away, a real work of regeneration could begin among
the white population. For "the lower classes . . . who . . . [were]
bound . . . as effectively as slaves," the war was "as truly a war
for freedom as for the blacks." [2] A Virginian, ready to cast his lot
with the Church North, saw ahead limitless vistas for Northern
Methodism. "When this rebellion ends, a great change will come
over the minds of the masses," he said and promised that his co-
regionalists would be ready for "new light and . . . true principles." [3]

Early tests seemed to prove valid the hypothesis of a "loyal,
conciliatory party" of whites in the South who could not resist
the blandishments of Northern Methodism. The Holston area
initially bespoke a group of people "wise enough to see the

96

changed condition of things" and "pious enough to humble themselves in the presence of lessons so great and impressive." There were additional favorable portents in other parts of the old slave domain. From West Virginia along the border to Missouri, relative pacification brought a steady trickle of white members into the church. The border accessions nowhere approached the large-scale variety except for a bloc of eighteen Kentucky preachers who, in October, 1865, renounced their allegiance to Southern Methodism and petitioned for admission into the Northern church. Throughout the Civil War these Kentucky clergymen had been blatant in their professions of loyalty to the federal government, and their sympathies were kept hot by Northern Methodist espionage. Seizing upon the refusal of the Church South to move decisively in the direction of Methodist unity, this Republican-Unionist faction packed itself off to the North and carried along several hundred laymen.[4] Also in cities of the lower South where the Northern Methodists clung to appropriated churches, they had a respectable enrollment of whites. In several urban areas the temporary suspension of Southern Methodist activity induced natives to attend Northern ceremonies, and often the Southerners had their names entered on the register by missionaries who were not above impressing superiors by padded statistics. These various auguries, modest though they were, kept alive a hope of large inroads among the white population.

However, missionaries who shouldered their way into the Southern states soon added confirmation to dissenting opinions which contended that aside from the border South white converts would be in a distinct minority. "Though conquered, they are as bitter, proud and arrogant as ever," wailed a gospel herald who tried his luck with the whites in Virginia less than a month after Appomattox. A chaplain in Alabama, who combined military duties and missionary work, uttered this pensive plaint from a half-year's experience around Huntsville: "The prejudice of the whites against . . . preachers of the M. E. Church makes

the position of a Methodist preacher a most delicate one." [5]
Rather than a discovery of many "true . . . men in all parts of the
South . . . waiting with anxious . . . prayers for the advent of the
old church" religious emissaries encountered "bitter, unrepentant rebels" with "a settled determination . . . to prevent the
growth of all national institutions, whether civil or ecclesiastical." Some Northern Methodists, slow to believe that they were
mistaken, pleaded with the fairer-hued folk of the South "for
a bold outspoken course," because "the opportune hour [was]
passing." But others, in view of the reluctance of Southerners
"to confess themselves wrong or to deplore their folly," proceeded to the less welcome but more solid conclusion that
Northern Methodism had "but a faint prospect of success with
the native white population." [6]

The popularity of the Northern church among the Southern
whites, both geographically and socially, was roughly in inverse
ratio to the earlier prevalence of slavery. In those regions and
among the level of the white population classified as nonslaveholding, the Methodism of the North gathered most of its recruits. The observation of one preacher that the Northern
organization held "none of the Negro aristocracy" is not open
to debate, although the church may not have been "better for
the fact." Exempting the states which remained with the Union,[7]
the warmest response from Southern whites was found in or
close to the Appalachian ranges and valleys which thrust from
the northeast in a southwesterly direction. According to a denominational census of 1881, thirty-three thousand of the fifty-
three thousand whites adhering to Northern Methodism in the
middle and lower South came from eastern Tennessee, far western Virginia and North Carolina, northern Georgia and northeastern Alabama. The Virginia-North Carolina Piedmont and
middle Tennessee accounted for another ten thousand. About
half of the remainder were settled along the northern and western fringes of Arkansas and the corner of Texas which abutted.
In addition, a smattering of white Northern Methodists lived in

east central Texas, generally within a hundred mile radius of Austin.[8]

Other islands of Northern Methodists existed in the larger cities of the South. The original strength of these usually depended upon Northern military personnel, civilian officials, merchants who had taken residence in the South, and a few native adventurers. A tourist who attended Sunday services at a Methodist Episcopal Church in New Orleans in 1868 saw in the audience the "Governor of the State, the mayor of the city, two generals ... a state Supreme Court judge and lesser luminaries." The board of trustees of the Nashville church, in the middle months of 1866, included the assistant commissioner of the Freedman's Bureau, the provost marshal of Tennessee and Kentucky, four merchants from the North, and the local postmaster.[9] The Northern Methodist society in Richmond was organized through the insistence of Governor Francis Pierpont and his wife and had among its other prominent attendants General and Mrs. E. R. S. Canby who were anxious for "a church where loyal people could feel they were among friends." In Virginia, the Richmond congregation and also those at Norfolk and Portsmouth were "largely made up of Northern people who [had] settled in the state since the war."[10]     *79097*

Methodists in the execution of their Southern strategy did not overlook "the honest Germans." During the *ante bellum* era the Northern church's greatest successes among non-British peoples had been scored amidst these immigrants. The German material was not remarkably abundant in the Confederate states, but the Northern Methodists counted more converts from this element at the end of Reconstruction than did their Southern rivals.[11] In some places Southern Methodism was left with only the husk of its prewar German membership. Two-thirds of the fifteen hundred German Methodists in Texas in 1876 were tied to the Northern branch and they composed the main body of the South German conference. In New Orleans, at the same time, the vitality of three Northern Methodist congregations con-

trasted sharply with the feeble state of Southern Methodist
work among Germans of the area, and the Southerners were
likewise in arrears in the courting of the German folk around
Nashville.[12] The Northern church, taught by experience that
English-speaking missionaries were coolly welcomed by the
Germans, sought to adapt its missionary methods to the tastes
of the potential converts. German preachers who had been dispatched from Louisville and St. Louis were largely responsible
for Northern Methodist gains in the farther Southwest. The
Northern denomination also made desultory attempts to entice
Germans in the eastern portions of the South. In early 1869,
German-speaking clergymen set out from Louisville and Nashville, respectively, to ferret out opportunities in Chattanooga,
Knoxville, Atlanta, Charleston, Savannah, and other cities in
the southeastern quadrant, but their explorations were without
tangible results. Despite a report of "favorable conditions" no
societies, except a transient one at Knoxville, ever were organized.[13]

The regional concentration of Northern membership in the
South authenticated a Methodist's comment that "our missionaries are successful just in proportion to the loyalty of the people." [14] In the districts (although not with all the population
therein) where the idea of a Southern nation had been met with
the least tenderness, the Church North gleaned its greatest
following of whites. Political antipathy in these areas spilled over
into a religious uprising against a sect which "went into the
rebellion . . . chafing and fretting and boasting and blowing that
the South would achieve her independence." William Brownlow's "religious patriotism" was outraged by the "canting hypocrites" of "a bastard Methodism" who would "propose to preach
to Union men the religion of Jesus Christ." [15] Southern Unionists
took no pains to shield the link between their political prejudices
and ecclesiastical preferences. The invitation to the convention
which met in Knoxville during July, 1864, to decide on secession
from the Church South was addressed to "all *loyal* Methodist

ministers and no others." [16] Before the Northern Methodist authorities took the revolutionists in East Tennessee in tow, the latter labeled themselves "the United States Church." A trifling movement in northeastern Alabama, which later merged with the Northern church, called itself by the same name and made "loyalty to the government . . . one of the tests of membership." The most accurate testimony a Methodist missionary in Alabama subsequently gave to a Congressional committee was the assertion that the Northerners "found the . . . loyal feeling . . . to a very great extent [and] did not create the necessity or demand [but] simply supplied it." [17]

Unionists of the South, by precept and example, winnowed the "treasonable and rebellious" chaff from their ranks before the Church North bestowed upon them formal organization. However, as the Southerners who sympathized with Northern Methodism had sifted others, so were they subjected to the same process. The Northern General Conference of 1864 wrote into the Discipline a provision that clergymen enlisted on Southern soil must "give satisfactory assurances . . . of their loyalty to the national government and hearty approval of the anti-slavery doctrine of [the] church." [18] That these prerequisites for entry into the pastorate were eminently political, Methodists denied because it was impossible in a season of stress to "distinguish between moral and political offenses." "We refuse the holy eucharist to liars and thieves, drunkards and adulterers," cried one Northern pastor. "What of men guilty of treason?" The conclusion was inescapable. Those who had been exposed to the contagion of "rebellion and slavery" were not to be invited into communion until they could come with "heart, head, and hands cleansed." "Let there be no door of entrance into our ministry except upon an open and honest renunciation of slavery and secession . . . and a declared acceptance of . . . the laws and constitution of the country," insisted one opinion maker. This screening technique, the ministerial force explained, guaranteed that no Southerners would take "refuge behind the pulpit and hurl . . . poisonous shafts at the heart of the Republic from among the vessels of the communion table." [19] To a church which believed that national unity was to be a major result of its expansion, it was indispensable to sink the Southern anchor in firm bottom.

Although the clause on slavery and loyalty was quietly dropped from the Discipline in 1868, prior to that time the restrictions were not allowed to lie inert. In every conference organized in the South before 1868, the sureties of orthodoxy were regularly required and faithfully given. The Southern abolitionists and Confederate-haters had their testimony duly recorded, and those who had endorsed slavery and supported the Southern side of the contest were required to confess "that they had gone astray, and had sinned grievously." [20] Most of the contrite probably arrived at their new beliefs through a peaceful evolution of ideas, but a few intimately revealed that their changed opinions came with the profoundness of a revival conversion. A Virginian, with a "mind . . . nearly unbalanced from brooding morbidly over his past" put a foot on the path to reclamation by crying from his anguish, "Brother . . . I have sinned against the Holy Ghost . . . I voted for secession!" More protracted was the wracking experience of John Caldwell, who wrote his name large on the annals of political and ecclesiastical reconstruction in Georgia. One day his "feelings were wrought upon with greater intensity than any previous day." He "spent a night of wakefulness and prayer, searching [his] heart" and "besought God's forgiveness for the part [he] had taken in . . . the war." Out of the "night of agony and penitence" Caldwell "received new light and life from above . . . and formed a resolution . . . to speak plainly to the consciences of the people on . . . the evils of slavery." [21]

The Church North never outlined a specific procedure for receiving Southern laymen into fellowship, and therefore the levying of political exactions depended upon the attitude of the individual pastor and his congregation. The charge that

Northern Methodist preachers opened their services with the malediction that "this is a loyal church and rebels are not wanted here" was rebutted by the shot that "rebels against God and their government are proper subjects for prayer and intercession." [22] Occasional preachers did instruct the laity to be politically correct before entering the sanctuary. A Methodist missionary bluntly told an Alabama audience, "If there is any man who is a secessionist, or in any way inimical in his feelings toward the United States Government, he ought not to join this church." [23] Nevertheless, since most students of the Southern scene recognized that the Methodist churches were "strictly partisan everywhere," and few congregations would sit under a man "who might differ from them in political sentiment," it was not necessary to probe too deeply into the politics of the laity. The Northern church was distinctively the church "for the radically loyal" and, by reputation, ferociously intolerant of either minister or member with "two drops of rebel blood in him." [24]

Southern whites who had come back to the church of the North "penitent and confessing" often brought "works meet for repentance" which they placed on exhibition. At a session of the Kentucky conference in 1866 "patriotism and religion got mixed up most thoroughly and patriotism appeared the more refreshing as it gushed forth from a heart full of religion." In the early years of Reconstruction in Virginia, amidst the joyous shouts arising from a revival meeting, was heard, "Glory, Glory to God . . . I always believed secession was wrong and the Old Church was right." [25] The cornerstone of a church for whites in Shelbyville, Tennessee, contained an American flag, Brownlow's *Whig* and the Constitution of the United States, while in the foundation of another structure at Knoxville was placed a "Life of Abraham Lincoln," "copies of the military Reconstruction Bill," "the Knoxville paper," and "a photo of Governor Brownlow." This, slyly murmured a Methodist, "seemed very political to our secession friends, but to us it was religion in one of its higher manifestations." [26] The premium put on right principles obtrudes from the pages of ministerial obituaries. "He was a true lover of his country, which . . . was the object of his veneration," read one memorial. A second preacher, perhaps unusual in that he "suffered a small degree of mental aberration," was wholly normal in his "undeviating . . . loyalty to the Government of the United States." [27]

The positive attractions of Northern Methodism, however, were sometimes little more decisive in recruiting Southern whites than the centrifugal pressures exerted by the Southern church. Admiration for one Methodism was indissolubly mixed with repugnance for another. "I would rather live and die out of the church . . . than to be in connection with the Church South," stormed one Tennessean.[28] This high bitterness nourished upon memories of the political inquisitions to which Unionists in the Southern states had been subjected by religious authorities. In the war years the Methodists of the South vied with those of the North in guarding against outbreaks of political disaffection. The Holston Annual Conference of the Southern church during 1862, 1863, and 1864 saw thirty-five separate indictments against preachers for deviation in their loyalty to the Confederacy. The trials eventuated in eight expulsions from the conference and one suspension. The outlawed preachers and many of those accused later slipped over into Northern Methodisms.[29] In several other states the summary handling of Southern Methodist pastors by their fellows lent an impulse to the trend toward the Church North. James Postell, of South Carolina, was left without an appointment by his bishop, whereupon Postell migrated to north-central North Carolina and founded the first permanent Northern Methodist societies in the state. Two of the founders of the "United States Church" in Alabama previously had been subjected to Southern Methodist censure; one was expelled, and one demoted to a lesser station. John Caldwell's excuse for a change of church relations was a demotion from his Newnan, Georgia, pastorate to an "obscure section . . . filled with ruffians, outlaws, and murderers." Whatever prompted the disciplinary measures taken in South Carolina, Alabama, and Georgia, all of them, like the visitations in East Tennessee, fell on men who had become rabidly Unionist.[30]

Northerners generally were quiet about other motives that decided Southern white clergymen to transfer to their denomination, but adversaries furnished additional explanations. Doubtlessly, a portion of the renegades were "broken down and soured men . . . discontented . . . and not appreciated," who hoped for an improvement in fortune from the change of environment. With greatest regularity, however, Southern Methodists complained that "salary was the main inducement" for treason against their church. The "notorious fact that generous offers from a full treasury were made to needy parsons" was dinned until it became uncritically accepted. To one layman a falling rate of pulpit exchanges signified that the Northern church had "secured about all the . . . Southern Methodists who went up to the highest bidder." [31] So common was the supposition of a "slush" fund to tempt clergymen that in the Southwest the pastors who went over to the Church North won the appellation of "Greenback Preachers." [32] Northern Methodists seldom validated these scurrilous rumors by publicizing the financial arrangements made with their clerical proselytes. Few were as candid as a high official of the Missionary Society who bared his conviction that unworthy men had been persuaded into the Northern ministry "because they imagined they had a . . . treasury behind them which would give them a . . . support." [33]

While Southern churchmen wrathfully rebuked the Northern descent on their pastorate, they denied that their church had been weakened by loss of the captives. One unregenerated Methodist thought that the Northern church acted the part of "a good smut machine to cleanse the Southern church." The ministerial apostates, it was said, were "not men of mark" and had won "positions in the M. E. Church they never could have obtained in the Southern church." [34] These strictures intentionally ignored the great body of turncoats with average abilities and the few of outstanding talent, but Wesleyans belonging to the Northern family often concurred in the view that "wet logs" had been "rolled out on them." Northern prelates realized that the church could not be too discriminating in the caliber of its clergymen during the first years of the tenure in the South. Bishop Clark warned missionary superintendents against demanding anything of preachers, white or Negro, beyond the very minimum set down by the Discipline. "We shall . . . have to admit some whose attainments would hardly win admission with our older conferences," [35] advised Clark. This compromise with expediency produced results which were severely censured in Northern quarters. Few, if any, condemnations of the white pastorate in the South, spoken by Southern Methodists, ever equalled the scalding appraisals put forward by preachers who themselves were affiliated with the Church North. "Money-grabbers, office-seekers, rum suckers, and hypocrites—who . . . sought . . . to replenish their coffers" ran one description of a parcel of clerics enrolled immediately after the war. A fastidious spectator at the Alabama conference lampooned its white members as "an ignorant, shiftless, incompetent class" while a Kentuckian complained that pulpits in his state were crowded with "third- and fourth-rate preachers . . . and . . . men of questionable clerical dignity." The modest endowments of many white clerics were sharply pointed up by an anecdote which had its locale in eastern Kentucky. There, a parson stilled the doubts of parishioners about his doctrinal soundness by remarking, "I am too ignorant to lead you astray." [36]

The animadversions on the white converts broadened to include the laity. From his editorial sanctuary, Edward Myers scoffed that "the Northern church in its Southern work is confined almost exclusively to . . . the most ignorant portion of the whites." [37] Myers' opinion was not greatly at variance with the observations of some Northern missionaries. The first Northern

agent in eastern Tennessee, after test samplings, said that because the "rich were rebels" he had been heard only by the
"poor" and "ignorant." "The people sympathizing with us are
very poor; the wealthy are very hostile," lamented a Methodist
in Virginia, and a North Carolina evangelist wrote that the only
whites accessible to him were of "the poorest class." Methodist
societies in northern and western Arkansas were likewise pronounced notably deficient in "principal property holders [and]
business men." [38] These individual statements, however, will not
support high-flying generalizations about the comparative social
strata to which the different Methodisms appealed. "Leading,
wealthy Southern white Methodists" were scarce in the
Northern church, but neither were they abundant in the territories where Northern Methodism penetrated deeply into the
white population. Each denomination in the Appalachian country drew its strength from the yeomen and mountaineers who
peopled the region. One traveler characterized the converts to
the Northern gospel in eastern Tennessee as "poor but comfortably living farmers," and his description also fitted the Methodists of the area who communed with the Church South.[39]

Methodists expected that their services would be needed not
only by the native white population but by the Northern immigrants who settled in the South. This movement along longi-
tudinal lines, many guessed, would swell to imposing proportions, and ecclesiasts therefore urged the church "to go along
with these men, finding them pastors, building them churches
. . . teaching them the duties of citizenship and the . . . blessings
of Christianity." [40] But churchmen did not supinely wait for
the southward-flowing tide to set in and bear their organization
with it. Instead, they became vigorous propagandists of emigration. In the dawn of peace, many Methodist spokesmen looked
upon the transplantation of Northerners as a means of rejuvenat-
ing the South and welding together the nation. Other champions
of migration acted from more obscure motives without being
less enthusiastic about the idea. When the church began to put

down roots in the South, Northern Methodists on that new frontier assumed the primary responsibility for exhorting the North to spray its citizens over the warmer latitudes. From Tennessee, Alabama, and Georgia, where the white membership was concentrated, came a flood of appeals for Northern residents. Some were directed only "to earnest religious men and women" but more asked for "mechanics, farmers and capitalists [to] put things in motion and develop the sunny South." The latter were informed that "the resources of the South [were] almost without limit" and that "no country on the globe . . . [had] greater natural advantages." Everyone was promised the benefits of a "salubrious and healthy climate" and "scenery grand and picturesque." [41] At first, this locally-sponsored publicity was confined to correspondence, conversation, and articles published in Northern journals, but with the location of the *Methodist Advocate* at Atlanta in 1869, the South had a capable organ of its own. And Editor Fuller, unco-operative as he was with some schemes of Northern members in the Southern states, completely agreed with this one. Fuller was industrious in inviting and answering inquiries about the region, penning propaganda and imploring the periodicals with which he exchanged "to direct the attention of the public to the advantages the South has to offer." [42]

The most earnest Methodist efforts to attract Northerners, however, issued from Missouri. Intended and unintended advertisements to lure immigrants to the state began to cram the columns of church journals many months before Appomattox. The solicitations from Missouri matched those from the lower South in promiscuously aiming at the moral and corporeal senses. One Missourian asked for "a host of good Methodists to come . . . and . . . dry up every grog shop and shut up every billiard shop, and stop the mouths of profanity, that are so plentiful hereabouts." [43] More neglected to mention chinks in the state's moral armor, and simply put in a request for "farmers, mechanics, laborers and school teachers," all of whom would "find ample space in which to work, and full remuneration for their labor." Methodist correspondents sometimes stooped to language to tempt the sensual man that does credit to modern advertising. Missouri, according to one blurb, had these exceptional advantages: "healthy," "soil unsurpassed in the world," "grass . . . equal to Kentucky," "cheap transportation," "much timber," "coal of good quality," "water [a]plenty," "short winters," "early springs," "pleasant summers," "beautiful . . . autumns," "kind, intelligent, peaceable citizens," and "superior educational facilities." [44] To forestall the dissipation of Methodist strength by random settlement, Missouri clergymen commonly urged that church members migrate collectively. "Emigration by colonies, bringing neighbors, church and ministers along is the true policy," was the advice given to prospective settlers by a St. Louis Methodist.[45]

The anxiousness to stimulate the population flow to Missouri quickly bloomed into organized forms. A group of Methodist clergymen and laymen met in St. Louis in June, 1865, to consult on measures for building up their church in the state. This conference dealt primarily with the problem of procuring suitable teachers and preachers for the expanding Methodist membership in Missouri. It voted the establishment of an agency to procure the needed types of professional people from outside the state and elected Benjamin F. Crary, editor of the *Central Christian Advocate*, to double as publicity director and enlistment officer.[46] Soon thereafter a much more ambitious scheme took shape at the opposite end of Missouri. During January, 1866, Methodists around Kansas City, impressed by "the large number of letters of inquiry," founded the *Missouri Methodist Board of Immigration* "to aid in disseminating such information as will be interesting to . . . members in the East who desire to come to Missouri." A full roster of officers was named, and subordinate boards were to be established in each county. The business of the local units was to harvest information on economic and social life in their respective areas and forward it to the parent bureau for condensation and publication.[47] Although the agitation of the St. Louis and Kansas City groups was only one of the complex of forces working for immigration, the Methodist clerical and lay population in Missouri rapidly increased. Within a year of the war's end, sixty-five new preachers had been gathered "from all parts of the nation," and in 1867 the white lay members of the church were nearly thrice as numerous as they had been in 1865.[48]

In no other state of the South did Northern Methodists profit to any extent from an influx of newcomers, for the folk movements of Americans continued to run along east-west lines. Furthermore, the Church North, outside the highland region, failed to retain the allegiance of many of its members who moved to the South. Preachers of the Northern connection criticized it as "disparaging to Christianity," but laymen persistently changed their Methodism with their residences. The pastor of a Southern Methodist church in New Orleans declared that he had taken into his congregation "enough members of the Methodist Episcopal Church to have made the [Northern] church a strong organization." These converted immigrants, he contentedly purred, were "some of the largest contributors." [49] The New Orleans parson ascribed his success to "kindness" but, Northern preachers doubted that all their lost constituents had fallen into this trap. A reporter in Memphis asserted that Southern Methodists never attached "South" to the listing of their churches in city directories, and that many strangers had "been hoodwinked in this way." Another asserted that Methodist Episcopal church houses were neither as conveniently located nor as commodious as the edifices owned by the Southern wing. But these statements paled beside the allegation that Northerners cast off their earlier religious affiliation "to secure business or social standing." From widely separated areas came mourning over "our friends . . . who come to the South and ignore their church relations . . . lest they may injure their business, or be despised by Southern society." [50] Northern Methodists often charged that the economic and social pressures exerted on their white members where the Church South had an ascendancy were not accidental but outgrowths of a studied plan. Clergymen of the North talked darkly of "proscription," "concealed threat[s] of ostracism," and "merchants . . . on the black list of Southern trades people." A veteran mission worker in New Orleans boldly arraigned Southern religionists for encouraging boycotts against entrepreneurs who communed with Northern denominations. "Southern churches," he said, "play upon the selfishness of [business men] . . . by efforts to persuade them that if they expect patronage they must attend unquestioned Southern churches." Nor did the writer omit the note that such tactics "succeeded." [51]

These accusations may have been manufactured from faulty intelligence, but laymen coming into the South as permanent residents inevitably felt the influences which played about them. Without embarrassment, one uprooted Northerner divulged how the prejudices confronting him affected his thinking. "I am urged every day to join . . . the church . . . South. I like to be social . . . I have frequently thought I had better . . . join in the . . . ranks and get back . . . my respectability . . . as I now stand they look upon me as an alien." [52] The forces compelling religious conformity in the Southern regions, no matter whether incidental or planned, not only siphoned off Northern strength but also cut down conversions among the native whites. Missionaries, in extenuation of their small successes, usually advanced the opinion that "many would join our church in this country, but they fear proscription." The Church South, once it had been revived, congealed into such a powerful front that sympathizers with the "Mother Methodism" were "afraid to open their mouths . . . or . . . extend any courtesies." [53] The "weak-kneed spineless souls" who remained fastened to Southern Methodism despite a reported conviction to the contrary were motivated by something more weighty than the simple "fear of being called by an odious appellation." Fidelity to a church with the suffix "South" was enforced in most Southern communities as a basal obligation for the locally-born white. For a Southerner to renounce a denomination bound up with a particularistic culture for one to which the South traced many of her ills meant a divorce with the past, with neighbors, and often with family. "Smiles," "popular recognition," and a sense of belonging outweighed, in the minds of numerous whites generously disposed toward the North, the impropriety of religious association "with the vilest secessionists." [54]

Methodists who had been colonized in the South often experienced the mortification of being more grossly traduced by native proselytes of the Church North than by announced enemies. Notwithstanding Bishop Clark's belief that "men from the North and from the South have met . . . and found that they were brethren," the mixing of dissimilar Northern and Southern elements in one denomination resulted in an unstable compound. Differences of taste and clashes of ambition, especially marked among the clergy, disfigured Methodism's great experiment in brotherhood and caused emotions to run over restraining barriers. "I . . . stand upon my lifetime work among the people . . . who have known me personally . . . and bid defiance to all . . . prowlers who have left their . . . native country . . . because the people had no further use for such scoundrels," roared a locally-reared Tennessean at the "exotics" of his church.[55] The appearance of what were inelegantly labeled "Negro-squeezing preachers" of abolitionist bent often violated Southern racial antipathies. An East Tennessee layman whose keenest sensibilities had been bruised raged, "I hope that our circuit will be freed from Northern men . . . who say they are willing to sit down and eat at a common table . . . with Negroes." Political rivalries between the old settlers and newcomers also tore at intrachurch harmony. In nearly every Southern state the unity of the Republican party was strained by nativist protests against carpetbag domination, and the Northern preachers who dabbled in politics frequently were caught in the unrest.[56]

The resentment of homegrown Methodists, however, flared up most often at their measly allotment of ecclesiastical spoils. The princes of the Church North earlier had been cautioned that the Southern Unionists were "particularly sensitive in regard to outside interference" and wanted their own men to "lead in the [new] organization." But the bosses of Northern Methodism, reportedly because of "a want of talent and preaching abilities" among the Southerners, stocked the better positions with Northern transfers. This practice engendered the "envy and suspicion of the native white brethren." [57] "Heart-burnings and dissatisfactions" at the arrival of "special transfers" to fill administrative vacancies and the lusher pulpits were continuing features of Southern conference sessions through the reconstruction period. A Missourian ventilated the prevalent dissatisfaction by whining that the "men who . . . ventured their lives for the cause [were] forgotten" while "raw recruits . . . occupied secure and comfortable quarters." Maryland malcontents in 1866 tried to force through their conference a remonstrance against the importation of Northern preachers, but the proposal was sidetracked after "an exciting debate." One Tennessean who returned to Southern Methodism because "the stations and presiding elders' districts were filled entirely by men who came from the North" compared the Northern church's policy "to carpetbag rule in the state." [58]

But tense as relations between them sometimes grew, Northerners and Southerners combined their energies to build up Methodist Episcopal institutions. The motif of the centenary year of American Methodism (1866) was an emphasis on education, and the church of the whites in the South, within its modest limits, entered into the spirit of the day. By a fortuitous juncture of circumstances, the Northern Methodist Holston conference during the hundredth anniversary of the church became the owner of a physical plant at Athens, Tennessee, adequate for the establishment of a seat of learning.[59] Though the school began as an academy, it emulated the tapeworm in the industrious addition of segments, and soon Methodists of the Church North were boasting of their "Loyal College . . . true to science, country, morality and religion." From this station the institution climbed to greater heights by the incorporation of law and theological faculties and had its exalted rank recognized in a charter from the state legislature which conferred the name of "East Tennessee Wesleyan University." [60] However, innuendoes circulated that East Tennessee Wesleyan was more shadow than reality. Academic activity was concentrated in a three-story brick building which also served as an administration center, a dormitory, and a refectory. The quality of instruction was officially placed at a level "as high and as thorough as any other literary institution in the land" but incurable iconoclasts contended that the intellectual offerings were akin to those of "a good village academy." Even Northern Methodists confessed to "a single drawback" in the "financial department." This shortcoming was blamed on the failure of laymen "to contribute money or students." [61] Since attempts to augment the enrollment and endowment of East Tennessee Wesleyan were handicapped by the school's distinctively local reputation, churchmen inferred that a prosperous institution of higher learning for whites needed the pooled resources of the whole Northern Methodist population in the South. Into the imagination of church people the design of a regionwide university began to scratch its way, and this ambition was goaded on by the competitive instinct, for the Central University of the Methodist Episcopal Church South scheduled its opening at Nashville for 1872.

The initial organized gesture for a central Methodist university was made in September, 1872, by the Knoxville Educational Convention, an informal assembly of Methodist clergymen, teachers, and laymen from Tennessee, Alabama, and Georgia. It recommended the appointment of a joint committee by the annual conferences of the South to "agree upon, locate, name, and procure a charter for . . . an institution" which would be the jewel of the schools for whites.[62] The Holston conference snapped up the suggestion and sent beseeching letters to other areas with a sizable population of white Methodists. Responding to the stimulus, representatives from eastern and central Tennessee, Alabama, and Georgia met in Chattanooga in January, 1873, and founded a committee first to locate the institution and then to get it launched. A hot race ensued among East Tennessee communities to win the prize, with Knoxville, Chattanooga, and Athens always in the lead. Because "such an institution would bring money into any place" Methodists were not bashful about asking for reciprocal treatment and intimated to the petitioning sites that the consideration given to their applications would be in ratio to their respective donations of land and cash. When the decision was announced in May of 1873 it was in favor of Knoxville, whose merchants and bankers had subscribed fifty thousand dollars and forty acres of land. A prayer for corporate status immediately went to state authority and the embryonic institution, at first called Central Methodist, was prechristened Knoxville University.[63] The projected school, with "its land . . . purchased, its trustees elected, its charter secured, . . . [had] everything but money." [64] For this want, Knoxville University was stillborn.

Originally the Methodists hoped to short-circuit the financial problem by the discovery of "some princely minded friend . . . of great educational enterprise, possessed of adequate means." However, even with the bait that the proposed university would "cheerfully change its name whenever any man . . . [would] make a donation sufficiently large to render it desirable," the Methodists failed to catch a Vanderbilt or a Peabody.[65] They were then compelled to gamble on the aggregate of smaller contributions, but ran into an ambush of ill fortune. Whites in the seaboard states and in the transappalachian border conferences of the South, vexed at the site of the projected school, stood sullenly oblivious to the pleas for funds. The killing blow fell with the business depression of 1873. The Knoxville subscribers and others defaulted on their commitments, and the expectations which had been placed in a collection to be taken during the centennial year of American Independence were disappointed. East Tennessee Wesleyan, until the middle of the next decade, remained the only Northern Methodist school "of high grade" for whites in all the broad expanses of the South.[66]

The university at Knoxville was intended as the capstone of an educational structure for white Methodists which rested on seminaries and academies as numerous "as territory and population may demand." A few of these "university feeders" had been established several years before the Knoxville enterprise began to mature, to give the rudiments of education to a clergy "suffering incurably for want of educated ministers."[67] When the movement for a central university gained headway, it carried with it a dilated enthusiasm for preparatory schools. "Each annual conference connected with our church in the South needs a seminary and should move in that direction at once," said a Methodist educator in 1873.[68] Despite the prevailing business dislocation, Methodists reacted affirmatively to the educational challenge. The published number of academies for whites in the middle and lower South reached six by 1875, seven in three more years, and continued on a slowly ascending spiral.[69] These seminaries were monotonously unimposing institutions, and often both the faculty and buildings showed fidelity to the injunction "to extemporize." The Alabama Conference Seminary, which may have been below average, was taught by the stationed preacher in a church thirty by forty feet. Inasmuch as the meetinghouse was in a rural area, no rooming or boarding facilities were available near the school, and the students "were living in camps."[70] However, the Northern Methodists who improvised their teaching staffs and shelters generally showed greater wisdom than those who plunged beyond their immediate means. Holston Seminary at New Market, Tennessee, was sophisticated enough to hire professional teachers, and soon found itself in debt to its employees. Members of the Church

North in Georgia purchased a large lot at Ellijay and erected "an elegant . . . brick building . . . supplied with furniture of the latest . . . styles, and many appliances for teaching." Hardly a twelvemonth elapsed before the property was in the throes of foreclosure, a fate from which it was rescued only by outside help. Northern Methodists in North Carolina were more unlucky. Their Annual Conference of 1876 recorded the unhappy end of High Point Seminary in a statement of liabilities and assets. The debits exceeded seven thousand dollars; the credits were "undetermined" and the school had to "be sold at public auction." [71]

The sum of regional plans for white education was judged in 1875 to have brought results "astonishingly meager." The shattering of the Knoxville enterprise, the plight of East Tennessee Wesleyan (which was almost pulled under by debt in 1875) and the floundering condition of the academies convinced Southern adherents that a reasonably efficient educational system for Methodist whites waited on assistance from the North. "It is a well-known fact that one-half of the whites are in a condition in reference to education in which it is . . . as much a Christian duty to aid them as the colored people," concluded a Tennessee observer.[72] Preachers in convocation endorsed the analyses of conditions of destitution and sought Northern help in grappling with the crisis. Arkansas clergymen, worried that "a great many white youths in the South [were] growing up comparatively ignorant," requested Northern subsidies for the location of "at least one institution of learning in each of the conferences of the South and Southwest." Northern Methodists in the Appalachian region were less specific in their appeals, but in 1875 asked that "the next General Conference . . . so adjust the educational . . . machinery of the church as to bestow upon the white schools . . . the . . . material aid which their importance demands." [73]

Although besieged from every side by solicitations, the church moved haltingly to assist educational work in the white conferences. The lone Methodist agency to entertain attentively petitions for aid before 1876 was the Board of Education. This bureau was authorized by the General Conference of 1868 to collect funds for the assistance of "men preparing for the ministry of the . . . church" and for the subsidization of "theological schools . . . universities, colleges, and academies." However, the financial inability of the board to afford a full-time secretary during the first eight years of its life hints at the amount of relief extended to the South.[74] The usual bureaucratic replies to applications for succor contained little more than expressions of sympathy and vacuous promises. A few officials even pompously rebuffed "the nurslings." A director of the Board of Education advised whites in the Southern outposts that "our seminaries have not been usually helped from abroad" and that "our pioneer conferences . . . are but repeating the history of all the older institutions." [75] Southern members were not hushed by the advice to use more "zealous efforts of their own" but the solid South was a political fact several seasons before whites of the section regularly received scraps from the church treasury for the furtherance of their educational programs.

The controversy over education was but one of the indices of stress between the Southern whites and the Northern wing of the church. Living in a minority section of the denomination and being even a minority within that section, Southern whites expostulated against other varieties of ecclesiastical neglect. The Methodist who wailed that "the church in the North has not and does not . . . appreciate either its responsibility or opportunity . . . with the white people . . . in the Southern states," summarized other conclusions extended over many years.[76] A Kentuckian wanted to know, "Where are our bishops . . . why cannot . . . our bishops give us a little of their spare time?" When the royalty of the Methodist Church came to the South, it was observed that their journeys of inspection resembled the "flying visitations of angels." A Georgia preacher who had watched several Northern prelates in action vouched that an official tour amounted to "a run from city to city and a reception or two; an address of welcome from the great to the great." Then "the great man returns home and the world is enlightened by his letters as to the true wants and conditions of the work." [77]

The disinclination of chief administrative officers to cultivate the white vineyard intensively, Southern communicants argued, was also demonstrated by the scarcity of bank drafts from the North for ministerial salaries and church construction. "The church has no right to ask . . . men who are . . . in this work to add to semi-apostolic labors . . . the bitter pangs of . . . penury," said one preacher who felt the pinch more sharply because he had come from a plush Northern pastorate.[78] Always the preferred remedy was "a great enlargement of the church's liberality as dispensed through the church boards." As these funds seemed to flow in a shallow stream and with a slow current, Southerners diligently searched for the fault and detected that it lay with the bishops, secretaries, and boards of managers who did "not fully appreciate the peculiar demands of the Southern field." A convention of white clergymen and laymen convoked at Athens, Tennessee, followed popular opinion in both its diagnosis and curative prescription. The Athens gathering protested that the religious colonies in the South did "not get all proper sympathy and aid from . . . officers," that "the claims of the West are urged at our expense," and menacingly pledged to "speak until we remove these obstructive authorities from their seats, or until they hear our cause." [79]

Whites of the Southern states did not rest their case for more attention upon the dictates of altruism. The "obstructive authorities" who "were not doing their duty to the white people of the South" were imperiling the expansion of Northern Methodism. A virile, self-sufficient organization in the South, said the remonstrants, had to be built on the white part of the population. "A church to be permanent must anchor itself to the soil," argued a Georgian, and this could result only from the formation of "societies among the owners of the soil." If the amelioration of Negroes appealed to the benevolence of the Church North, mundane necessities ought to make it seek after the "landholders and influential citizens." [80] The perceptiveness of this reasoning sometimes won public assent in the North. Daniel Curry, old abolitionist that he was, declared in 1871 that "the question whether or not we . . . effect a lodgment for our church among the ruling classes of the South is . . . one of life or death with us in that region." The alternatives before Northern Methodism, as seen by the cantankerous editor, were "to go forward in that direction or . . . be compelled to retreat from [the] present position." [81] Nevertheless, the main body of Methodism did not admit the bare choices posed by Curry. Throughout most of the Reconstruction era, the North continued to entertain the wistful query "Is nothing to be done for . . . white people?" without a radical alteration of its policies.

## NOTES

[1] *Christian Advocate*, March 14, 1865.

[2] Dunham, *The Attitude of the Northern Clergy*, 203ff; *Central Advocate*, October 18, 1865.

[3] *Christian Advocate*, March 21, 1865.

[4] *Ladies Repository*, XXV (August, 1865), 702; "Journal of the Kentucky Conference, 1866," "Journal of Daniel Stevenson," I, (Typescripts, in the private library of John O. Gross); [A member of the Kentucky Conference] *The Methodist Churches, North and South, An Address to the Members of the M. E. Church and to all Friends of Law, Peace, and Right* (Cincinnati, 1866), 5ff.

[5] *Western Advocate*, May 10, 1865; January 17, 1866.

[6] *Central Advocate*, September 13, 1865; *Christian Advocate*, June 7 and November 22, 1866.

[7] The border states of the South were, of course, the richest in Northern Methodist whites. Maryland, Delaware, West Virginia, Kentucky, and Missouri held 112,798 of them in 1881.

[8] This analysis of the distribution of whites has been correlated from *Minutes of the Annual Conferences, 1881.*

[9] *Christian Advocate*, August 30, 1866, and January 30, 1868.

[10] Ridgaway, *Life of Bishop Janes*, 318; Myrta Avary, *Dixie After the War* (New York, 1906), 108; *Methodist Advocate*, March 16, 1870.

[11] Macum Phelan, *A History of the Expansion of Methodism in Texas, 1867–*

*1902* (Dallas, 1937), 42ff; Paul F. Douglass, *The Story of German Methodism* (New York, Cincinnati, Chicago, 1939), 127ff.

[12] Extension Society, *Tenth Annual Report* (1875), 14; *Eleventh Annual Report* (1876), 23.

[13] *Methodist Advocate*, May 19, 1869; J. A. Klein to Simpson, January 9, 1869, Simpson Papers.

[14] *Central Advocate*, November 7, 1866.

[15] Knoxville *Whig*, September 6, 1865; October 30, 1867.

[16] *Ibid.*, May 24, 1865. Italics in the original.

[17] Price, *Holston Methodism*, IV, 476; Fuller, *An Appeal to the Records*, 217; *Report of the Joint Committee to Inquire into the Condition of Affairs in the Late Insurrectionary States*, 42 Cong., 2 Sess. (13 vols., Washington, 1872), *Alabama*, 126. Hereinafter cited as *Ku Klux Conspiracy*.

[18] *Discipline of the Methodist Episcopal Church, 1864*, p. 85.

[19] *Central Advocate*, April 12, 1865; *Northern Advocate*, June 21, 1865; *Christian Advocate*, June 22, 1865; Knoxville *Whig*, August 23, 1865; *Northwestern Advocate*, August 29, 1866.

[20] *Journal of the General Conference, 1868*, p. 547; *Northwestern Advocate*, June 28, 1865. The Holston conference was a model for subsequent procedures. The native preachers who maintained that they had been neither proslavery nor proconfederate gave the following samples of evidence: William H. Rogers —"I was taught to hate . . . slavery. I was among the first in favor of allegiance to the government." John W. Mann—"As far as slavery is concerned my skirts are clear. I was called 'Lincoln' . . . proscribed and persecuted." Jonathan L. Mann—"I have ever been an original unmitigated simon pure abolitionist . . . for sixteen months I served God and my country in the army." Those whose previous life made them suspect on the critical issues witnessed these statements of contrition: J. N. S. Huffaker took the oath to the Confederacy but admitted that "in this view and course he was mistaken." J. Albert Hyden "had been educated to believe that slavery was . . . right . . . but . . . had come to see differently." However, "he was never suspected of being loyal to the Confederacy." Erastus Rowley "had been a slaveholder . . . but regarded slavery as removed by the war and accepted the fact as a blessing for the whites." Pearne, *Sixty-one Years of Itinerant Life*, 289–92.

[21] Conser, *Virginia After the War*, 31; Caldwell, *Reconstruction of Church and State in Georgia*, 3.

[22] Knoxville *Whig*, April 4, 1866.

[23] *Ku Klux Conspiracy, Alabama*, 758.

[24] *Pittsburgh Advocate*, July 27, 1865; *Northwestern Advocate*, May 30, 1868; *Methodist Advocate*, February 10, 1869.

[25] *Central Advocate*, March 28, 1866; Conser, *Virginia After the War*, 48.

[26] *Western Advocate*, September 19, 1866; July 10, 1867.

[27] *Minutes of the Kentucky Annual Conference, 1868*, pp. 24, 25.

[28] Pearne, *Sixty-one Years of Itinerant Life*, 291–92.

[29] Martin, *Methodism in Holston*, 75–77; Knoxville *Whig*, November 1, 1865.

[30] Missionary Society, *Forty-Eighth Annual Report* (1866), 143–44; *Christian Advocate*, May 21, 1868; Caldwell, *Reconstruction of Church and State in Georgia*, 3–7.

[31] *Nashville Advocate*, September 18, 1869; September 3, 1870; Fuller, *Appeal*

to the Records, 283, quoting *Southern Christian Advocate; Methodist Advocate,*
September 25, 1872, quoting St. Louis *Christian Advocate;* Thomas O. Summers,
ed., *Life and Papers of A. L. P. Green* (Nashville, 1877), 512.

[32] Phelan, *Expansion of Methodism in Texas,* 143.

[33] *Southwestern Advocate,* February 12, 1874.

[34] Summers, ed., *Life of A. L. P. Green,* 512; *Methodist Advocate,* April 17,
1872; *Northwestern Advocate,* September 9, 1874.

[35] Curry, *Life of Clark,* 229.

[36] *Western Advocate,* April 6, 1870; August 28, 1872; *Methodist Advocate,*
April 6, 1870; *Southwestern Advocate,* December 4, 1873.

[37] *Methodist Advocate,* September 11, 1872, quoting *Southern Christian Advocate.*

[38] Calvin Holman to Simpson, February 1, 1864, Simpson Papers; *Central
Advocate,* July 19, 1865; *Western Advocate,* May 17, 1869; Missionary Society,
*Forty-Seventh Annual Report* (1865), 161.

[39] *Southwestern Advocate,* May 7, 1874.

[40] *Western Advocate,* May 31, 1865.

[41] *Methodist,* February 9 and June 1, 1867; *Western Advocate,* January 26,
1870; *Zion's Herald,* February 29, 1872; *Methodist Review,* LX (April, 1878),
234.

[42] *Methodist Advocate,* March 17, 1869.

[43] *Central Advocate,* May 9, 1866.

[44] *Ibid.,* March 1, 1865; May 23 and August 8, 1866.

[45] *Northern Advocate,* July 19, 1865.

[46] The origins of the St. Louis movement can be found in the *Central Advocate,*
June 7, June 21, and August 2, 1865.

[47] *Ibid.,* January 31 and February 7, 1866.

[48] *Western Advocate,* March 28, 1866; *Annual Cyclopedia, 1865,* p. 550; *1867,*
p. 494; *Minutes of the Missouri Annual Conference of the Methodist Episcopal
Church, 1865,* p. 23; *1867,* p. 49.

[49] John Mathews, *Peeps into Life: Autobiography of Rev. John Mathews* (n.p.,
n.d.), 205.

[50] *Methodist Advocate,* March 17, 1869; *Western Advocate,* August 28, 1872;
*Central Advocate,* September 19, 1872.

[51] *Ibid.,* August 23, 1871; *Methodist Advocate,* September 13, 1871; *Northern
Advocate,* June 22, 1876.

[52] *Methodist Advocate,* August 17, 1870.

[53] *Pittsburgh Advocate,* December 1, 1866; *Methodist Advocate,* May 26, 1875.

[54] J. H. Caldwell to Clinton B. Fisk, September 1, 1865, B.R.F.A.L.; *Zion's
Herald,* September 24, 1874; *Northern Advocate,* March 16, 1876.

[55] Knoxville *Press and Messenger,* August 20, 1868; *Methodist Advocate,*
January 6, 1869.

[56] Indianapolis *Journal,* December 31, 1865; *Methodist Advocate,* April 29,
1867; Knoxville *Whig,* April 11, 1869; Knoxville *Press and Messenger,* April 14,
1869.

[57] Joseph Jones to Simpson, February 22, 1864, Simpson Papers; Knoxville
*Whig,* July 23, 1864; November 6, 1867; Nashville *Advocate,* September 10,
1870.

[58] *Northwestern Advocate,* March 29, 1865; *Zion's Herald,* March 7, 1866;

*Methodist,* March 19, 1866; *Nashville Advocate,* September 10, 1870; "Journal of Daniel Stephenson.", I, (Typescript, in the private library of John O. Gross).

[59] Southern Methodists freely alleged chicanery in the transactions surrounding the purchase of this property, but the many mysteries involved in the sale remain buried with the participants. The Southern Methodist Church established a female seminary at Athens before the Civil War and appointed Erastus Rowley, a native of New York, as president. During the war the school became burdened with debts, a large proportion of which were owed to the president of the institution. In 1865, Rowley renounced the Church South and became a preacher in the Northern organization. With the change of religious connection, Rowley instituted suit in chancery court for payment of his claims against the seminary. The judiciary ordered the school property sold for the satisfaction of debtors, and it was purchased by Rowley for a small fraction of its estimated value. Rowley then sold the ground, buildings, and equipment to the Holston conference of the Church North. These weird dealings are traced and interpreted in Knoxville *Whig,* August 1 and October 24, 1866; March 13, 1867; *Nashville Advocate,* September 4, 1869; *Methodist Advocate,* September 2, 1874; Martin, *Methodism in Holston,* 94–97; Price, *Holston Methodism,* IV, 403ff; D. Burt to William P. Carlin, May 14, 1867, B.R.F.A.L.

[60] Knoxville *Whig,* March 27, 1867; *Minutes of the Holston Annual Conference, 1869,* p. 27; *1871,* p. 36.

[61] *Ibid., 1870,* pp. 23, 24; *Nashville Advocate,* May 22, 1869.

[62] *Minutes of the Tennessee Annual Conference of the Methodist Episcopal Church, 1872,* p. 27.

[63] The best source for this educational movement is the files of the *Methodist Advocate,* especially the numbers of February 12, March 26, and April 9, 1873. Also, *Minutes of the Holston Annual Conference, 1873,* pp. 30–33, and *Minutes of the Georgia Annual Conference of the Methodist Episcopal Church, 1873,* p. 27.

[64] *Zion's Herald,* July 16, 1874.

[65] *Methodist Advocate,* April 23 and October 15, 1873.

[66] *Minutes of the Kentucky Annual Conference, 1874,* p. 35; *Minutes of the Holston Annual Conference, 1876,* p. 24ff.

[67] *Ibid., 1871,* p. 24ff; *Methodist Advocate,* October 28, 1874.

[68] *Ibid.,* February 12, 1873.

[69] In 1878, white preparatory schools were found at New Market, Hollow Rock, Tullahoma, and Fullens, all in Tennessee; Collinsville, Ala.; Ellijay, Georgia, and Asheville, N. C. However, these schools faded, re-emerged and combined so bewilderingly that a recitation of their location at a given time means little. *Methodist Review,* LX (April, 1878), 22.

[70] Extension Society, *Tenth Annual Report* (1875), 18.

[71] *Minutes of the Holston Annual Conference, 1875,* p. 25; Hammond, *Methodist Episcopal Church in Georgia,* 134; *Methodist Advocate,* September 20, 1876; *Minutes of the North Carolina Annual Conference, 1876,* p. 21.

[72] *Methodist Advocate,* September 1, 1875.

[73] *Journal of the General Conference, 1876,* p. 197; *Minutes of the Holston Annual Conference, 1875,* p. 33.

[74] *Journal of the General Conference, 1868,* pp. 534ff; *1880,* pp. 629–635.

[75] C. C. Stratton, ed., *Autobiography of Erastus O. Haven* (New York and Cincinnati, 1881), 194.

[76] *Methodist Advocate*, July 7, 1875.

[77] *Western Advocate*, October 7, 1868; *Methodist Review*, LIII (January, 1872), 126; *Methodist Advocate*, May 21, 1873.

[78] *Methodist Review*, LVI (January, 1874), 43–44.

[79] *Proceedings of the Southern Methodist Convention, 1871*, pp. 42, 54.

[80] *Methodist Advocate*, January 10 and April 3, 1872.

[81] *Christian Advocate*, December 15, 1871.

# V

# The Mission to the Africans

There are two Africas. One is beyond the seas,
the other is at our door.

*Ninth Annual Report of*
*The Freedmen's Aid Society*

JOHN NEWMAN, deputed to direct Northern Methodist activity
around New Orleans, climaxed his inaugural sermon in early
1864 with the assertion "that if the Caucasian should reject the
gospel and refuse to fill the churches . . . we turn to the sons of
Africa." [1] No matter whether he intended his descant primarily
for the sprinkling of curious white Southerners in the lower audience room or for the Negroes crowded into the galleries, Newman propounded a stubborn riddle about his church's intentions
in the South. The enigma is composed in one part of the statement that Methodism "was called . . . into the South in behalf
of the oppressed blacks" and in the other of the contention that
"the first call [was] to the whites." During the *ante bellum* period the Methodist Episcopal Church had conducted no energetic campaigns to proselyte Negroes, and official policy toward
the inclusion of colored members, at its best, can be described
as indifferent.[2] Many church folk thought that this bland unconcern for the spiritual welfare of the blacks carried over into
the early days of Reconstruction.

The first missionaries detailed to service in the South were
freely charged with neglecting to seek after colored members.
Methodist agents, so the arraignments ran, "fondled" the whites
"and virtually repelled multitudes of blacks." [3] The accused may
have been instructed "to act as missionaries to the people without respect to color," and by their own choice may have exposed
themselves to censure, but Methodist scouts often said that
administrators had given no advice about the conversion of

Negroes. "When I came . . . I had no instructions to do anything among the colored people," avowed a Methodist representative in western Tennessee, while a worker in the vicinity of Baton Rouge impatiently demanded of his superiors, "What is the church going to do with or for the colored people?" [4] To the negrophile faction of Methodism these omens looked "very like an expedient to get rid of an unwelcome call to duty" by forfeiting the opportunities for Negro converts to the African churches.

The suspicions of proponents of Negro conversion were augmented by remarks from responsible churchmen. John Reid, in the *Western Advocate*, editorially declared that whites and blacks alike were subject to "the inevitable tendency not to amalgamate, but to separate, even in church relations," and he maintained that his sect had "no motive . . . sufficient to stem this tide of African independence." Without the Negroes, commented Reid, Northern Methodism would "be free from . . . perplexing questions." [5] The views of the *Western*, rather than novel, were but an echo of those previously advocated by Samuel Nesbit. Writing from a confidence yet untarnished by experience, the Pittsburgh journalist forcefully enunciated his peculiar program for the religious conquest of the South. About procedure toward the whites, Nesbit unhesitatingly wrote that it was the duty of Northern Methodism to "gather them into the fold . . . educate them [and] evangelize them." He was nearly as emphatic in his attitude toward the recruitment of Negroes. "The gathering of whites and blacks indiscriminately into the same church," the Pittsburgher pronounced "hazardous and dangerous," open "to formidable objections" and a "doubtful experiment." The most convenient (therefore the wisest) policy, according to Nesbit, was to leave the freedmen to be harvested by the African Methodist churches. [6]

To assume, however, that the Church North originally hoped to build the Southern projection on a white base and took up the pursuit of Negroes only after that aspiration was shattered is a myopic interpretation. A large segment of the Northern membership, from the awakening of interest in the South, wanted to attend exclusively to the freedmen; others urged that the Methodist mission be executed without reference to color. Pulled to and fro by conflicting recommendations and poorly briefed on conditions in the South, Methodist officials waited to evolve a policy until the "leadings of Providence" became apparent. Then men and money were sent to assist. Bishop Janes tacitly acknowledged the prelacy's adherence to this line when he said that he and his associates "were watching their opportunities and just . . . as . . . Providence opens . . . the door, we are re-entering and recommencing our pastoral services." [7] In the lower and middle tiers of Southern states, the omens quickly loomed on the time horizon. Missionaries, in the van of Methodism's expansion, resorted to many different phrases to convey the idea that "the colored . . . people [would] form the only material for the M. E. Church as a rule," and their reports resolved the uncertainty and confusion over which color of the Southern population should be the most assiduously pursued. Northern enthusiasm, held back by a barrier of white resentment, flooded into the more accessible channels. As a woman Methodist observed, "It is not only the African who needs uplifting but it is the African alone that can be reached." To win the blacks went about four-fifths of the funds expended on the South during Reconstruction.[8]

Although the colored membership of the Methodist Episcopal Church was much more widely spread over the South than was the white, it also showed an inclination toward spottiness. Almost eighty percent of the fifty-five thousand colored Northern Methodists found in the border South in 1881 lived east of the mountains. At the same time, one hundred four thousand of the one hundred thirty-four thousand Negro communicants in the lower latitudes claimed residence in South Carolina, Georgia, Mississippi, Louisiana and Texas. Crass realists, who condemned the bicolored evangelistic campaign in the South as impractical, discovered support for their arguments in the contrasting geographical distributions of the Negro and white disciples of Northern Methodism. Aside from the border states, only in those sectors of the Southland where the Appalachian ridges flatten out to the east, south, and west did appreciable numbers of Negro and white Methodists live in proximity to each other. Elsewhere, either the blacks were heavily outnumbered or, as more often happened, they constituted an overwhelming majority of the membership. In 1881, the Negro membership of the Church North in the Tennessee uplands was hardly more than ten percent of the Methodist total for the area. At the opposite extreme were Louisiana, Mississippi, and South Carolina. Louisiana reported ninety-nine whites (excluding Germans) contrasted to more than ten thousand blacks and in Mississippi the counts were two hundred seventy-five and twenty-four thousand five hundred, respectively. The most remarkable disparity of all was in South Carolina. The Palmetto state listed about thirty-six thousand Northern Methodist adherents in 1881, and an inconsequential sixty-nine of them were white.[9]

To imaginative churchmen the South was a more accessible Africa, but the host of freedmen were not unfamiliar with the lineaments of Protestant Christianity. The churches of the *ante bellum* South, and Methodism was chief among them, had been important agents of the Negro's slow acculturation. This unforeseen conditioning of the blacks for conquest by the Northern gospel was quickly recognized by responsible ecclesiasts. The Northern General Conference of 1864 ruminated that the Negroes "who have been until recently under the care of the Methodist Episcopal Church, South, will . . . seek a home with some other branch of the Methodist family.[10] What might have been meant as a veiled suggestion was implemented by missionary activity. "It would be an unpardonable error," said a prominent clergyman, "if these . . . colored members belonging to the Southern Methodist Church . . . are not received into our church."[11] Capitalizing on the religious fluidity which prevailed among the Negro population in the flush days of liberation, Northern missionaries organized congregations in wholesale lots out of renegades from Southern Methodism. In a number of major urban communities, the Church South was stripped bare of its colored following. Stark statistics relate an eloquent story. Southern Methodism, which had enumerated a black membership of two hundred eight thousand in an 1860 census, saw that figure melted down to forty-nine thousand within a year after the end of the war.[12] While several denominations profited from the ravishment of the Southern church, Methodists of the North came off with a generous share of the spoils. Lucius Matlack, an abolitionist of much antiquity, belatedly remarked that emissaries of his church had found in the South "thousands and tens of thousands of . . . converted . . . freedmen . . . all ready to [Northern] hands." For "such a preparation of material" Matlack rightly and considerately thanked "the Southern Methodists."[13]

Northern Methodism had solid appeals to the Negro shopping for a denominational home. Not all of these attractions were of a ceremonial or doctrinal nature. Students of the Reconstruction scene regularly commented on the freedman's disposition to choose his religion according to his politics, and the whispered association of the Church North with the political party which paraded under the motto of "justice to the Negro" produced transitory benefits for both organizations. With deadly effect, the rumor got abroad that the Methodist Episcopal Church was "Massa Linkum's church." The governor of Alabama, Robert Lindsay, told congressional inquisitors in 1871 that Negro Methodists in his state were clearly divided along party lines, with Republicans entering the Northern church, Democrats the Southern.[14] Although they attributed the phenomenon to the preaching of "the Gospel principles . . . that underlie all just government and good society," Northern apostles unblushingly acknowledged the uniform political preferences of their black disciples. "The colored people in church fellowship with us are almost wholly Republican," wrote one religionist. A colleague characterized Negro Northern Methodists as "natural Republicans." The Southern church, on the other hand, held "some of the vilest Democratic Negroes in the South." [15]

Northern Methodism's vaunted promise to "stand up as the guardian of the Negroes" was sugared by assurances of immediate equality in ecclesiastical rights. Bracing against the onslaught from the North, the Southern bishops foretold "defections [of Negroes] to churches offering greater social inducements from their adhesion." [16] Representatives of the Church North worked to fulfill the prediction of the Southern episcopal committee. As a corollary to the argument that "freedmen have no right to remain in connection with any church that sympathizes with slavery," Yankee evangelists presented the liberal policies of the Northern organization in sharp relief. Timothy W. Lewis, negotiating in Charleston with freedmen who had assembled to decide on their future church relations countered the pleas of Southern Methodist clergymen "to stay with us in your old places in the galleries" with the declaration that "there will be no galleries in heaven [and] those who are willing to go with a church that makes no distinction as to race or color, follow me." Lewis's valiant effort won him the field.[17] The most effective device for the ingathering of the colored population, many Methodists maintained, was the announcement "that there was no distinction in the Methodist Episcopal churches; that colored people have the same privileges as whites." "The equality of relations enjoyed by black and white was the rallying cry which gathered the people to us," reminisced one missionary veteran of the Southwest. Freedmen who had apostatized to the "Mother Methodism" periodically confirmed the observations of whites. The Methodist Episcopal Church was the "only church for black men," averred one prominent Negro convert, because "it . . . welcomes all Americans, white or colored . . . to the equal enjoyment of its privileges." [18]

The lures dangled before the freedmen, however, often were more tangible than pledges to support programs of civil and religious equality. A Southern Methodist clergyman, quizzed about his church's loss of its Negro communicants, replied with asperity, "We have quit buying niggers; we leave that now for others to do." [19] The intemperance of this utterance should not blot out a fact readily admitted and often regretted by Northern pastors. "Special inducements to persuade . . . by promise of pecuniary . . . advantages, cannot be employed without compromising our own integrity and that of others also," warned one missionary whose experiences in the South had given him new insights into the frailties of mankind. [20] For Negro pastors there were material advantages in connecting themselves with the Northern church. Clergymen, like lower orders of mortals, had to face up to the hard business of caring for the natural man, and the missionary treasury of the Methodist Episcopal Church, although not bloated with money, offered the possibility of a reasonable wage. John Newman, enrolling colored preachers in the Lower Mississippi country, promised the recruits "four hundred dollars per annum." This prospective income, modest as it was, could be matched by few freedmen at any time in the era of national reconstruction. The considerations which led an Arkansas Negro to don the mantle of Northern Methodism were doubly persuasive with less-sophisticated freedmen. After refusing several calls to the ministry because of "a large family to support," the reluctant Arkansan related that his objections wilted when a Methodist Episcopal presiding elder pledged "a salary which . . . would enable me to support my family and educate my children." Partly on the theory that once the head was won the members would follow, colored pastors were most favored with pledges of aid, but congregations, too, were similarly enticed. A society of Negroes at Griffin, Georgia, voted to join the Church North after the solemn oath was heard "that . . . they should have help to build a church, [buy] Sunday School books, and [pay] a teacher." [21]

Methodist agents, in roaming over the South, occasionally took advantage of the freedman's ignorance to swell membership totals. The chicanery of a Northern legate in Huntsville, Alabama, was facilitated by the illiteracy of a Southern Methodist Negro preacher. The representative of the Church North arrived in the city, interviewed the Negro parson, appropriated the membership rolls, and informed the preacher-in-charge that he and his congregation were a part of "the old Methodist Church." When the white trustees of the property confronted the black clergyman with a demand to evacuate the meeting-house because he had changed his Methodism, the deceived parson explained how he had gotten himself and his congregation into jeopardy. "I did not know I had joined a new organization," he said, "and I did not know . . . until this fuss . . . [that] there is a Church North and a Church South." [22] The imperious attitude, demonstrated by the white missionary in this one instance, was often an object of complaint by competitors of Northern Methodism. Northerners were tempted to view the freedmen's fumbling quest for a sectarian haven as an invitation to precipitate action, and their haughtiness in settling the religious affiliation of Negroes was deemed by an African churchman to more closely resemble "Barnwell Rhett with his slaves . . . .than . . . ministers of Christ." [23]

Gentle-souled laymen, unused to the intricacies of ecclesiastical politics, saw "no need for the churches to quarrel over the Negro whom they were trying to elevate," but their admonitions were not always heeded. Denominational rivalry flared in the race to exploit the Southern bonanza. Abreast of the Wesleyan families in outdistancing competitors were the varied breeds of Christians lumped under the head of Baptists. One computation, no more inaccurate than others, had the number of Baptists and Methodists in excess of eight-five percent of the churched population of Negroes. [24] Reciprocally aggressive and opportunistic, these bumptious denominations indulged in duels of varying intensity. Federal bureaucrats, their designs for the freedmen's amelioration foiled by religious strife, vexatiously exclaimed at "the sectarian prejudice which runs so high between . . . the Baptists and the Methodists." [25] The contemporary opinion that sectarianism was more pronounced among blacks than whites is not of proven accuracy, but Methodist missionaries were calloused by stings from faithful Negro Baptists. One crusading Wesleyan who approached too closely to a choleric freedman got the ejaculation, "D-m . . . Methodist preacher . . . Methodist religion ain't no good." "The Methodists ain't to be trusted," avowed another partisan of immersion. "They are a low, mean set and have no authority in the Bible." [26]

Methodist clergymen, however, had long been cutting their pastoral teeth on quarrels with the Baptists, and the bickering over the Negroes merely perpetuated one phase of a historic relationship. Absorbing more Northern Methodist attention was the competition for black proselytes afforded by other Wesleyan families. To the profound humiliation of Northern ecclesiasts, virtually all of this interMethodist rivalry came from the African denominations. The Southern church never exerted itself to keep intact its *ante bellum* monopoly among the Negroes. A declining enrollment and a recognition of the problems involved in adjusting the relations between whites and blacks under the new order of things quickly convinced Southern Methodists that the most workable plan was to cut loose the Negro communicants. Without official sanction, Southern Methodist preachers encouraged the freedmen to enter one of the African denominations and, to reduce the likelihood of their lately-freed parishioners wandering into the Northern fold, white clergymen often went to elaborate lengths to transfer their Negro membership *in toto* to an African church.[27]

For the black folk who had not abandoned Southern Methodism with or without the advice of whites, the General Conference of 1866 mapped out plans. It directed the establishment of separate Quarterly and Annual Conferences for Negroes and when these had matured sufficiently the Southern bishops were instructed to assist the blacks "in organizing a . . . separate jurisdiction for themselves." By 1870, the evolutionary process had advanced far enough to warrant the formation of the Negro adherents into an independent church, and in December of that year the fledgling was launched on its career at Jackson, Tennessee.[28] The new denomination, identical in doctrine and discipline with Southern Methodism, was popularly known as "de chu'ch set up by de white foke" but legally named the Colored Methodist Episcopal Church of America. The enmity entertained by various Northern clergymen toward the Church South was readily transferred to its creation. "Shame!" screamed a parson at the "few weak colored men who love masters and are too lazy to be free." They had fallen in with a movement that was "doing active service against the welfare of their race." [29] Negro affiliates of Northern Methodism joined their white brethren in slinging mud. Those who took communion in the offspring of Southern Methodism lamented that they had "been harassed, persecuted, and abused" by fellow freedmen, and they remonstrated against being labeled followers of a "Rebel Church," a "back-kitchen church," and an "Old Slavery Church" designed "to lead the Negroes back into slavery." [30]

Beyond the Colored Methodist Church loomed still more formidable opponents to the Northern campaign for capturing Negro Southerners. These huskier adversaries were the older independent Negro denominations, the African Methodist Episcopal Church and the African Methodist Episcopal Zion Church. Each had behind it more than forty years of practice in ecclesiastical statecraft. While the fraternal bonds between individual Zionists and Church North pastors sometimes stretched to tautness, it was at the hands of the "Mother Church" of Negro Methodism that the Northerners received their most unkind treatment. "Our church in its advance southward . . . is greatly embarrassed by the misguided opposition to us of the African Methodist Episcopal Church," moaned a member of the editorial corps. Regardless of whether they acted "without provocation" or had been "opposed, insulted and misrepresented [by] missionaries of the Methodist Episcopal Church," [31] African churchmen indifferently disguised their dislike for Northern white competition. The *Christian Recorder*, the official organ of the African Methodists, many times hinted that the Church North ought to remove itself completely from the Southern field.[32] That such intimations coincided with official reasoning was evinced by Jabez Campbell, one of the bishops of the African church. "We would like to have all the ground," wistfully sighed the black hierarch.[33]

Faced with requests to leave Negro Southerners to another sect, Northern prelates protested that they had "no right . . . to devolve . . . responsibilities in this matter upon another set of men," especially since their own church was "much better qualified to accomplish the work of universal evangelization." When pressed to specify the deficiencies which rendered the African establishment incompetent to care for the freedmen, white spokesmen averred that the black brethren had "neither the men nor the means needed to carry on the work." [34] African Methodists, although they heatedly denied any shortage of manpower, acknowledged the want of "means." But the Negro ecclesiasts had a bold plan for surmounting the handicap of poverty. They proposed that the Methodist Episcopal Church subsidize African missionary projects among the freedmen. Bishop Campbell paraphrased the proposition this way: "We . . . did hope that as the mother . . . of Methodism had means without men, and the African M. E. Church . . . had men without means, . . . our mother would furnish the means, and let us furnish the men." [35] The returns from this religious share-cropping were to go exclusively to the laborer. The plea "for Christian assistance" melted the hearts of some Northern clerics, but it tapped the vinegar in the personalities of others. "Matters of 'brotherly love' and 'fraternal relations' are all very well," read one acidulous comment, "but they have nothing to do with subsidies of money." [36] The Northern officialdom seemed to agree.

However, the religious sweepstakes were not run under rules that disqualified the poor, and the African Methodists owned an effective counterbalance to the white church's incontestably superior wealth. "It is natural . . . for . . . Negro . . . people to come to us," boasted an African publicist, because "blood is always more potent than money." Thrown into the pit with a denomination that "had the money," black Methodism hammered home the reminder that it "had the blood" and consequently was "the church for all the colored Methodists of this country." [37] With convincing constancy, white apostles atoil in the Southern field vowed that they were kept busy rebutting African Methodist precepts to the Negroes "not to give their support to a white man" and to "set up for themselves, and have no preachers . . . but persons of their own color." "The . . . wholly colored churches are as intensely prejudiced . . . against the white race as the Confederate element is against the colored," exploded a Northern Methodist journalist.[38] In introducing the volcanic racial issue into the sectarian wrangle, African missionaries exhibited the purest of motives. A selfless concern for Negro interests compelled them to urge "the colored people to separate from white preachers and teachers." Past and present unarguably proved, Negro religionists said, that the freedmen "could not have their rights accorded to them in the Methodist Episcopal Church." The black folk, previously the "slaves of the Southern white people, . . . now were slaves of the Northern people" who denied their "full and true manhood . . . in both practice and law." [39] It is a mark of the temerity, if not the wisdom, of white Methodists that they did not shift the grounds of controversy. The debate joined on the subject of skin; it was aggressively taken up by the Northerners. White preachers industriously plied the thesis that African Methodism was founded "on the mere distinction of complexion" and that it was "wrong to build any church on the basis of color [or] race." Realizing that Negro clergymen were apt to be heard where white men encountered rebuffs, the Northern Methodists shoved darkskinned converts into the breach whenever opportunity offered. In the lower South the main burden of disabusing the freedmen "of the idea that they have no need . . . of white friends" was shouldered by Negro controversialists. These apologists not only acted as living shields against the jibe that the Northern church was "a church for white men only" but made convincing witnesses for the counterargument that "the A. M. E. Church [was] wrong in . . . building up a church on the strength of caste." [40]

Out of the interMethodist competition for African proselytes emerged a denominational coalition that alternately baffled and angered Methodists of the North. Missionaries quickly uncovered a deliberate combination of Methodist bodies athwart their road southward. The new allies—"without social affinities to unite them [and] with a quarter of a century of mutual antagonism to separate them"—were the Southern Methodists and the African Methodists. "The African . . . Church endorses every slander breathed against the M. E. Church and its functionaries . . . by the M. E. Church South," grieved a Mississippi correspondent. A Georgian, probing into "the illiberal spirit of proscription" in this state, traced its source to "the ministers and members of the M. E. Church South together with the African Methodists." The two denominations, he wrote, were united in "violent . . . opposition to the Methodist Episcopal Church." [41] The sectarian partnership became quasi-official when African Methodist delegates to the Southern General Conference of 1866 joined with the whites in drafting a joint address to their respective churches. "It is vitally important," rumbled the manifesto, "that we unite in an unbroken phalanx to oppose . . . the aggressions now being made upon us both by the Methodist Episcopal Church, North." [42] The apparent enmity of African Methodists toward the Northern church, contrasted with the bliss existing between the Negro sect and

Southern Methodism, enabled a disciple of the latter persuasion
to preen while explaining a condition which "has perplexed our
Northern friends amazingly." African Methodism's behavior, he
asserted, demonstrated that "the Southern people are better
friends to the . . . Negro . . . than any other class in this
land" and "the colored people have found it out." Nor could the
writer forbear a parting volley at the routed Methodists. "The
Negroes prefer the logic of facts to the sophistry of empty pro-
fession, and judging each section by its own works . . . give
their verdict in favor of the Southern branch." [43]

This construction of African Methodism's conduct, however,
is nearly as shallow as a Northerner's statement that the Negro
church was an innocent tool of the South "for . . . driving the
Methodist Episcopal Church from the Southern territory." [44]
Black ecclesiasts had weightier motives for friendship with the
Southern church. Gratitude for the members who had been
funneled from the Church South to the African organization,
the knowledge that Southern Methodism was not a serious
competitor for Negro converts, and the pragmatic wisdom of
living in harmony with the dominant Methodism of the section
each shaped the thought of Negro religious leaders. Capping
these considerations was an ambition to inherit the property
which Southern Methodism, as a hangover from slavery, held in
trusteeship for Negro congregations. Its evangelistic program
hobbled by insufficient housing, the African Church covetously
pursued every possibility for correcting its deficiency. Many
Northern preachers, themselves acquainted with the strange
workings of opportunism, understood the end contemplated by
African Methodist diplomats. Remarked one observer: "In order
to secure the lease of . . . churches . . . for . . . colored
Methodists . . . legally held by white trustees the African
Methodists . . . have entered into close . . . relations with
the Southern Methodist Church, and have . . . assumed an attitude of bitter hostility to the Methodist Episcopal Church." [45]
The African ambassadors to the Southern General Conference

of 1866 were instructed to ask that realty retained by Southern Methodism for the use of Negroes "be permanently and peacefully transferred to the . . . African . . . Methodist Church." Although the Southerners declined to transfer ownership in 1866, politicians of the Negro denomination persevered in their tortuous diplomacy with the hope of beating down resistance. Displays of affection, however, became noticeably fewer after 1870 when the Southern Methodists organized a separate church for their black residue and bequeathed to it the property which African Methodists had expectantly eyed. Bitterly disappointed, and threatened by an additional rival, some African ecclesiasts executed a neat turnabout and urged that the Negro church and Northern Methodism "lock arms and have no concord" with the new denomination.[46]

The cutthroat bidding for Negro recruits, a bystander declared, had brought about "confusion confounded" and "ignorance crowded into the vortex of passion and strife." The Southland was littered with local skirmishes between black and white Methodist clergymen, and individuals of the second species abundantly commented that they were shown less "Christian courtesy" by African Methodist representatives than by those of any other sect. "I never thought that Christian professors could be possessed with so much evil and underlurking venom," cried one mission laborer whose forbearance had been exhausted by the tactics of African religionists.[47] Ill-feeling sometimes fermented into violence. A Northern evangelist in Natchez, after having a succession of meetings broken up by "pious roughs," plaintively wrote, "The African M. E. Church . . . cannot endure the thought that we should have anything to do with the colored people.[48] But reciprocal jealousy and suspicion and the ugly outbursts they fathered were evanescent products of interdenominational friction. More sinister in portent was the racial issue which skulked close to the surface of relationships and willingly yielded itself to use. No one institution can be blamed for the fact that "after the war the colored people were more than ever to themselves religiously" but the eagerness to exchange accusations of racism strangely paralleled the emergence of religious segregation. Certain it is that neither African nor white Methodism, by its choice of argumentative weapons, did anything to alleviate a condition both professed to deplore.

For all the prodigal expenditure of strength, however, Methodism's chief business in the South was attendance to the religious needs of the freedmen. From this work the Northern church never allowed its main energies to be diverted. In the generation of Negroes which awoke from slavery, missionaries found a people uniquely receptive to Protestant evangelism. "The religious side is always an open one with the Negro," observed the worldly-wise John W. DeForest.[49] Unsophisticated to the point of primitiveness and unsure of the possibilities of freedom, the Reconstruction black was tailored for consumption by the revivalistic machine. "We have found nowhere . . . over the world," reported a commission of Methodist inspectors, "a people more susceptible of the . . . influences of religion." [50] Except for fidelity to superficial forms, the freedmen's emotive reactions followed a pattern which sliced across denominational lines. Uninitiated whites often were uncertain whether they were witnessing Baptist or Methodist ceremonies or those of any other evangelistic sect. Their bewilderment, however, apparently sharpened their interest. It was the rare literary sojourner in the South who did not pause to comment on the religious life of the Negro. By so doing, these white raconteurs put a later age much in their debt because the freedman was ill-equipped to chronicle his own experiences.

The religious organizations which wooed the freedmen prospered in direct ratio to their tolerance of uninhibited worship. Northern Methodism, rich in Negro converts, eminently illustrated this rule. Sunday services, prayer meetings, love feasts, class meetings, and revivals alike were featured by the unrestraint of the black participants. "If the Negro is indolent . . . there is no want of energy about his religion," tartly remarked a perambulating parson. Newcomers to the South blinked in amazement at the freedmen's ebullient religiosity. "Such . . . shouting and other physical and spiritual manifestations I have never before witnessed," spoke an immigrant to Mississippi.[51] It was often affirmed that there was no way to measure the height of the freedmen's enthusiasm, but one white preacher advanced this tentative formula: "Multiply the excitement of any . . . revival among the whites by any factor you please and you will not measure the intensity of these manifestations among the browns." Mission supervisors daily analyzed narratives that told of "many shouting . . . and in ecstacies," "fifty or sixty lying as dead at one time in the . . . praying circle," "sighs and lamentations and shouts of praises going up . . . throughout the city at all hours of the night," and "twenty or more leaping at once." [52] The religious demonstrations were not only ardent but also sustained. Missionaries agreed that Negro members did not "know anything about protracted meetings, for all [were] such." Abel Stevens, the historian of nineteenth century Methodism, returned from a survey of the South to relate that "the frenzied noises" and "incoherent outcries" emitted by worshipping freedmen usually continued "till after midnight and sometimes all through the night." [53]

Amidst the seeming anarchy of Negro worship, however, lived the rudiments of a ritual, dimly recognizable and highly flexible, because it was unencrusted by the accretions of centuries. Truceless enemy though it was of form, the freedmen's vigor fitted into an embryonic system that would wither away only with a broadening of social and economic horizons. It is questionable if anything happened during a religious ceremony, for which the blacks were unprepared. The missal of habit governed the unfolding of devotional rights, and surprise was left to innocent whites. The meeting schedule with its "time for talk [and] time to sing and shout" was arranged to allow the communicant an opportunity to manifest his joy while Negro clergymen were deliberate in the procedure to lift the emotions of their auditors. Their homiletic technique was outlined by the preacher who informed his congregation that he would "first explain the text, secondly . . . argue it, and thirdly . . . put on the rousements." An onlooker happily defined the last term as that "by which sinners are alarmed and made to flee from the wrath to come." [54] Prayer and congregational singing blended with exhortation until some "got took." Their bodily well-being protected by brawny and phlegmatic "holders," appointed specifically to the duty, the penitents were finally "struck down" and the assembly subsided, "panting, quaking and sighing." [55]

The Negro was besieged with admonitions that "the pursuit of happiness is not to be found in the emotional part of religion," but he good-naturedly accepted warmth as a meet substitute for the refinements of a learned gospel. Investment "with the Holy Spirit" not "larnin'" was the criterion venerated among black Christians. "I don't want de 'ligion of quality people—I got de 'ligion of Jesus," boasted one black saint.[56] "Book religion" took an inferior rank to that which "came from God in the wilderness." In the crude ascription of a priority to faith over reason, the emancipated slave was truer to the Wesleyan tradition than some of his critics, but he skirted one pitfall in the path of orthodoxy only to fall into another "false view of experimental religion." Saved by naïveté from the heresy of skepticism, the freedmen, to the bewildered ire of Methodist theologians, shortcircuited the tenuous connection between reason and revelation and adjured the commentaries of man to "follow the spirit of the Lord without a will of their own." Said one Negro in the evening of life: "I know nothing of writing, but I know what God has said to me." Among the newly-made citizens, God had a reputation for never "leaving His own in ignorance." [57] This persuasion, staved by certainty to the status of dogma, turned aside the scorn of whites as well as rendering detailed metaphysical explanations needless to its beneficiaries.

The meaning of religion to the Negro, however, is not summed up by a recitation of physical excesses or by attention to an unquestioning belief in elementary dogmas. No less than the nineteenth century white, the freedman bent his faith to utilitarian ends. Christianity imparted muscularity of outlook and variety to the humdrum of life. It gave clear-cut answers to questions which troubled the noble and lowly alike. As one greyed "uncle" uttered his awareness of intellectual sufficiency, "Others say what they think but I talk what I know." [58] The spirited nature of his religious exercises also purged the freedman's pent-up feelings probably better than an athletic contest does those of perpetual sophomores. "I feel I am on a mountain top," "I feel as if I growed a foot and a half tonight," and "I feel like a barrel with new hoops" were attestations of the tonic of release unsystematically gathered from Negroes leaving a Texas meetinghouse. Of steadier pulsation was the religious solace which sucked the sting from disappointment, drained the gall from dreary hours and sweetened lives that otherwise might have been barren. The black folk expressed the thought with multiple ingenuity. The gist of a refrain heard by a missionary in a bush-arbored shelter conveyed as accurately as any language a motive for the assent to simple doctrines. While "we have hard trials every day—we are going home to live with Jesus" where "there'll be no more Monday mornings." [59] Besides religion's assuagement of the psyche, the church building, or whatever was pressed into service as a substitute, furnished a core for social activity. A traveler who stopped at a Negro church in Virginia recorded that "it occupied the minister a long time to give out the notices . . . and there was not an evening or afternoon that had not . . . some occasion of religious sociability." [60] Cut off from the choicest avenues of edification and recreation, the freedman had in the meetinghouse a news agency, a fraternal order, and, in bachelorhood, a matrimonial bureau.

The Negro cloaked his religious faith in a verbal symbolism that had the rich smell of earth. The abstract emptiness of eternity was filled with word images fabricated from the stuff of mundane existence. In "Hebben" God lived "in a big House . . . wid cherubims and seraphims to tek' care ob him an' de place." The triumphant Christian went "to that land where there's no fever, or ager [sic], or cholera," where "cawn and po'k" could be had for the asking and "where . . . sorrow, pain or death . . . never enters." [61] Even the knottiest problems of dogma and sacred history were untied by the freedmen's ingenious symbolism. The serpent which caused man's undoing was "like de rattlesnake dat Jim Brown cotched and put in de tin bucket" while a windlass manned by angels explained the physics involved in the ascension of Jesus. A colored parson defined original sin in a way that must have gone straight to his hearer's understanding and paid oblique tribute to Lucifer's cunning. The devil had a kitchen, explained this preacher, in which he left the door ajar and original sin was "de circumstance of being born [near to] dat open door . . . wid . . . de smell of dem savry meats and drinks dat be in dat ar kitchen." [62] In the days following hard upon the war, a white chaplain, preaching to Negroes around Charleston, discovered from a personal adventure that the black folk assimilated Christian teaching in proportion to its relevance to their circumscribed environment. He tried first to alarm his congregations by depicting "the Place of Torment after death as being hot" but his endeavors called forth merely happy countenances. Only after he told them that "Hell is a place where men freeze to death" did he get the coveted ejaculation, "Ah, Mister, me nebber wants to go dare." [63]

The freedman, in his reactions to the Christian gospel, was not wholly without the sympathy of whites, but even his friends were annoyed because "religion [was] not always followed by the virtue of morality." Or, as one bold accusation read, "morals and religion are practically distinct." [64] The counts against the liberated people can be grouped under a few indices: "the consumption of valuable time in idleness," incapability "of uttering a truth," "tarry[ing] too long at the wine," invasions of smoke houses and watermelon patches other than their own, and "throwing all semblance of chastity to the winds." [65] That "some genuine . . . apostolic examples of piety" were found among the freedmen does not impugn the validity of the indictment, for the testimony in its behalf is impressively heavy. However, Northern Methodism can hardly be blamed for the chinks in the moral armor of professing Negro Christians. Clerical gatherings uniformly took pained note of ethical lapses and exhorted black Methodists to "habits of industry, sobriety, and strict economy." The first pastoral letter of the Mississippi conference spelled out an ethical code of sterling respectability. It admonished members "to depend upon their own strong hands for support," "to procure at once employment," "to not squander a . . . penny . . . on . . . extravagances" and "to lead quiet and peaceful lives in all Godliness and honesty." [66] The keenest search will not turn up any contrary Methodist advice to the freedman. Disciplinary resolutions aimed at overt breaches of propriety backed up the entreaties to "Christian self-denial." Methodist councils regularly promised the extreme penalty of excommunication for "habitual intemperance," "living in concubinage," and "thievery." The continuing war for uprightness sporadically put believers under anchoritic regimens. The affiliates of Northern Methodism in South Carolina not only were expected to forego "dram drinking, tobacco and loose women" but, under threat of dismissal, "stay away from the dance, the theater, the horse race, the card table, [and] the opera." [67] These occasions of sin, spiritual monitors argued, were conduits to the malignancy itself.

The formidable task of grass-roots instruction and reproof fell largely upon the Africans who had been licensed to preach under the Methodist canon. Exacting onlookers doubted that divers personal shortcomings rendered "Negro preachers . . . the best men to lay the foundations of a great work," but, apologized a missionary superintendent, "they are the best instruments we can get." [68] What appeared an ineluctable necessity probably was a fortuitous advantage. The raw manness that wanted polish and was resistant to clergymen of artificially fostered talents and experience seemed to vindicate the wisdom of "making freedmen the pastors of freedmen." "No one is so well adapted to pastoral labor among . . . the freedmen . . . as these preachers who have arisen among them," wrote a veteran missionary. They had, maintained this reporter, "a practical shrewdness and . . . under[stood] better how to manage their . . . race than anyone else." [69] Nor were the abilities demanded for successful ministerial direction of the ex-slaves deserving only of deprecation. The preacher needed a discriminating insight into the many frailties of his wards, a Joblike patience to bear with them, and—to exert clerical prerogatives effectively—a knack for playing the parts of actor, diplomat, prophet, and philosopher.

At the outset of Reconstruction, the gifts which black parsons brought to their office were usually of the rudest sort. Of the first thirty colored clergymen enrolled by Northern Methodism in the states of South Carolina, Mississippi, and Texas, only four could read "simple large print" and none could write.[70] In lieu of scholarly attainments the colored pastor relied on his natural repertoire of a strong diaphragm, graphic volubility, and uncomplicated faith. Disdainful of prepared homilies "because it [was] only the letter of the word where a preacher gets up . . . and cries out firstly, secondly, thirdly," he customarily opened his mouth and "let the Lord do the rest." "As it comes up, so it comes out" was a pulpiteer's crusty epigram. The African clergyman's wild gesticulations, rude diction, barbarous grammar, and facility for manufacturing theology, grated on chaste sensory organs; but, reasoned a student of forensics, "if eloquence must be measured by its power to effect and persuade, then . . . colored preachers stand pre-eminent." [71] African preaching was a specialty, and those who dispensed it considered the capture of an audience a fair trade for the immolation of "logic, grammar and other incumberances." Recurrent

Methodist experiments designed to appease the freedman's excited hunger by more sedate means often met with dismal failure. A Negro who listened to the practised phrases of a fair-skinned Methodist disclosed a cause when he prayed that "the Lord would loose the . . . tongue of the white brother who brought the Gospel from afar." [72] The man of "learned stupidity" was likely to go unheard while a colored colleague, innocent of bookish lore, but earnest in his address, and "keen in appreciation of the motives of the heart," bulged out the meetinghouse. To the common-run freedman, a sermon on the "uncircum-scribed heart" or a rendition of "Jews, screws, de, fi, dum" from an original of "Jews crucified him" were perfectly orthodox if uttered with sufficient unction. [73]

While the unlettered Methodist parsons performed important services during the difficult years of transition, they were cease-lessly faced with agitation for their extinction. Few beside their own parishioners seemed satisfied that an able use of native talents was a valid qualification for clerical parchments. The Methodist invasion of the South had scarcely gained headway when clerical associations, prodded by Northern missionaries, began to tilt against "the extravagant utterances . . . of ignorant, misguided, and . . . egotistical preachers." Although without consistent displays of unanimity, the proposition slowly put down roots that "one who cannot read cannot be a safe teacher." [74] Confronted by appalling illiteracy throughout the Reconstruction period, Methodist governing bodies had no choice, short of imperiling the supply of clerics, but to ask of ministerial candidates qualifications that were archetypes of modesty. The most lenient standards expressed a vague desire for licensees with "some knowledge . . . of the elements of theology" and those of maximum strictness merely wanted preachers who could "understandingly read the Bible and Discipline." [75] These restrictions did not prevent educationally naked novices from romping in the clerical estate, but the hedge-rows around holy orders were patrolled as they grew. Conference journals are sprinkled with inscribed rejections of "good Christian" aspirants for ordination. "Not having brought up their studies," they were declared "not competent in the duties of a minister of the Gospel." [76] As a further witness of the evolving order, the Methodist educational system in the South was designed primarily to give the freedmen "a more intelligent comprehension of Christianity."

Consonant with the injunction that "ignorance felled hundreds but vice counted its thousands," the Methodist scrutiny of clerical conduct also grew more strict. The Negro ministry had its licentious minority, but the assertion that "the lives of most . . . [colored] preachers [were] shameful in the extreme" is forgetful of the many who toiled with stern morality and unremitting industry. For those who made light sport of the latter ideals, Northern Methodism's record does not have to be ignominiously buried. In the Annual Conference the Methodists had an efficient agent for plucking out ministerial smut, and they used it enough to deserve recognition. In a predominantly Negro conference, the examination which ensued upon the disciplinary question "Are all the preachers blameless in life?" was not the routine affair that it often was among whites. Auditors at many ministerial business sessions noted that "the close questionings after bigamy, rum, debt, and tobacco showed commendable anxiety for the purity of the body." [77] At the Mississippi conference in 1875, thirteen of the eighty-five preachers connected with Northern Methodism in the state were indicted for misconduct, and the next year "a middle-aged brother of respectable talents" was expelled because "he took a little in his pepper tea quite regularly." During a session of the Louisiana conference, impeachment of character became so free that the few Northern whites present persuaded the assembly to adopt a resolution recommending "fewer promiscuous charges" and "more charity toward brethren." [78] If clerical wrongdoing was not eradicated by such inquests as these, at least it should have been made more surreptitious.

The religion of the Negro, for all its peculiarities, had proto-types on the domestic scene. Notwithstanding interpretations which hold that the freedmen's Christianity was conditioned by "memories of Africa," the religious forms of the Negro resembled those of other Americans in a comparable stage of development. In no salient feature (not excepting moral truancy or "gross superstition") was the freedman's faith radically different from that of the farmer-frontiersman of the earlier West. The freed-men, said one commonplace estimate, were "fervent but igno-rant; religious yet enthusiastic; devotional, but apt to be vision-ary; shrewd, yet narrow conceptioned," and so were the white components of Methodist societies up and down the Mississippi valley during the earlier nineteenth century.[79] Charles Nordhoff, whose insights into the postwar situation always merit consider-ation, was repelled by "the violent and ghastly" demonstrations in Negro worship; but he thought them little different from what he "had seen in Western camp meetings among white people in [his] younger days." [80] Less equivocally, others vouched that the "gospel showers" which fell upon the blacks recalled "the grand displays of heavenly favor . . . seen in the West in years gone by." "The present status of the colored ministry is . . . equal to that of the whites fifty or sixty years ago," remarked an ancient Methodist soon after the war, and he might have included the laity without great violence to fact.[81] Both the freedman and the pioneering white, though perhaps for different reasons, were poor in worldly goods, insulated against the cross winds of ideology, and exposed to the tempests of nature and fortune. In this crucible of a hard environment were forged analogous religious psychologies.

In summations of their work with the freedmen, Methodists often forgot that humility is a Christian virtue. The Northern church, said some of its partisans, was "the strongest moral force among the freedmen" and had a paramount influence in keep-ing "the Negroes from acts of desperation and violence." How-ever, before these extravagant claims can be fairly dealt with, the whole body of evidence from which Methodists appraised the role of their church should be reviewed. And the Northern project for making "the poor of this generation, the rich in the next generation" rested on the school as well as the church.

## NOTES

[1] Fleming, ed., *Documentary History*, II, 240.

[2] Carter G. Woodson, *History of the Negro Church* (2d ed., Washington, 1921), 190ff.

[3] *Christian Advocate*, June 22, 1865; July 20, 1866; *Zion's Herald*, August 30, 1865.

[4] *Methodist*, May 13, 1865; *Christian Advocate*, August 10, 1865.

[5] *Western Advocate*, July 12, 1865.

[6] *Pittsburgh Advocate*, March 12, 1864.

[7] *Christian Advocate*, August 31, 1865; *Western Advocate*, May 24, 1865.

[8] *Christian Advocate*, June 8, 1865; *Western Advocate*, March 15, 1876; *Methodist Review*, LIX (July, 1877), 472.

[9] These figures have been culled from *Minutes of the Annual Conferences, 1881.*

[10] *Journal of the General Conference, 1864*, p. 485.

[11] *Christian Advocate*, June 29, 1865.

[12] Paul H. Buck, *The Road to Reunion* (Boston, 1937), 64.

[13] Freedmen's Aid Society, *Tenth Annual Report* (1876), 69–70.

[14] *Christian Advocate*, July 18, 1867; *Ku Klux Conspiracy, Alabama*, 180.

[15] James Lynch to Simpson, December 3, 1868, Simpson Papers; *Methodist Advocate*, May 18, 1870; *Southwestern Advocate*, February 24, 1876.

[16] *Annual Cyclopedia, 1865*, p. 552.

[17] Lawrence, *Centenary Souvenir*, ix; *Western Advocate*, April 12, 1865.

[18] *Methodist*, June 17, 1865; *Christian Advocate*, April 4, 1872; *Methodist Advocate*, March 5, 1873.

[19] *Methodist*, October 26, 1867.

[20] *Methodist Advocate*, May 19, 1869.

[21] Missionary Society, *Forty-Seventh Annual Report* (1865), 139; *Central Advocate*, April 18, 1865; *Western Advocate*, September 26, 1866.

[22] *Ku Klux Conspiracy, Alabama*, 959.

[23] *Methodist*, June 17, 1865.

[24] Freedmen's Aid Society, *Eleventh Annual Report* (1877), 5.

[25] Louis W. Stevenson to John W. Alvord, June 30, 1870, B.R.F.A.L.

[26] Conser, *Virginia After the War*, 73; *Northwestern Advocate*, August 23, 1865.

[27] David Sullins, *Recollections of an Old Man, Seventy Years in Dixie* (Cleveland, Tenn., 1910), 327; *Methodist*, January 23, 1875.

[28] *Journal of the General Conference of the Methodist Episcopal Church, South, 1866*, pp. 58–59; *1870*, pp. 168, 183, 252.

[29] *Methodist Advocate*, April 7, 1869.

[30] *Ibid.,* May 18, 1870; Fleming, *Documentary History,* II, 261; Woodson, *History of the Negro Church,* 193–94; *Southwestern Advocate,* February 26, 1874.

[31] *Western Advocate,* March 13, 1866.

[32] A collection of suggestions along this line can be found in the *Christian Advocate,* June 29, 1865.

[33] *Central Advocate,* August 30, 1871.

[34] *Christian Advocate,* August 10, 1865; *Northwestern Advocate,* October 3, 1866.

[35] *Central Advocate,* August 30, 1871.

[36] *Christian Advocate,* August 10, 1865.

[37] Benjamin T. Tanner, *An Apology for African Methodism* (Baltimore, 1867), 369, 397.

[38] *Christian Advocate,* July 5, 1866; *Methodist Advocate,* September 16, 1874; March 15, 1876.

[39] *Western Advocate,* January 2, 1866; *Methodist Advocate,* April 3, 1872; Tanner, *Apology for African Methodism,* 67; Josiah Beardsley to E. M. Wheelock, January 24, 1865, B.R.F.A.L.

[40] *Central Advocate,* April 18, 1866; *Northwestern Advocate,* October 3, 1866; *Zion's Herald,* March 7, 1872; *Methodist Advocate,* March 5, 1873.

[41] A. W. Caldwell to J. F. Chalfant, April 16, 1867, B.R.F.A.L.; James Lynch to Simpson, December 3, 1868, Simpson Papers.

[42] *Methodist Review,* XLVIII (July, 1866), 441.

[43] *Western Advocate,* March 20, 1867, quoting *Texas Christian Advocate.*

[44] *Western Advocate,* August 15, 1866.

[45] *Methodist,* March 30, 1867.

[46] *Journal of the General Conference of the Methodist Episcopal Church, South, 1866,* p. 73; *1870,* p. 183; *Western Advocate,* March 20, 1867; *Methodist Advocate,* April 28, 1869.

[47] *Ibid.,* April 7, 1869; *Southwestern Advocate,* May 21, 1874; *Minutes of the Tennessee Annual Conference, 1875,* p. 32.

[48] *Western Advocate,* April 25, 1866.

[49] John W. DeForest, *A Union Officer in Reconstruction.* Edited by James H. Croushore and David M. Potter (New Haven, 1948), 113.

[50] *Methodist,* January 3, 1874.

[51] *Northwestern Advocate,* November 7, 1866; *Methodist,* October 19, 1867.

[52] *Christian Advocate,* May 23 and July 18, 1867; *Zion's Herald,* March 21, 1872; *Methodist Advocate,* May 22, 1869; September 18, 1872.

[53] *Western Advocate,* July 11, 1866; *Methodist,* February 14, 1874.

[54] *Northwestern Advocate,* November 7, 1866; *Western Advocate,* October 12, 1870.

[55] Samples illustrative of the bare description above can be found in *Ladies Repository,* XXV (June, 1865), 339; Whitelaw Reid, *After the War: A Southern Tour, May 1, 1865 to May 1, 1866* (London, 1866), 522ff; *Christian Advocate,* July 18, 1867; New York *Evangelist,* April 3, 1873.

[56] *Northern Advocate,* September 24, 1868.

[57] *Western Advocate,* November 16, 1864; *Zion's Herald,* March 21, 1872; *Christian Union,* July 10, 1872; Freedmen's Aid Society, *Twelfth Annual Report* (1878), 84, 91.

[58] *Western Advocate*, February 21, 1866.

[59] *Northwestern Advocate*, December 18, 1872.

[60] Charles D. Warner, *On Horseback. A Tour in Virginia, North Carolina, and Tennessee* (Boston and New York, 1888), 9.

[61] *Northern Advocate*, October 11, 1866; *Northwestern Advocate*, November 7, 1866; September 9, 1868; *Methodist*, February 19, 1870.

[62] *Zion's Herald*, February 8, 1872; Simkins and Woody, *South Carolina During Reconstruction*, 411.

[63] John H. Franklin, ed., *Civil War Diary of James T. Ayres* (Springfield, Ill., 1947), 50.

[64] E. W. Mason to John W. Alvord, January 1, 1870, B.R.F.A.L.; *Methodist*, February 14, 1874.

[65] *Western Advocate*, May 17, 1865; *Central Advocate*, June 6, 1866; Mitchell, *Life of Levi Scott*, 197; Frances B. Leigh, *Ten Years on a Georgia Plantation Since the War* (London, 1883), 238.

[66] *Northwestern Advocate*, June 28, 1865; *Minutes of the Mississippi Mission Conference of the Methodist Episcopal Church*, 1865, p. 7; *Methodist*, February 14, 1874.

[67] *Methodist Advocate*, April 21, 1869.

[68] Freedmen's Aid Society, *Sixth Annual Report* (1872), 16; James D. Lynch to Simpson, December 5, 1868, Simpson Papers.

[69] *Christian Advocate*, March 31, 1864.

[70] *Methodism and the Republic: Uncorrected Proof Sheets Sent Out in Advance to Ministers Intending to Take Collections for Home Missions and Church Extension* (n.p., n.d.)

[71] *Western Advocate*, February 7, 1866; *American Missionary*, XXII (January, 1868), 27; *African Methodist Episcopal Church Review*, I (October, 1883), 140.

[72] *Methodist*, April 27, 1867; *Christian Union*, July 10, 1872.

[73] *Zion's Herald*, October 8, 1868; February 8, 1872.

[74] Freedmen's Aid Society, *Twelfth Annual Report* (1878), 15.

[75] *Western Advocate*, January 22, 1874; *Southwestern Advocate*, December 31, 1874.

[76] *Minutes of the Louisiana Annual Conference of the Methodist Episcopal Church*, 1877, p. 11.

[77] *Christian Advocate*, June 20, 1867.

[78] *Minutes of the Mississippi Annual Conference*, 1875, p. 8; *Minutes of the Louisiana Annual Conference*, 1875, p. 8; *Southwestern Advocate*, January 28, 1875; *Zion's Herald*, May 4, 1876.

[79] *Minutes of the Texas Annual Conference of the Methodist Episcopal Church*, 1874, p. 25.

[80] Charles Nordhoff, *The Cotton States in the Spring and Summer of 1875* (New York, 1876), 73.

[81] *Western Advocate*, June 7, 1865; *Southwestern Advocate*, July 2, 1874.

# VI

# The Education of the Freedmen

De old church . . . put clothes on our backs, and
shoes on our feet and hats on our heads, and . . .
they's put brains in our hats, bless the Lord.

The Reverend Henry Green
of New Orleans

THE FREEDMEN'S HUNGER for education became something of a
legend as the nation commenced to sweep away the debris of
war. An interpretation of great currency in the North had the
Negro in a "rush . . . for the spelling book" and in "a perfect
blaze of enthusiasm to learn." [1] Promulgated with persistency
and volume, it almost drowned out dissenting voices which
cautioned that the ex-slaves' attitudes toward learning fluctu-
ated widely. Whitelaw Reid came back from a Southern journey
to announce that "feeling among the Negroes about education
varied . . . with the locality." "Wherever . . . the place was
remote from the towns, there was at least an indifference to
education," Reid said. He also remarked that the young seemed
more eager for schooling than their elders. One freedman, filled
with years, expressed what Reid took as an idea familiar to the
older generation. "Wat's de use ob niggers pretendin' to larnin'?"
soliloquized this hoary fieldhand. "Wat'll dey be but niggers
wen dey gits through?" [2] The divided opinion of oldsters on
the benefits of learning manifested itself in occasional outbreaks
of parental unconcern for the education of children. One Negro
father, advised that his offspring should be in a classroom, re-
torted, "I neber got any lu'nin' . . . let de chilluns do as I'se
done." [3]

However, the hostile or indifferent constituted only an uncertain proportion of the liberated population, and there was
no dearth of freedmen ready to undergo the experience of formal

153

schooling. Their alacrity in offering themselves for academic conditioning more than taxed the resources of the North. In satisfying their appetite for knowledge, the Negroes met Methodist influences which infiltrated the educational process through a variety of apertures. Numerous affiliates of the Northern church found places in the Freedmen's Bureau. A congressional report of 1872 remarked that "many of the agents of the Bureau were preachers and had been selected as being the most devout, zealous and loyal of that religious sect known as the Northern Methodist Church." [4] A few Methodists passed beyond the common ranks in the Bureau's administrative structure to reach stations of power and dignity. Clinton B. Fisk, who demonstrated his devotion to the Church North in every way except taking clerical orders, directed Bureau affairs in the combined jurisdiction of Tennessee and Kentucky. At different times, Methodist Episcopal clergymen held State Superintendencies of Education under the Freedmen's Bureau in the states of Virginia, Florida, Tennessee, and Alabama. Another was Assistant Superintendent in South Carolina.[5] Clerics likewise appeared in state and local school systems as teachers and administrators. Some were county or city superintendents, and three received election or acted as presidents of state universities in the South.[6]

Beside public appointments, other important avenues of approach were available to Methodists. These were in the nonsectarian benevolent societies which arose by the score to give the crusader his big chance. Responding to intelligence about "hordes of uneducated, ignorant and improvident blacks," Northern teachers began work in eastern Virginia before the end of 1861 and, as other parts of the Confederacy were opened by federal armies, pedagogues from the North extended the field of their operations. To support and systematize the educational efforts, a bewildering proliferation of charitable organizations ensued in the Northern states. One student, audacious enough to count their number, has listed seventy-nine without making a

claim to finality.[7] Initially the benevolent associations, founded
on a local or state-wide scale, acted autonomously, but in 1863
a trend toward consolidation set in, which passed from regional
unions to the formation of the American Freedmen's Union
Commission in 1866. This organization was a federation of the
larger nondenominational philanthropic societies, except the
American Missionary Association.[8] With other Protestant denominations, Northern Methodism at first co-operated with the
various Freedmen's associations. The Northern church officially
endorsed the activities of the benevolent groups, encouraged
laymen and preachers to seek employment as teachers and relief
workers, and opened pulpits to appeals from the societies for
funds. Methodist clergymen also occupied some of the top ranks
in the hierarchy of benevolent endeavor. Church North clerics
were particularly prominent in the officialdom of agencies whose
main strength was in the Old Northwest, and in 1866 the Methodist contributions were tacitly acknowledged when Bishop
Simpson was honored with the presidency of the Freedmen's
Union Commission.[9]

Northern Methodists, nevertheless, were not content to let
others act as trustees for their time and treasure. The churches
had always been restively yoked to the nondenominational
Freedmen's Commissions, and as early as 1863 they had begun
to withdraw and organize agencies of their own for education
and relief work among the Negroes. The process of denominational atomization, by the summer of 1866, had evolved to a
stage where Northern Methodism was left as the single major
ecclesiastical unit which had not confined its energies on behalf
of the freedmen within narrower evangelistic limits.[10] Provided
with this plausible excuse, a few Methodists concentrated
around Cincinnati, who had gained some notoriety by their
earlier philanthropic work, quietly issued a call for a meeting
in early August, 1866, to consider the church's future policy on
the education of the colored population. The convocation which
assembled in Cincinnati in answer to the summons numbered

a scant eleven persons, and remained in session only briefly, but it sufficed to impart a new direction to the Church North's educational program. From the Cincinnati convention, in answer to burgeoning sentiment for a separate Methodist educational agency, came the organization of the Freedmen's Aid Society of the Methodist Episcopal Church.[11]

A complex of motives was responsible for the founding of the Freedmen's Aid Society. To say that some of them did not spring from disinterested benevolence does not impeach the genuine concern of churchmen for the Negro's uplift, but merely recapitulates what Methodists themselves divulged. In a message to the clergy and laity of the Northern church, the founders of the Freedmen's Aid Society sought to justify their enterprise by remarking that "nondenominational societies have not been careful as to the Christian sentiments and standing of their teachers" and such unconcern had imperiled "the purity of [the] Gospel taught to freedmen." [12] The criticism contained in the address was intended, in part, as propaganda in an ideological war that had recently erupted into the open. The nonsectarian Freedmen's Commissions had long been split into wings of opposing educational philosophies. One group, in which the Methodists were important, if not leaders, contended that a special and intense effort should be made by teachers to indoctrinate the pupils with specific religious beliefs. A "regular work" of instruction was to "save souls from ignorance, sin, and perdition" and "win them to Christ." A contrary opinion, proclaimed most loudly by the Unitarians, drew a distinction "between the teacher and the missionary, the civilizer and the evangelizer." Advocates of the second view believed that the teacher should impart secular information with only an embroidery of broad moral precepts. Religious instruction was to be retailed by a preacher, and outside the classroom. The factions agreed that the freedmen needed "both education and religion," but their differing attitudes were summed up this way: "The question is . . . shall these two general interests be cared for by the same organization or by different organizations? The [non-sectarian] societies . . . say 'by different organizations.' The religious societies . . . say . . . 'the two interests should be joined.' " [13]

At headquarters and in the field, protagonists of the opposing doctrines vigorously jabbed at each other. A missionary in Galveston, Texas, proud that he was a "Liberal Christian," castigated sectarian-minded employees of the Freedmen's Union Commission as "hungry, wolfish bigots" who misused the Commission's funds "for narrow proselytism" and "small denominational ends." [14] The smoldering controversy came to a head in July, 1866, when O. B. Frothingham, a New England Unitarian, published a scathing attack on "the sectarians." Frothingham demanded that teachers sent to the South be admonished "to have nothing to do with churches, creeds or sacraments, . . . not to inculcate doctrinal opinions, or take part in sectarian propagandism of any kind." He asserted that if "speculative and ceremonial religion" were not kept distinct from pedagogy "the danger must be that mental instruction will be warped." Frothingham likened his Protestant opponents "to Romanists." [15] The upshot of the dispute was that Methodists, with Bishop Simpson in the train, began to retire from participation in the American Freedmen's Union Commission. Less than a month after Frothingham's outburst, a separate Methodist society was born.

While the argument over curriculum content furnished the Methodists with an occasion for flight from existing benevolent organizations, there were positive attractions in a denominational Freedmen's Aid Society. Many Methodists believed, as did members of other Christian churches, that education should be bent to serve sectarian ends. "It was a mistake that Methodists even united at all with any outside agency," declared one clergyman. He believed that "from the start . . . Methodist hands should have handled Methodist funds . . . to found Methodist schools." [16] An educational society, churchmen said, was a neat complement to the missionary and church extension societies in building Northern Methodism in the South. Methodist educators wisely recognized that parochial schools, in the absence of publicly-supported systems, would bring a mass of potential converts within grasp of the Church North. "Schools give access to the people which we can get in no other way," rightly asserted a religious journalist, and his thesis found lodgement in the official mind of the church. Methodism's most august assembly baldly stated that "whoever shall educate the freedmen will also possess them ecclesiastically." Consequently, "the duty of educating . . . this people belongs peculiarly . . . to the Methodist Episcopal Church." [17]

Once the freedmen had been corralled by the Northern establishment, the religiously-dominated school would perform a double function. Through the enlightenment of Negro clerics and laymen, the worship of colored folk would be cleansed of "fanaticism and the wild vagaries of enthusiasm" and become something beyond "the largely emotional . . . visionary type . . . attended with much bodily exercise." One solemn intonation observed that "the schoolhouse and the meeting-house—the former furnishing cultivated intellects to minister . . . at the altar of the latter—are the true emblems of Christian civilization." [18] Concomitant with the purgation of Negro religious habits, a Methodist educational system furnished potential safeguards to orthodoxy, for the business of denominational schools was "to teach not science alone, but science impregnated by religion." The Church North, as one of its foes said, did not "believe in the policy of leaving the character to be molded by circumstances after the arts of reading and writing [had] been supplied." "The Methodist Episcopal Church should patronize its own schools, and educate its youth to love the church of their fathers," was the advice given to freedmen. Institutions supervised by others were "satisfactory," but "they did not train up Methodist[s]." [19]

The subordination of education to denominational purposes, legitimate as Northern Methodism regarded the practice, came to be widely reprehended by public servants. Its advantages, numerous public educators argued, were overbalanced by its deleterious effects. Amory Mayo, a reputable educational administrator of the period divided by 1900, maintained that the admixture of profane learning and denominational dogma fed to black students resulted in "a development of the sectarian spirit in the Negro race." [20] Mayo did not clinch the causal connection between religious bigotry and the work of denominational societies, but to Freedmen's Bureau agents sectarianism, whatever its origin, was a formidable impediment to the founding of Negro schools. "The great obstacle of establishing schools in country towns," announced one federal employee, "is the dissatisfaction between the Methodist congregation and the Baptist . . . Church, there being no co-operation between them." [21] Inasmuch as the church building often housed a school, quarrels arose among the freedmen over which denomination was to have the distinction of an educational plant in its meetinghouse. Baptists often boycotted schools conducted on Methodist property, and the Methodists reciprocated the ban. Leaders of one branch of Methodists even cautioned their affiliates against attending institutions supported by another Methodist church. Sectarianism also entered into the selection of teachers for the freedmen. A perplexed Bureau agent in Louisiana reported that "in many instances, the [Negroes] refuse to send their children to school unless the teacher is of their . . . religious belief." [22]

The impulses of humanitarianism, Christian orthodoxy, and sectarian advantage guaranteed the eventual organization of a distinctively Methodist society for Negro education. However, some onlookers thought that a mutiny within the columns of Methodism hastened its emergence. Their arguments had an outward plausibility. Seven of the eleven men who attended the birth of a Freedmen's Aid Society in Cincinnati were reckoned as abolitionists and two, Richard S. Rust and John M. Walden, had amassed considerable renown for their roles in the antislavery crusade. Prior to the launching of the Freedmen's Aid

Society, Methodist efforts in the South were largely guided by the Missionary Society. The Society's secretary, John P. Durbin, was heralded as indifferent or even hostile to the evangelization of the freedmen, and held in constant suspicion by the negrophile element.[23] From the dissatisfaction with the executive of the Missionary Society and the earlier antislavery records of most of the new agency's charter members grew the surmise that the Freedmen's Aid Society was a device by which radical Methodists meant to circumvent the inept policies of conservatives. Angry in the conviction that existing agencies were proceeding too slowly in the conversion of the freedmen, the negrophobes, some argued, decided on a bold stroke. Significantly, no invitations to attend the Cincinnati meeting were extended to executives of the Missionary Society. This discourtesy was pardoned by the comment that "there was no time to call in . . . our brethren from the East," but to those who recollected that conversations directed toward a denominational society had been going on for a year, the excuse was lame.[24]

The whole sum of money and energy spent on Negro education by Northern Methodism cannot be credited to the Freedmen's Aid Society. Before the establishment of this bureau, the Missionary Society paid the salaries of a few men whose time was given entirely to teaching, besides supporting many more who divided their labor between the sanctuary and the schoolroom. Also, the original properties of New Orleans University and of Central Tennessee College at Nashville were purchased by the Missionary Society. Another Methodist agency which contributed slightly to help the Negro to literacy was the Sunday School Union. The Bible, the hymnal, a spelling book (generally for the use of teacher and pupil), and literature "with plenty of small words and large pictures" were prescribed as standard equipment for the Methodist Sunday School in the South.[25] Moreover, numerous attempts originated with Methodists in the South to multiply educational opportunities for the freedmen. The most ambitious proposal issued from Mississippi and Louisiana; there the clergy in 1866 suggested the formation of a Methodist parochial school "in each circuit or station." On a less-elaborate scale, other conferences urged colored clergymen and lay members to improvise academic factories. Evidently, many locally-sponsored projects got out of the blueprint stage. Throughout the Reconstruction period, Methodist surveys of the educational picture in the South consistently noted that "most of our churches are used for school purposes" and that "nearly all of the preachers teach school in connection with their church work." [26] However, after the formation of the Freedmen's Aid Society, sectarian activity was increasingly pulled together under the canons of a central authority and, beyond doubt, this society made the most enduring Methodist contributions to Negro education.

When the Freedmen's Aid Society opened operations, a number of schools under Methodist auspices were already engaged in imparting the barest fundamentals of formal learning. Some of these the Society absorbed, and new ones were established at desirable locations. During the first years of its life, the Society concentrated upon the maintenance of schools for the most elementary instruction, and the educational units were much more distinguishable for quantity than quality. Primary schools under the Society's control reached a high of sixty in 1868, but after that date their number declined as the church gradually shifted emphasis to what were proudly labeled institutions of higher learning. The departure from kindergarten training followed the realization that the enlightenment of the whole population of freedmen obviously exceeded Methodist means. The best use that could be made of limited finances and personnel was to educate a few freedmen and hope that they would become the saviors of their race. The African was told that "the colored man . . . must be his own regenerator" and that the Church North proposed only "to educate . . . a number and send them forth . . . to regenerate their own people." [27]

However, while the idea that the blacks must leaven themselves was speculatively correct, it took on practical validity a few years after the war. By this time many freedmen had picked up enough primary knowledge to afford customers for instruction above the primer level. Richard Rust, for more than three decades the secretary of the Freedmen's Aid Society, subsequently recalled, "Our work commenced with primary study and . . . gradually advanced with the progress of the pupils until we . . . reached the higher branches." [28] The rise of carpetbag governments in the South, under the Reconstruction Acts, offered another reasonable excuse for greater attention to higher learning. Regularly the state constitutions drafted by these Republican regimes carried imposing sections on public education. The influence of such action on Methodist educational plans was demonstrated by the South Carolina conference of 1869. The South Carolina preachers aired the notion that "our new state constitution wisely provides for a . . . system of common schools . . . which . . . will relieve the church of this portion of her responsibilities." [29] That this conclusion reposed overmuch confidence in the rectitude of political adventurers did not prevent churchmen elsewhere from expressing similar convictions.

A final incentive to the quantitative retrenchment and qualitative improvement of schools was revealed in the Freedmen's Aid Society report for 1870. The document mentioned Methodism's "deep regret that no additional appropriations [could] be expected from the government" because the Freedmen's Bureau had closed out the main chapters of its controversial history.[30] The favors that the Church North had received from the federal agency were the same as those conferred upon other benevolent organizations busy at the education of the freedmen. By the original act of 1865, the Bureau had no funds with which to aid the educational work of the many Northern societies. Its initial help was confined largely to furnishing confiscated or abandoned structures for school purposes, co-ordinating the efforts of Northern associations, and under War Department vouchers providing transportation for teachers hired by the private organizations.[31] However, when Congress prolonged the life of the Freedmen's Bureau in 1866, it directed the commissioner "at all times to co-operate with private benevolent associations . . . in aid of the freedmen" and appropriated a half million dollars "for . . . schools . . . including construction, rental and repairs." [32] From the time of this legislation until 1870, the material donation of the government to Methodist schools, as well as those sponsored by other bodies, was larger. Beside the earlier assistance given through the transportation of teachers and the use of shelters, the Bureau expended money for the refurbishment or construction of buildings whose titles were vested in churches or nondenominational aid societies. For most of 1867 and 1868, additional federal aid came to the Northern groups through quarterly subsidies graduated according to the number of teachers employed by them.[33]

In lending assistance to the educational projects of Methodism and other sects, the federal government came close to outright subsidization of religious endeavor. The Freedmen's Bureau willingly aided in the construction of churches, provided the buildings doubled as schools. From the government's policy, Northern Methodism derived considerable denominational profit. As one educational supervisor wrote: "The Bureau helps largely in building . . . school houses and whenever we get a school house we get a meeting place." [34] However, the crumbs which fell to Northern Methodism apparently whetted its appetite for more. With so many churches and aid societies drinking from public revenues, jealousy at the distribution of assistance inevitably reared its head, and Northern Methodists chronically whined about discriminatory treatment from the government. "The Freedmen's Bureau in its . . . appropriations seems invariably to slight claims pressed . . . in the interest of Methodism," wrote the clergyman-politician James Lynch, and he went on to predict that "the history of the Bureau will show that it has always given the cold shoulder to Methodism."

Churchmen carried their protests to the highest echelons of the Bureau. Bishop Ames complained to Commissioner Oliver O. Howard that the Methodists "were not treated fairly," "that they could receive no assistance whatever from the Freedmen's Bureau," and "that Methodist agents were repulsed with . . . coolness." [35]

In the alleged neglect, discontented Methodists discovered the bogey of sectarianism. Never forgetful that both Howard and John W. Alvord, chief of the Bureau's educational division, were vigorous Congregationalists, Wesleyan spokesmen saw a settled design to "place the whole work of educating the colored men . . . under Presbyterian and Congregational influences" [36] through federal encouragement of the American Missionary Association. Bishop Ames, speaking from information supplied by Methodist missionaries, groaned that the sympathy of the Bureau was "altogether for the Congregationalists." Difficult though it is to convict Howard and Alvord of gross favoritism, some of their subordinates in the field were unquestionably guilty of the behavior criticized by Methodists. The Superintendent of Education for Louisiana, remarking that the Congregationalist-dominated American Missionary Association had "done more educational work than all other . . . agencies combined," declared that he had made it "a favorite channel for Bureau aid." [37]

Inscrutable bookkeeping methods hide the extent to which Methodism benefited from public funds, but the aid was sizable enough to make the church feel its loss acutely. Richard Rust, whose position lent weight to his opinion, wrote that "the failure of the bureau to render additional aid . . . will greatly embarrass our schools." While the Freedmen's Aid Society planned "to sustain normal schools and colleges . . . as heretofore," Rust said that the "common schools [would] be diminished nearly one half" by the cessation of federal grants.[38] The prediction was fulfilled as the primary school numerical curve, slanting downward since 1868, dipped sharply in 1871. In the spring of 1870, the Society was maintaining sixty schools of various grades which employed one hundred and ten teachers. One year later the totals were thirty-five and seventy-five, respectively. All the casualties were on the lower educational levels.[39] Northern Methodism did not supinely accept the deprivation of federal subsidies. Its tiffs with the Freedmen's Bureau were over matters of policy rather than theory. Church educators deeply regretted that "the clamor against the Freedmen's Bureau was allowed to . . . cripple and . . . destroy it." For a half decade and more after appropriations had been discontinued, churchmen of the North entreated "Congress to aid the educational societies . . . whose special object is to educate and Christianize the Freedmen." And on the off-chance that the ears of politicians would be trained toward Methodism during an election year, the General Conference of 1876 threw its weight behind the idea that parochial schools for colored Southerners deserved "liberal support from the government." [40]

Once the die was cast for higher-grade education, Methodist labors proceeded apace. By 1878, the Freedmen's Aid Society was the patron of sixteen "boarding schools" for freedmen, variously designated as universities, colleges, institutes, normal schools, and seminaries. Every state of the old Confederacy, save Virginia, was favored by one or more Church North institution.[41] The label of a school bore no correspondence to the caliber of its academic offerings. The Methodists had the mischievous habit of magnifying the character of institutions by the magnificence of their titles. After ten years of operation, New Orleans University had "about twenty little colored boys and girls . . . studying the common school branches" and the whole establishment did "not amount to anything more than a fair district school." Claflin University, chartered in 1869, announced in 1872 that "college classes will be formed the present year." Notification of intention was reiterated in 1874 and 1876, before the actual accomplishment in 1878. Applicants for admission to Clark University in 1872 were informed that "none are admitted lower than the Fourth reader" and Shaw University likewise wanted "proficiency in the third reader" from its matriculants. A New Englander who surveyed Central Tennessee College in 1874 decided that it was "a school which . . . is no more like a university than an egg is like a full-sized rooster." [42] Critical Methodists admitted that no matter what name was conferred by a charter, the best of their institutions were no more than equal in rank to "an academy or a high school . . . considered from a New England point of view." [43] In the education of a people "with the stink of slavery still upon them" it could not be otherwise.

In extenuation of churchmen, it can be said that the institutional titles were bestowed with a look toward the coming years when circumstances would allow the gap between aspiration and hard fact to be closed. But through the Reconstruction period Methodist colleges and universities tried to accommodate in the same plant scholars in every stage of advancement. A student with diligence and money could pass from the primary grades through intermediate and college preparatory instruction to a liberal arts degree and even take some professional training without ever changing his post office address, always with the reservation that to none of these "terms were attached the comprehensive meanings . . . assigned in . . . other parts of the country." The advertised curricula on the different levels duplicated Northern models. Clark University in Atlanta, one of the few schools able to bear the publication costs of a catalog, was typical of equivalent Methodist institutions. Instruction in the "lower English branches" at this school in 1879 included "reading, elocution, spelling, penmanship, composition, English grammar, arithmetic, [and] U. S. history." Pupils who planned for college were further subjected to the rigors of "Latin, Greek, . . . and Mathematics from Algebra to Quadratics." The four-year liberal arts course provided for still more "Latin . . . , Greek, Mathematics, [and] English" spiced by study in "Natural, Moral and Political Science . . . [and] Metaphysics." [44]

The Freedmen's Aid Society, guided by the theory that the black man had to lift his own race, focused its attention on professional training, especially for the ministry and teaching. Methodist schools were designed as factories to hammer out the future leaders of the freedmen. Every church-supervised institution which pretended to any rank boasted of its normal and theological departments, and Central Tennessee College by 1877 had surpassed these usual adornments. Beside owning a law faculty, this college had connected with it Meharry Medical School.[45] A breakdown of the Negro enrollment in the sixteen Methodist schools of "upper grade" in 1878 indicates that professional preparation was the paramount, if not exclusive, business of education. From the combined student bodies, which totaled two thousand five hundred ten in the year 1878, almost one thousand five hundred enrollees said that they were preparing for careers in teaching or preaching. The paucity of facilities helped to keep down the sum of scholars studying law and medicine, but even their number approached a hundred. Of the other nine hundred pupils enigmatically called either "primary," "intermediate," "academic," or "collegiate," most also would become teachers and preachers to the black folk.[46]

There was discernible Methodist feeling that the formal disciplines did not fully meet the educational needs of the colored population. Because freedmen were "the merest children," some thought that they should be "taught how to work . . . as much as to read and write." The great mistake of Methodist educators, said one correspondent, was the "too universal attempt to educate the freedmen . . . in the higher branches of learning when they should be taught . . . the useful arts and agriculture." [47] But to talk of industrial education was much easier than to institute a program. While the movement toward training the Negro in applied skills faced diverse obstacles, financial difficulties were foremost. Far less money was required to pre-empt a shelter and install a few chairs than to buy a farm or to equip a carpentry or printing shop. However, the Church North was not wholly a laggard in the field of mechanical and agricultural education. The South Carolina legislature, by an 1872 statute, enlarged Claflin University to include the State Agricultural College and Mechanics Institute. Under this arrangement, which continued until 1896, appropriations were made by the state legislature to the Claflin authorities, who administered the industrial department as a part of the university. Within five years, a two-hundred-and-fifty-acre farm was in operation, with facilities for the schooling of carpenters and blacksmiths. A program more comprehensive than that of Claflin's began to mature at Clark University in 1880, with Henry Warren, a Boston clergyman and later a bishop, as the moving spirit. Before 1885, schools of carpentry, agriculture, printing and domestic economy had opened. An agent of the United States Office of Education who began annual visits to the South in 1880 subsequently paid a tribute to the latter program by declaring that "in . . . Clark University . . . he found the most successful attempt to introduce industrial training . . . outside the Hampton Institute." [48]

Measured against any criteria, Methodist schools for freedmen had the same marks of material poverty as the students who attended them. The first teachers detailed to work in the South often had their inventiveness taxed to locate shelters. Some momentarily failed to find any and used the "outdoors, under the trees." Many others lodged their schools in "old shanties." One teacher who volunteered for early duty in Maryland said that she and her pupils were on "the most friendly relations with pigs that . . . are visible through the floor and . . . come up and dip their long noses in the school waterpail." A pedagogical sister in Augusta, Georgia, was "obliged to give up sick" after her first day's work because the January "wind blew in all around and from beneath . . . the school." [49] Even when the Methodist role in Negro education began to assume permanent airs, the transformation of physical equipment was painfully slow. Clark University in 1874 was housed in a single building which had "no plaster, paper, nor ceiling." Crevices in the walls gave light and ventilation, but the president of the institution declared that he "could not keep it comfortably warm during the coldest weather." The next year the principal of Haven Normal School reported that his students had "suffered during the winter months from cold" even though a "hundred . . . were crowded into one room." Walden Seminary opened at Little Rock in 1877 "in . . . an open, dilapidated church, entirely unfit for a schoolroom" but after a year moved up to the splendor of "a suite of rooms on the second floor of a building, the lower part of which [was] used as a store." Not without justification, the Freedmen's Aid Society, with more than ten years endeavor behind it, looked over its schools and was "humbled at their poor equipment in buildings, . . . furniture, apparatus . . . and endowments." [50] However, signs of improvement appeared. Central Tennessee College, in somewhat exaggerated fashion, symbolized an evolution that was penetrating to other Methodist units. Central Tennessee opened in the unplastered basement of a Negro church in Nashville in 1866. The Freedmen's Bureau quickly put it into possession of an abandoned Confederate gun factory, and from here the school purchased land and began to erect buildings. By 1875 the institution took pride in its "four edifices of brick" which housed administrative offices, recitation rooms, dormitories, a dining hall, music studios, a science laboratory, and a library.[51]

For the staffing of its schools, the Freedmen's Aid Society depended upon the reservoir of learning in the North. The employment and the assignment of pedagogues was the prerogative of the Society's secretary. During the summer preceding the school terms, which usually opened in October or early November, advertisements were circulated for applicants to fill vacancies in the Methodist schools of the South. It occasionally happened that the volume of Northern response was inadequate and church officials, after they had failed in the gentle arts of persuasion, reluctantly had to turn to Southern converts to complete faculty rosters.[52] The financial arrangements made

with teachers had a pleasantly informal character. The Freedmen's Aid Society took care of the transportation of personal
and household effects, but salaries both in amount and peri-
odicity depended upon collections taken from the church membership. Educational missionaries were warned in advance that
the "salary . . . may not exceed fifteen dollars a month in addition
to . . . boarding." [53] Apparently remunerations often fell short of
this quotation, and were remitted irregularly. Cries that the
Freedmen's Aid Society was "seriously handicapped by a lack
of funds with which to meet teachers' salaries" lost their novelty
early in the Society's history. An evangelist-educator in Georgia,
frustrated by months of vain promises, irately wrote, "If I don't
get help soon I shall consider that I am in the employ of nobody
as nobody pays me anything." [54] The paucity of Northern assistance often pushed instructors to desperate measures. One
woman teacher, "reduced . . . to beggarly poverty," was "compelled to part even with articles of clothing . . . to avoid . . . cold
and hunger." A colleague, without convertible wealth, wrote
that she had spent all her means and was "without a single
dollar, depending upon the charity of a colored family for a few
things to sustain life." [55]

Fortitude, however, was not the attribute Methodists prized
most highly in a teacher. Schools controlled by the Northern
organization were expected to inculcate "sound doctrines and
pure principles" and be made "to subserve the great cause of
vital religion." Parallel with this dogma, Methodist assemblies
decreed that "the conversion of the student is an object most
earnestly to be sought for by those in whose hands his education
is placed." [56] In the appointment of personnel, the Freedmen's
Aid Society tried to live up to the mandate put before it. Application forms asked prospective hirelings to "state the . . . religious advantages you have had." The Methodist membership
received assurance that "special care [was] had to the religious
. . . qualifications of teachers" and "such only [were] employed
as [were] men and women of deep and fervent piety." With a

few years of experience behind his department, the secretary of
the Freedmen's Aid Society was able to say that the precautions
had yielded results. Methodist faculties were crowded with persons "scarcely less distinguished as missionaries than as teachers"
who "sweetly blended the work of imparting instruction and
leading souls to Christ." [57] Fidelity to a trust shines through the
published correspondence of Methodist teachers in the South.
Almost as frequently as they noted the academic progress of
their students, the teachers commented on an "ambition to win
souls to Jesus," "a . . . gradual but sure reformation of morals,"
and "conversions . . . deep and excellent. . . ." [58]

However, teachers were only part of the blanket of religion
and morality covering Methodist education. "All our instruction
proposes to show . . . God. . . . Daily in every branch of study we
teach and preach Christ," announced one university executive.
Freedmen who entered Clark University were *ipso facto* "considered as morally pledging themselves against intemperance,
lewdness, idleness, and all kinds of vice." [59] Once the student had
been caught in the educational mill, he was constantly shaped
by materials and methods of instruction. Daily chapel sessions,
a prayer meeting each day, three doses of church on Sunday,
and special convocations "for the promotion of holiness" helped
to keep pietistic fervor high.[60] Lest moral alloy creep in between
the covers of printed pages, Methodist educators were also "held
responsible for the character of the books used." Approved texts
should not hide "the God of the Bible . . . from view" and "not
only recognize the facts of the Bible but be filled with its spirit."
John Braden, president of Central Tennessee College, in 1875
went to a logical extreme in selecting reading material when
he ordered the use of "the Bible . . . as a textbook . . . throughout
the college." [61] The slant toward evangelism in Methodist
schools was so pronounced that the Superintendent of Education in Mississippi alleged that the Northern church "had done
nothing in the secular branch of education" but had devoted its
whole resources "to religious or denominational work." He found

Northern Methodists "very dogmatic . . . in . . . their efforts to elevate the . . . Negro." [62]

If the concatenation of pedagogical influence, ceremonies, and textual matter did not transform Methodist institutions into the "perpetual Pentecosts" wished by some, exhibitions of religiosity were common enough to satisfy the less demanding. Items of educational news ordinarily carried tales about "manifestations of the Divine presence." The director of Bennett Seminary in Greensboro, North Carolina, thought that the most rewarding part of his work was "to see strong young men bow at the altar" and mentioned that he had often been satisfied. Central Tennessee College in 1873 reported a "revival of . . . increasing power" with the mourners' benches filled "as fast as . . . they . . . [were] cleared." Somewhat shortened classes were kept up at Central Tennessee despite the diversion, but a revival which had broken out at Shaw University the preceding year had completely shattered the academic routine. Here "the recitations were suspended for several days . . . and the time was occupied in praying and advising those . . . earnestly groaning after redemption." [63] Some experts, "by careful inquiry," determined that relatively the classroom was the most effective proselyting instrument owned by the church. A Methodist auditor who listened to a speech by Bishop Thomas Bowman in 1875 recounted that the prelate "said that twice as many were converted in the seminaries, in proportion to number, as in . . . Sabbath schools, and four times as many as in . . . congregations." [64] That Bowman's samples were taken unscientifically does not belie the gist of his conclusion. The resources spent on freedmen's schools were being repaid by accessions to Methodism.

The excellence of educators at expanding church membership lists spearheaded a Freedmen's Aid Society drive for a bigger share of Methodist money. An augmented income, argued the Society's officialdom, would eradicate the most obvious weaknesses of the parochial school system. It would repair and enlarge property, regularize teachers' salaries, create endowment and scholarship funds, and relieve understaffed faculties. However, the claim that "where our schools have failed, the church has failed also" had very indifferent success in prying wider the pocketbooks of the Northern membership. The campaign for a fuller educational treasury stalled partly on the unconcern of the laity and even of the clergy. Richard Rust charged that in 1873 fewer than half the Methodist preachers in the land had put forth any effort to take collections for the freedmen's schools.[65] A difficulty of at least equal magnitude came from the competition of five different Methodist agencies for contributions. In this race, the Freedmen's Aid Society could place no better than third. During 1873, when the educational bureau's income was above average for a ten-year span, its gross receipts were only two-thirds as great as those of the Church Extension Society and about eight percent of what the Missionary Society collected. The disparity was to grow with each year. The conclusive blow to an enlarged academic program fell with the financial depression. In 1874, disbursements to schools were cut back to seventy percent of the preceding year and, although expenditures gradually recovered, the Freedmen's Aid Society in 1878 was still spending less than it had spent in 1873.[66]

The Methodist dominion over the process of formal learning, however, was very incomplete. Exhortation of the North for redoubled effort could not change the character of the raw stuff which the educational manufactories were supposed to turn into different products. Inevitably, the freedman's economic and social background strewed obstacles along the way of his education. To the great disgust of Methodist educators, they sometimes ran into opposition from the colored membership of the church. The enmity to schools had its focal point in the elder Negro clergymen who could effectually silence critics with the question, "Did Christ ever go to college?" No riddle attached to the thinking which molded this view. The old Negro preachers, observed a Freedmen's Bureau employee, were "shrewd enough to see that as the people become enlightened . . . their occupation is gone." The following of the unlettered preachers may have been small, yet the dispatch asserting that a parson's diatribe against " 'book larnin' . . . brought down the whole house with a triumphant 'amen' " was far from an oddity.[67]

Nevertheless, the prejudice which regarded nescience and virtue as synonomous was a small bar to the colored man's rejuvenation beside the inability to keep him consistently exposed to instruction. "With most of them . . . attendance is quite irregular," wrote a Methodist teacher in the opening years of national reconstruction, and to a slightly diminishing degree a comparable condition prevailed through the remainder of the era.[68] Some freedmen were merely curious about the mysteries of education and, upon the discovery that the intellect did not grow osmotically, departed with the shot, "I ain't learnin' nuffin' 'tall." The teacher's work was also made "disheartening" by "the readiness with which the . . . pupils were led astray" by pleasurable diversions. But overriding all the explanations for spasmodic attendance was "the pupil's want of means to continue study." The deep poverty that impressed every tourist in the South took its toll in the education of the Negro. Officials of the Freedmen's Aid Society agreed that the majority of students of adolescent age and beyond annually had to interrupt their education and teach, preach, or do manual labor "till they had saved enough of their earnings to pay for a few more months of schooling." [69]

Churchmen sought by many paths to skirt the deterrent of indigence. Tuition at Freedmen's Aid Society schools was low, varying from ten cents to rarely more than a dollar a month, dependent upon the institution and the course of studies pursued. Ministerial students were relieved of these fees, and other pupils were seldom pressed by school authorities for payment. One or another of the church bureaus also provided small sums for student support and church members were urged to become the patrons of particular freedmen and contribute toward keeping them under instruction for an academic year.[70] The larger Methodist schools also had accommodations for scholars to board themselves and sometimes even granted "the use of a small plat of ground from which to raise vegetables." The sight of a Negro student arriving for the impending scholastic term "with a mulecart of provisions, meal, bacon and cowpeas" awakened no surprise, because the items were merely for his personal larder.[71] From an awareness of the link between economics and persistence in the chase for knowledge, several schemes were floated to enable colored pupils to earn a living conveniently without a break in their studies. The only venture of this kind which attained even passing success was at Bayou Teche, Louisiana, where John Baldwin, a wealthy Ohio layman, purchased a rundown plantation and deeded it to the Freedmen's Aid Society. Before the enterprise was involved in bankruptcy in 1877, Methodist freedmen farmed the land on shares, and had the benefits of a school, church, and other community institutions.[72]

The breadth of Methodist educational work among the freedmen is a little more certain than its depths. In 1879 the schools of the Freedmen's Aid Society claimed to have enrolled sixty thousand pupils in the preceding dozen years and estimated that another two hundred twenty five thousand had been taught by trainees of Methodist institutions.[73] These figures, although a compound of loose computation and guessing, are possibly a reasonable approximation of fact. The question of how many were really infected with the contagion of education can be answered only by subjective testimony. Since the church intended merely to educate a select number, this question was of vital importance. Intermittently, sour notes were sounded. A federal inspector in Georgia scoffed that Methodist teachers "play[ed] school very successfully without imparting any instruction whatever." A ministerial educator concurred in the above evaluation, and boldly added that his church had made "the past misfortunes of the race an excuse for a rapid unsystematic half culture." [74] Nevertheless, adverse appraisals were predicated upon severely traditional maxims, and deprecated the many small piecemeal gains. The teachers who measured the freedmen's rise from a dead level of zero were enthusiastic about his progress and prospects. They showered the North with glowing accounts of colored students who "during the evenings of . . . one month advanced . . . from the primer to become . . . tolerable readers, good penmen and . . . masters of the fundamental rules of arithmetic" or "who passed from ABC's through First, Second, and Third Reader . . . well into the Fourth Reader . . . in only four months." [75] To tough-minded Methodists such things were painfully small dividends for a generous investment of men and money, but patient churchmen could take them as signs of the yeasty ferment of Negro culture.

The collision of opinions among those engaged in the cultural elevation of the Negro should warn the historian to refrain from an estimate of Methodist accomplishments. The amelioration of the freedmen was a job too big for Methodism alone, nor could it be done in the years between 1865 and 1880. However, it is due to the educational and religious endeavor of the Church North to say that sectarian rivals sometimes admitted that Methodist energies were not cast to the wind. No tribute was more rewarding than the one of a Southern clergyman who spoke from long experience to tell Northern churchmen that "the colored Methodists in the South who have had the advantage of your . . . training are far in advance of any [other] colored people in that section." [76] That this was simply the belief of a fallible mortal did not make the words any less sweet to the ears of Methodists.

## NOTES

[1] *Christian Union,* July 10, 1872; Freedmen's Aid Society, *Eighth Annual Report* (1874), 7.

[2] Reid, *After the War,* 510–11.

[3] *Western Advocate,* July 5, 1876.

[4] *Ku Klux Conspiracy, Majority and Minority Reports,* 442.

[5] The State Superintendents were, respectively, R. M. Manly, H. H. Moore, J. F. Ogden, and R. D. Harper. The Assistant Superintendent was B. F. Whittemore. *Western Advocate,* September 19, 1866; Swint, *Northern Teacher,* 91–92, 125; Walter L. Fleming, *Civil War and Reconstruction in Alabama* (New York, 1905), 459.

[6] Henry Fox acted as president of the University of South Carolina. Arad S. Lakin and R. D. Harper, both immigrants from Ohio, were successively elected to the presidency of the University of Alabama. Because of the hostility of the whites, however, Lakin could not be inaugurated, and Harper, taking a lesson from his predecessor's difficulty, declined the post. Knoxville *Press and Messenger,* October 8, 1868; February 17, 1869; *Methodist Review,* LVI (January, 1874), 41; *Ku Klux Conspiracy, Alabama,* 111–115; Fleming, *Reconstruction in Alabama,* 611–13.

[7] Julius H. Parmalee, "Freedmen's Aid Societies," in United States Department of Interior, Office of Education, *Bulletin* No. 38 (1916), 268–295.

[8] The American Missionary Association was the only important agency which antedated the war. Founded in 1846 to do missionary work among the slaves, its most notable *ante bellum* accomplishment was the establishment of Berea College. The A. M. A. drew its primary strength from New England and, although nondenominational, was strongly Congregationalist in its composition.

[9] *Independent,* October 4, 1866; Swint, *Northern Teacher,* 143–170.

[10] Amory D. Mayo, "The Work of Certain Northern Churches in the Education of the Freedmen, 1861–1900," United States Department of Interior, *Annual Report of the Commissioner of Education, 1902* (Washington, 1903), 293–94.

[11] For the proceedings of the convention and the constitution of the new church bureau, see Freedmen's Aid Society, *First Annual Report* (1867), 3ff.

[12] *Northwestern Advocate,* August 15, 1866.

[13] *Independent,* July 12, 1866; *Zion's Herald,* July 18, 1866.

[14] Clipping from Boston *Recorder,* Scrapbook "C," Simpson Papers.

[15] *Independent,* July 12, 1866.

[16] Freedmen's Aid Society, *First Annual Report* (1867), 11.

[17] *Ladies Repository,* XXX (March, 1870), 240; *Journal of the General Conference, 1876,* p. 310.

[18] *Northwestern Advocate,* February 19, 1873; *Minutes of the Texas Annual Conference, 1874,* p. 25; Freedmen's Aid Society, *Fifth Annual Report* (1871), 6.

[19] *Western Advocate,* May 31, 1865; *Methodist Advocate,* September 8, 1875; *Christian Union,* December 22, 1875.

[20] Mayo, "Northern Churches in the Education of the Freedmen," *Annual Report of the Commissioner of Education, 1902,* p. 293.

[21] Charles F. Myers to A. G. Studer, May 21, 1866, B.R.F.A.L.

[22] H. R. Pease to J. W. Alvord, July 14, 1868, B.R.F.A.L.; *Western Advocate,* March 3, 1869.

[23] *Zion's Herald,* June 28, 1865; *Christian Advocate,* May 25, 1866.

[24] *Central Advocate,* August 15, 1866.

[25] *Christian Advocate,* April 18 and July 11, 1867; *Central Advocate,* July 19, 1871; Freedmen's Aid Society, *Eighth Annual Report* (1874), 38; Stearns, *Black Man of the South,* 63.

[26] *Minutes of the Mississippi Mission Conference, 1867,* p. 14; Freedmen's Aid Society, *Eighth Annual Report* (1874), 35; *Minutes of The Tennessee Annual Conference, 1876,* pp. 22–23.

[27] Freedmen's Aid Society, *Third Annual Report* (1869), 7; *Fourth Annual Report* (1870), 30; Richard S. Rust, ed., *Isaac M. Wiley: Late Bishop of the M. E. Church* (Cincinnati and New York, 1885), 125.

[28] Freedmen's Aid Society, *Eleventh Annual Report* (1877), 22.

[29] *Methodist Advocate,* February 24, 1869.

[30] Freedmen's Aid Society, *Fourth Annual Report* (1870), 7.

[31] Luther P. Jackson, "Educational Efforts of the Freedmen's Bureau and the Freedmen's Aid Societies in South Carolina," *Journal of Negro History,* VIII (January, 1923), 15.

[32] *Statutes at Large of the United States of America,* XXXIX (Boston, 1866), 92, 176.

[33] Technically, the grants were made for the rental of school buildings, but the standard rate was $10 per month for each person engaged in teaching an average of thirty or more pupils. R. S. Rust to Col. Edwin Beecher, August 31, 1869, B.R.F.A.L.; *Methodist Review,* LV (January, 1872), 105; Oliver O. Howard, *Autobiography,* 2 vols. (New York, 1908), II, 271.

[34] *Missionary Advocate,* XXIII (April, 1867), 7.

[35] O. O. Howard to W. P. Carlin, March 6, 1868, B.R.F.A.L.; James Lynch to Simpson, December 5, 1868, Simpson Papers.

[36] *Methodist Advocate,* June 8, 1870.

[37] O. O. Howard to W. P. Carlin, March 6, 1868; E. W. Mason to O. O. Howard, June 30, 1870, B.R.F.A.L.

[38] Richard Rust to John W. Alvord, September 12, 1870, B.R.F.A.L.

[39] Freedmen's Aid Society, *Fourth Annual Report* (1870), 11; *Fifth Annual Report* (1871), 13.

[40] *Ibid., Eighth Annual Report* (1874), 5, 77; *Journal of the General Conference, 1876,* p. 624.

[41] These schools were: Central Tennessee College, Nashville; Clark University, Atlanta; Claflin University, Orangeburg, S. C.; New Orleans University; Shaw University (soon changed to Rust College), Holly Springs, Miss.; Wiley University, Marshall, Texas; Centenary Biblical Institute, Baltimore; Bennett Seminary, Greensboro, N. C.; Cookman Institute, Jacksonville, Fla.; Dadeville Seminary, Dadeville, Ala.; Haven Normal School, Waynesboro, Ga.; Lagrange Seminary, Lagrange, Ga.; Meridian Seminary, Meridian, Miss.; Rust Normal School, Huntsville, Ala.; Walden Seminary, Little Rock; West Texas Conference Seminary, Austin. In addition, two Biblical Institutes and Meharry Medical College, Nashville, were being operated in conjunction with one or the other of the above named schools. Freedmen's Aid Society, *Twelfth Annual Report* (1878), 11.

[42] J. H. McCarty to Simpson, December 30, 1876, Simpson Papers; Freedmen's Aid Society, *Sixth Annual Report* (1872), 22–24; *Tenth Annual Report* (1876), 20; *Twelfth Annual Report* (1878), 19; *Zion's Herald*, September 24, 1874.

[43] *Methodist Advocate*, July 19, 1871.

[44] *Catalog of the Officers and Students of Clark University, Atlanta, Ga., 1879*, pp. 14–17.

[45] Freedmen's Aid Society, *Tenth Annual Report* (1876), 13, 25.

[46] Ibid., *Twelfth Annual Report* (1878), 12.

[47] *Northwestern Advocate*, June 28, 1865; *Christian Advocate*, June 10, 1875.

[48] Lewis, *Centenary Souvenir*, xvii; Howard, *Autobiography*, II, 406; *Catalog of Clark University, 1883–1884*, pp. 16–19; Mayo, "Northern Churches in the Education of the Freedmen, 1869–1900," *Annual Report of the Commission of Education, 1902*, p. 299.

[49] *Zion's Herald*, March 14, 1866; Emma S. Taber to Richard Rust, January 7, 1870, B.R.F.A.L. Freedmen's Aid Society, *Eighth Annual Report* (1874), 33.

[50] *Methodist Advocate*, March 24, 1875; Freedmen's Aid Society, *Eighth Annual Report* (1874), 33; *Eleventh Annual Report* (1877), 14; *Twelfth Annual Report* (1878), 54.

[51] *Methodist Advocate*, October 20, 1875.

[52] The Freedmen's Aid Society employed fifty-two teachers in its first year of operation. The number rose above a hundred in 1868, achieved a momentary level with a high of one hundred and ten in 1870, dropped steeply the next year and thereafter maintained an average of about seventy-five. However, the teachers paid by the Society were not the only ones who taught in its schools. Possibly half of the instructors in the Society's schools drew their salaries from other sources. Nor does this exhaust the list of Methodists engaged in teaching in the South. A greater number labored in schools supported by state aid or private subscription than in those under the jurisdiction of the church.

[53] *Christian Advocate*, August 29, 1867; Curry, *Davis W. Clark*, 227.

[54] M. E. Pruett to J. R. Lewis, May 20, 1870, B.R.F.A.L.; *Zion's Herald*, February 22, 1872.

[55] *Western Advocate*, January 29, 1868; Mrs. C. F. Brim to J. R. Lewis, n.d., B.R.F.A.L.

[56] *Minutes of the New Jersey Methodist State Convention, Held in Trenton, New Jersey, September 27–29, 1870* (Trenton, N. J., 1870), 77; *Minutes of the Texas Annual Conference, 1874*, p. 19; *Methodist Advocate*, June 23, 1875.

[57] *Christian Advocate*, August 29, 1867; Freedmen's Aid Society, *First Annual Report* (1867), 2; *Sixth Annual Report* (1872), 13.

[58] *Western Advocate*, June 10, 1868; February 3, 1869; June 15, 1870.

[59] Freedmen's Aid Society, *Eighth Annual Report* (1874), 30; *Catalog of Clark University, 1879*, 19; *Zion's Herald*, November 5, 1874.

[60] This was the fare at New Orleans University in 1874, but it was not unique. Freedmen's Aid Society, *Eighth Annual Report* (1874), 34.

[61] *Proceedings of the Southern Methodist Conference, 1871*, p. 32; *Methodist Advocate*, June 23, 1875.

[62] H. R. Pease to O. O. Howard, January 1, 1869, B.R.F.A.L.

[63] *Methodist Advocate*, April 10, 1872; December 3, 1873; Freedmen's Aid Society, *Twelfth Annual Report* (1878), 39.

[64] *Methodist Advocate*, October 20, 1875.

[65] Freedmen's Aid Society, *Eighth Annual Report* (1874), 54.

[66] Ibid., *Seventh Annual Report* (1874), 17; *Twelfth Annual Report* (1878), 24.

[67] Conser, *Virginia After the War*, 74; Freedmen's Aid Society, *Twelfth Annual Report* (1878), 27; H. R. Pease to John W. Alvord, July 14, 1868; J. R. Lewis to O. O. Howard, July 17, 1869, B.R.F.A.L.

[68] *Christian Advocate*, March 21, 1866.

[69] *Methodist*, March 2, 1867; Freedmen's Aid Society, *Tenth Annual Report* (1876), 33; *Journal of the General Conference, 1876*, p. 309.

[70] Freedmen's Aid Society, *Eighth Annual Report* (1874), 42; *Twelfth Annual Report* (1878), 52.

[71] *Christian Advocate*, April 9, 1868.

[72] *Minutes of the Louisiana Annual Conference, 1876*, pp. 19–20.

[73] Freedmen's Aid Society, *Twelfth Annual Report* (1878), 14.

[74] O. H. Howard to J. R. Lewis, April 5, 1869, B.R.F.A.L.; Freedmen's Aid Society, *Eighth Annual Report* (1874), 39.

[75] *Christian Advocate*, March 21, 1866; April 9, 1868.

[76] Quoted in *Methodism and the Republic*.

# VII
# God's Controversy with Methodism

The Methodist Church, in forwarding her work in the South, [is] bowing too deferentially to the Southern spirit of caste.

*Independent,* January 4, 1866.

There is no church in Christendom that more heartily despises caste than the Methodist Episcopal Church, but she must use common sense in dealing with this . . . question.

*Central Advocate,* January 31, 1866.

ONE OF THE SETTLEMENTS to come out of the age of Radical Reconstruction which Southerners never tried to undo was the strict separation of religious worship along racial lines. During the *ante bellum* era, whites and Negroes in the South held membership in the same denominations and very generally in the same congregations. Segregation was enforced in the allotment of pew space and the administration of the sacraments, but members, irrespective of color, "all sang and shouted together." On the heels of the war, however, came a revolution of practice in the evangelical churches of the South and not only did mixed congregations pass into limbo, but entire denominations also became exclusively white or Negro as the ex-slaves crowded into colored Baptist or African Methodist churches. The only major Protestant organization that made a strenuous effort to run counter to the trend and accommodate large numbers of whites and Negroes in the same religious body was the Methodist Episcopal Church. In undertaking "this most difficult work, hedged about with prejudices on both sides" Northern Methodists were to fall into mutual reproach. The hope that "points of race would not be sprung" or, if they were, that members would let "matters of difference go, and work for Jesus" met with frustration again and again.[1] The correctness of a Southerner's indelicate prediction that "the almighty nigger will . . . do the work of Beelzebub in the . . . church" was subsequently confirmed by the high tribunal of Methodism. The General Conference of 1876 ruefully remarked that the attempt to adjust relations between white and black members had "been the cause . . . of much excitement and discussion, and . . . of considerable personal feeling."[2]

The most outspoken champions of an unsegregated Methodism were found among the clergymen of New England. Frequently by resolutions, often by sermons, and constantly through their journal, *Zion's Herald*, preachers of this area demanded that the church bear "clear, unequivocal, and emphatic testimony . . . with respect to what is known as the spirit of caste." "We want no . . . unrighteous distinction of color in the church of God," keynoted a Massachusetts Methodist convention.[3] The Church North was "to ignore all distinctions of color in the membership and ministry" and "never allow their introduction into any organizations or movements in the Southern field." The highest service for which Methodism was called into the Southern states, said some New Englanders, was "to abolish . . . all thought and feeling . . . that distinctions arising from color . . . [were] intended to separate members of the same human family." They wanted the church to be "God's great tidal wave . . . to sweep away caste from the South."[4]

Foremost of all the vocalists on the subject of race relations was Gilbert Haven. Stocky, red-haired, intimately known in the coterie of professional reformers, and strongly veined with sensuality, Haven was the *bête noire* of conservatives, as he tried to obey his code that "the way to break to pieces this abominable folly of caste is to live it to death" by talk and action.[5] Had not the firebrand of racial antagonism been hurled into church affairs, Haven might have remained an obscure figure, but his fame grew as these differences became more intense. Blessed with a peculiar gift for "insult, detraction, and exasperating insinuation," the Massachusetts cleric vaulted to renown, if not adoration, by his unremitting attacks on "colorphobia." "It is a stench in the nostrils of the Almighty . . . that brethren in Christ are set apart because of their color," Haven ranted, and he insisted that Methodists "pay no more regard to the color of one's skin than to the color of his eyes or hair. . . ." [6] Haven, and the fringe which sided with him, sought not only an equality of ecclesiastical privileges for blacks and whites, but also an intermingling of the colors in the enjoyment of those privileges. The composition of congregations and conferences should be a blend of the two races.

For adjustments "founded on inevitable necessities," Haven had no respect. If Southern whites communing with the Northern church should object to an admixture of races, either "let them conquer their prejudices" or, if they "refuse to worship . . . with the blacks, there should be no other provision made for them." [7] Nor was the New Englander amenable to the oft-repeated suggestion that indiscriminate groupings might also be distasteful to the Negro. "We know the colored people," Haven confidently asserted, "and we know they want neither a Negro car, a Negro pew, nor a Negro conference." Sometimes forced to deal with evidence to the contrary, Haven took refuge in transcendant norms which he freely interpreted to his advantage. Even if "the colored people desire . . . separation," Haven once wrote, the request "must be answered by the question 'Is it right?' " And since "Christ is not divided . . . Christianity does not require a white Methodist Church and a black Methodist Church." Even though the adoption of his policies might involve the risk of repelling Methodists of both hues from the Northern denomination, Haven maintained that "the church above all things must do right." No matter how great the loss, "let the word and idea of black and white be expelled from the heart of the church." [8]

Haven's blasts at the color line overshot the province of religious politics. He counseled Americans to carry interracial fraternity beyond the sanctuary. From a Boston pulpit, Haven yearned for the day "not far off" when "the white-hued husband shall boast of the dusky beauty of his wife, and the caucasian wife shall admire the sun-kissed countenance of her husband." [9] Ruffled contemporaries received notice that it was fruitless to oppose "intermarriage of the two races." "Amalgamation is God's word," opined Haven, and "who art thou that fightest against God?" [10] The Bostonian's observations on miscegenation were often slanted to grate on the most tender of Southern sensibilities. Charleston residents learned that in their city was found "the coming race in all its virile perfection." "Here is amalgamation made perfect," said Haven. In the "exquisite tints of delicate brown" he saw the fusion of the African with the "Pinckneys . . . Rhetts, Barnwells and Calhouns." Southerners were further advised that this process would be accelerated by emancipation and "the daughters of . . . haughty Southerners . . . shall yet gratefully accept the offers of the sons of their fathers' slaves, and their parents . . . shall feel their house exalted by the alliance." Ten years was set, in 1865, as the time when "such marriages will be frequent." [11]

The proposition for "mixing and intermingling all colors" was converted into a flail with which foes tried to beat back the Methodist challenge in the South. Northern missionaries grappled continuously with the accusation that "the Methodist Episcopal Church was so shaping its course as to compel a mixture of both races in . . . churches" or "that its preachers advocate[d] a promiscuous commingling in the marriage relation." [12] Nevertheless, Haven spoke for few Methodists in the North besides himself. Even on the isolated question of religious segregation, the weight of Northern opinion lay somewhere to the right of the Haven extreme. An abolitionist in good standing, Daniel Curry, although he admitted that "the view . . . in favor of the equality of all men in the church . . . is the correct one," labeled it "an ideal to be aimed at . . . rather than a practical reality to be suddenly effected." [13] To other Methodists, the proposals for a color-blind church were "wild and foolish," "senseless," and "hopeless and preposterous." "Haven and . . . his particular kind may spend their sweat . . . to coerce the freedmen into . . . loving intercourse with the Anglo-Saxon race, but it is an . . . effort for which no thanks will be given," snapped one leading church-man.[14]

Northerners who believed it "useless to talk about ignoring all distinctions of color in the church" had a moral anchor for their argument in the thesis that "there was in each race a . . . prefer-ence for its own color." This, said moderates, was "a rightful basis for social separateness," and could "not . . . truthfully [be] called caste." [15] John Reid, one of the most energetic proponents of racial division in Methodism, defended his position by the contention that he was catering to the wishes of the Negroes no less than the whites. "The force that operates on the races is that of repulsion as much on the one part as the other," he wrote. "The peculiarities of each are so marked that they will always tend apart." [16] Stephen Merrill, Reid's successor on the *Western* and a bishop after 1872, did not camouflage his thought in the language of a pseudo science yet reached a similar conclusion. Merrill was unsure whether the alleged exclusiveness of the blacks resulted "from an instinct of nature, a mere prejudice or . . . inhuman treatment from the whites," but he had no doubt that they "want[ed] churches . . . of their own." [17] Reid, Merrill, and the many who teamed with them, were scrupulous to stay clear of any taint of racial discrimination. But inasmuch as there was "not more prejudice amongst the whites against the blacks than . . . of the blacks against the whites," to compel the Negroes to "mingle in white congregations when they desire[d] churches of their own would be a species of ecclesiastical tyranny not to be tolerated." [18]

Northern disagreements over segregation, in themselves wide enough to insure intradenominational friction, were intensified by the Unionist, nonslaveholding Southern whites who adhered to the Methodist Episcopal Church. Of this class of Southerners,

"Parson" Brownlow confided to an interviewer that "it is hard to tell which they hate the most, the Rebels, or the Negroes." [19] These antipathies the yeomen and mountaineers carried with them into the Northern church. "Inasmuch as God has made the two races of different color and scent it is but reasonable . . . that our social taste . . . be respected," read a familiar reply to pleas that Southern whites show more interracial tolerance. "Separate the African from the white race and we care not how high he is elevated," wrote an Arkansas disciple of Northern Methodism, "but we hold that it is unnatural to raise him to equal . . . standing with whites in white society." [20] Whites on the Methodist frontier of the South seldom rationalized their attitudes beyond the truism that "the white man is white and the colored man colored." But upon whatever rock their case was built, they clung to their "deep and inexpungeable prejudices" and warned "that neither national nor church legislation can force social equality upon us." In the long run their inflexible resistance was as determinative of church policy as any view held in the North. Irrespective of what some ecclesiasts wanted, Northern Methodism finally had no choice but to "let the work . . . develop according to the character of the people" and the whites made it known that they were "capable of managing their own church affairs without any interference [from] Boston." [21]

Despite the insistence of radicals that missionaries sent to the South be instructed to discriminate "only on grounds of moral fitness," the question of mixed or segregated societies originally was left to the judgment of each Northern preacher. In the border states and the Appalachian country no encouragement was given to uniting blacks and whites in congregational organizations. The lower South, however, witnessed several instances in the days of returning peace in which communicants of different colors worshipped together. Sometimes, in these interracial gatherings, no distinction between Negroes and whites was officially recognized. A missionary in the Sea Islands reported that in his flock "both races find such seats as please them in any or all parts of the house." [22] But, more often, the Northern denomination adopted the custom of Southern churches in the prewar period and provided communicants with separate accommodations. An unrepentant Confederate ungraciously noted that Northern Methodists in New Orleans made "the colored brothers and sisters roost like a flock of . . . blackbirds in the gallery, instead of occupying seats among the white folks." [23]

Nevertheless, the inclusion of whites and Negroes in the same societies proved a transient phase of the Church North's activity in the South. The mortifying reversal forced upon Timothy Lewis in Charleston exemplified the experiences of numerous missionaries. Four months after Lewis had won over a bloc of Negroes with assurances that Northern Methodism knew no color lines, he had to work out with the newly-won converts an agreement which specified that "the blacks worship in their churches and the whites in theirs." With boundless glee a native Georgian correctly recorded that "the brethren who have . . . tried to set up a mixed arrangement have signally failed." [24] Their sensitivity enhanced by a lack of success in reordering Southern prejudices, missionaries bore with ill grace insinuations that they had deferred "to the old spirit of caste." They sneered at the churchmen whose lives were "spent in the safe retreats . . . of the north studying abstract principles of social science and indulging in airy flights of rhetoric." One parson, thoroughly disabused of his prior fancies, wished that "all . . . northern . . . preachers who insist on mingling the two races in . . . church ministrations be sent South to practically develop their theories." "Ere half their allotted time expired, they would hasten home . . . wiser . . . men." [25]

The barrier which quickly went up between Negro and white congregations withstood subsequent efforts to breach it. Those who tried met with sharp rebuffs. In Atlanta, during 1874, an episcopal mandate ordered the union of the Negro and white churches in the city. In the furore, nearly half of the whites renounced their ecclesiastical allegiance, and the remainder relinquished the existing property to the Negroes and built a new church. A Northern transfer who asked his Tennessee parishioners in 1868 to admit Negroes to communion disturbed the "unity and brotherly love of the membership" and, said an outraged white, "started a commotion that he can never quiet." In the preceding year, at a Maryland church, the preacher's announcement that "colored people were invited to seats in the gallery . . . stirred up such a spirit of rebellion and riot that the trustees . . . had the meeting stopped." [26] Occasionally, however, it was the initiative of colored folk, rather than of anxious whites, that led to riotous incidents. A Freedmen's Bureau agent who attended a Methodist Episcopal meeting in Shelbyville, Tennessee, related that "a general stampede . . . for the door ensued" after "a dozen colored people . . . made their appearance in the . . . back of the church." [27] Northern Methodists of different colors in New Orleans clashed at least twice during the Reconstruction period on the issue of mixed congregations. A few Negroes in 1868 and again in 1874 petitioned for admission to Ames Church, which was attended exclusively by whites. Both applications were denied by the pastor and lay officials who decided "that no person of color should be allowed in the . . . church." Reportedly, the first controversy was hushed, but the second refusal brought "intense excitement among the colored people . . . and . . . throughout the city." Distressed clergymen in Louisiana sent out calls for episcopal advice, but when it arrived it was not distinguished for its novelty. Bishop Randolph Foster, after hearing arguments by the contestants "advised the colored members to consider the circumstances and not seek membership where they are not wanted." [28]

Routed from the advanced position of nonsegregated congregations, opposition to the color line in Methodism retreated to another station of defense. Unable to impress individual societies with the necessity for a bicolored membership, Methodism's left wing hoped to apply the principle to Annual Conferences. Even though the laity might succumb to the prejudice of race, they were determined that the itinerant ministry should conduct its regular business unconscious of such distinctions. In assuming a stand against the separation of conferences according to color, the adversaries of segregation gained in numerical strength and respectability. Clergymen who curtly dismissed the demand for promiscuous groupings on every level of religious activity were ready to concede that division should not be permitted to infiltrate the Annual Conference. Arthur Edwards, of the *Northwestern Advocate,* did not regularly travel in radical company, yet he contended that "there should be but one kind of conference organization" and asked Northern Methodism "to preach the truth without consultation . . . with the erroneous prejudices held by either whites or blacks inside our membership in the South." [29] Edwards and his companions were eventually disappointed in their opinions, but conference division was not achieved with the rapidity or ease of the racial divorce in congregations. It was the movement for unmixed Annual Conferences that aroused the most prolonged and bitter debate in the multisided struggle over segregation.

The General Conference of 1864, confronted with an influx of Negroes from the border districts, directed the bishops, "where in their . . . judgment the exigencies of the work . . . demand it," to "organize among . . . colored ministers, for the benefit of . . . colored members . . . one or more . . . mission conferences." [30] Armed with this authorization, the episcopal committee quickly formed Negro Methodists in the eastern border states into two administrative units under the names of the Washington and Delaware conferences. What was presaged by the establishment of these new jurisdictions for Negroes, Methodists did not agree. Those who appointed themselves "to watch jealously over ecclesiastical policy . . . that the prejudice of race . . . may no more appear" proclaimed "with heaviness of heart" that the Washington and Delaware conferences foreshadowed the Northern Methodist program in the remaining areas of the South. Others, however, spoke of the creations as "temporary expedients" which would "inevitably die at the next General Conference." [31] The view of neither side was completely substantiated by the 1868 General Conference, but that assembly took an additional step in the direction of a divided church. Replying to petitions from the white and colored clergy in Kentucky, Methodism's high tribunal delegated permission to the "bishops who may preside in the Kentucky Conference . . . to organize the colored ministers within bounds of said conference into a separate annual conference if said ministers request it." [32] Already aware of the tastes of the Negro parsons, the performance of episcopal duty in the Bluegrass state was merely perfunctory. With the coming of a third conference for black members the battle between Methodist brethren was squarely joined, as one side attempted to stay or roll back the forces of separation, and the other exerted itself to extend the precedents of 1864 and 1868 to the middle and lower tiers of Southern states.

In the territory of the deceased Confederacy, proposals for conference separation had varying degrees of relevance. After 1868, the question was most acutely practical in central Tennessee and the northern portions of Alabama and Georgia. Here sizable numbers of white and Negro Methodists lived side by side to amplify the painful difficulties of reconciling Christians of contrasting colors. The native whites of this region were nearly unanimous in their dislike "for the damaging and unpopular policy of mixed conferences," and agitated for the church to proceed toward division "without regard to speculation, exploded errors or millennial theories." Otherwise, "the white work in the South is a failure." [33] They were quick to notice that the church, by its legislation in 1864 and 1868, had become committed to an ambiguous policy. Along the border, where Northern Methodism had footholds before the war, separate conferences had won canonical sanction, but farther South mixed organizations continued in force. This situation, complained Southern whites, amounted to "one policy for the North and one for the South." [34] The native partisans of segregation heaped up their defenses by advertising that the South was required to perform what Methodists themselves balked at in the North. Negro membership, they reminded critics, was a thing so rare in the churches and conferences of Northern whites that it was looked upon as a kind of wonder. "The chief difference between our excellent friends [in New England] and ourselves," said one Georgian, "is that they disclaim against caste at a safe distance; we practice where we have to bear the odium." [35] The volume of propaganda for segregated conferences swelled out of proportion to the number of whites in the South when Erasmus Fuller brought the Atlanta *Advocate* into the lists. Although Fuller conscientiously opened the *Advocate's* columns to arguments on both sides, his editorial iterations that "our mission in the South . . . is . . . to preach the gospel not amalgamation" seemed wondrously impressive to Northerners.[36]

The Negro clergymen of Tennessee, Alabama, and Georgia in the segregation fight conducted themselves with a decorum that white Methodists would have done well to imitate. Black preachers in these areas were largely muted by illiteracy, but they manifested, through occasional spokesmen, considerably less enthusiasm for conference division than the whites. The brunt of opposition to a segregated Methodism, however, came not from the regions in which the problem was of greatest practical concern, but from South Carolina, Mississippi and Louisiana, where so few white Methodists resided that religious racism could be argued on principle without the distractions of reality. In the states of the lower South, white teachers and preachers, usually of extended abolitionist reputations, combined with a few highly-competent Negroes to general the battle against segregation in the name of the freedmen. Ardently and doggedly they scourged "all artificial distinctions in society." "The question . . . of equal rights . . . among men, irrespective of . . . race, is not one to be argued, but accepted by those who believe in the Bible," announced a convocation of New Orleans Methodists.[37] The Southern enemies of racial division, rather than being content with the preservation of the *status quo,* finagled to wipe away any church legislation which smelled of discrimination. They coalesced into something of an informal bloc on the basis of the "Louisiana Platform." This set of doctrines, advanced at the 1872 General Conference by the veteran anti-slavery crusader, Lucius Matlack, called not only for "no more separate conference organizations for colored people" but "the absorption . . . of those now existing . . . by . . . other . . . annual conferences." Antipathies ignited by the white-hot contest over segregation mingled with regional jealousy over the location of the *Methodist Advocate* in the middle South to conceive a new journalistic enterprise. With an obvious slur at Fuller, Louisiana Methodists lamented that "too many . . . church papers [were] giving their influences to the perpetuation of wicked castes" and the Louisianians fully communicated their objections in 1873 by unveiling the *Southwestern Christian Advocate* at New Orleans. The new paper had the stated purpose of producing "no uncertain sound on the great questions of equality between the races"—a vocation which its white editors eagerly pursued.[38]

While the argument over the relations of black and white Methodists droned on, the process of racial separation in mixed conferences was carried as far as possible without actual division. Built upon the basis of segregated congregations, presiding elders' districts soon came to consist exclusively of either white or colored preachers and communicants. The color line was likewise drawn through the Annual Conference sessions. "The noble body of white ministers" always occupied the front seats and "somewhat to the rear sat [the] colored ministers." Intermittent suggestions that it would be well "to ignore caste in all sittings of the conference" usually brought "men leaping to their feet . . . all of them greatly excited." [39] The seating arrangements indicated the Negro preacher's role in managing the business of the church. Sympathetic commentators observed that black clergymen in association with whites "rather hung timidly on the edges of the assembly than formed a part of it." They admittedly had "the inferior places," were "seldom consulted and not . . . asked to take any part in the work." [40] Nevertheless, partial segregation did not prevent eruptions of clerical antagonism. At the meeting of the Holston conference in 1867 the presiding bishop's attempt to administer communion simultaneously to ministers of both races was answered by cries of the whites about the "new and unnatural conduct of our leaders," "an unnatural and disgusting practice," and "a strike for Negro equality." Another bishop who later indulged in an identical experiment in Georgia declared that it resulted in "a fearful exposure of . . . caste" because "the white brethren would not partake of . . . the sacrament . . . and . . . left the house." [41] The ordination of Negro and white preachers in the same ceremony engendered more friction. Some Northerners felt that this matter was "altogether too trifling an affair to quarrel about," but Southerners persisted in the opposite notion. A preacher in East Tennessee complained about "Negro equality" after he "was ordained to deacon's orders . . . with . . . the colored brethren." A Georgian, one of a mixed class of candidates for clerical parchments, "refused to be ordained . . . and left the conference without ordination, saying he could never meet the opposition at home should he be thus ordained." [42]

To allay the excited passions of Church North members in the South would have taxed the wisest head and gentlest heart in Christendom, but the Southern field did not always get oversight from men with those qualities. After his election as bishop in 1872, "the hell-raising" Gilbert Haven took up residence in Atlanta and began the supervision of Northern Methodist endeavor in the middle and lower South. Methodist whites in these states reacted bitterly to this development. "Our people repudiate Bishop Haven [and] . . . will not receive him," wrote an indignant East Tennessean. Intelligence was widely disseminated "that the location of Bishop Haven . . . as the chief pastor of the Southern work would seriously embarrass the white

work in . . . the entire South." An Atlanta layman predicted that
Northern Methodist merchants in the South, because they were
"dependent upon the patronage and support of the Southern
people," would be compelled by Haven's arrival "to abandon
the church of their choice or give up their business." [43] Haven,
who privately said that he hoped to "infuse New England ideas
into the South," endeavored to rule the members of the Church
North in that section in a manner consistent with his precon-
ceived plans. He had indifferent success in changing Southern
opinion, but his announcements that "miscegenation is the word
for today" lighted up a trail of animosity. "Bishop Haven,"
wrote Charles Nordhoff, "appears . . . to have quite a genius for
keeping alive a subject which naturally stirs up rancorous feelings." One cautious editor, alarmed by the intensification of the
racial controversy in the South after 1872, found in Haven the
perfect scapegoat. "The election of such a man as Gilbert Haven
to the episcopacy, and giving into his charge the Southern work
. . . is sufficient . . . to account for much of this increase," he explained.[44] There were others, in and out of Northern Methodism,
who agreed.

The South, although it was the laboratory for Methodist experiments in racial relations, did not hold within itself the power
of a definitive solution. The decision for or against segregation
belonged to the General Conference which was dominated by
Methodists in the Northern states. In the North, arguments for
an unsegregated church had never been more than half convincing, and as the postwar pattern of custom in the South began
to clarify, they rapidly spun downward in popularity. Most importantly, the advocates of segregation won strong support in
the highest circles of the Methodist hierarchy. "The union of our
white and colored work throughout the South is a serious mistake," asserted the secretary of the Missionary Society in 1876,
and, at the time, he spoke for most of those of comparable rank.[45]
Methodism's managers did not forget that they were entrusted
with the direction of a mammoth corporation which had to be

kept in smoothly functioning order. Faced with what neutrals called the alternatives of "theoretical right" and "practical necessity," they decided on "practical necessity." Conference division seemed an immediate way of extricating the Southern project from serious embarrassments. Fewer displays of racial antagonism between Methodists, an end to "the jeers of bad men," and an accelerated rate of conversions among both colors were officially announced as the expected results of separation.[46] What Methodist leaders did not quite say was that they reckoned it more profitable to quit struggling against the usages of the South.

Also shuttling through Northern thought on segregation was the desire to cultivate better relations with Southern Methodism. Within the Church North were few exceptions to the rule that the warmest proponents of fraternity between the Methodisms were also very partial to setting apart the Negro. The Southern church had proclaimed in distinct terms its position on interracial religion. "You need never come to us with a proposition that the blacks be members of the same Annual . . . Conferences," cried one clergyman of the South. The Southern General Conference of 1870 echoed his words and listed "mixed conferences" among the impediments to interdenominational harmony.[47] Many Northern Methodists did not look upon these objections as unreasonable and, said opponents, were ready to offer "the dark brother as a sacrifice for the fraternal fellowship of the Methodist Episcopal Church, South." The *Methodist*, the organ of the reconciliationists, industriously tried to convince Southerners that "the subject of color is viewed in the same light . . . in both churches." "We really recognize the color line," orated David H. Wheeler, Crook's replacement as editor of the *Methodist*. Wheeler termed "racial lines . . . matters of Providence." [48] The readiness to buy Southern Methodism's loving clasp at the Negro's expense sometimes went to extreme lengths. Erastus O. Haven, a cousin of the incorrigible Gilbert and at different times president of the University of Michigan, Syracuse, and Northwestern, evolved a plan which would completely have cut off Northern Methodism's Negro membership. He recommended that the Northern denomination transfer its Negro communicants to the Colored Methodist Episcopal Church and then subsidize the latter's future missionary activity. This, Haven felt, would impress Southerners as "a real act of fraternity." [49] That Haven's proposition was quashed is unimportant beside the fact that it betrayed the thinking of a clique respected for its wealth and intellectual prestige.

The General Conference of 1876 testified to the ability with which the forces of segregation had softened Northern opinion. Conference division in the lower South, rebuked in 1872, was realized four years later. However, the great body of Methodists were not unmindful either of their earlier promises of equality to the freedmen or of the bitter-end opposition to segregation. Through the weary proceedings of 1876, delegates groped for a formula which would satisfy Southern whites yet afford the minimum of offense to the Negro and his friends. The settlement finally hit upon by the General Conference was not exceptionally heroic but, as one preacher said, it was the best attainable balance between "a true Christian expediency" and "the eternal principles of truth and righteousness." Sanction for the division of mixed Annual Conferences was at last given with the important proviso that such action in each conference had to "be requested by a majority of the white members and also a majority of the colored members." [50] Essentially, this solution handed the fretful problem of color back to the South, but Methodists found the doctrine of popular sovereignty more workable than had professional politicians a few decades before. By logic, cajolery, and threats, the black preachers were dissuaded from using their right of veto despite die-hard advice that they were throwing away a last chance to register a protest against "caste." Permissive authority given by Northern Methodism, the colored and white preachers of its faith went their separate ways after 1876. Within five years the South was covered with two networks of Methodist Episcopal Annual Conferences, one for whites and one for Negroes.[51]

The "burning Negro question" flooded over into the Northern Methodist educational system. Amidst the instability of Southern society immediately after Appomattox a considerable number of whites had attended Methodist schools in company with blacks, but this condition was no more permanent than that of mixed congregations.[52] When the color line hardened, it stretched across education as well as religion. However, the church was hardly more anxious to own up to a formal truce with segregation in the classroom than it was in the sanctuary. The institutions maintained by the Freedmen's Aid Society consistently advertised that their facilities were available "to all . . . students . . . without regard to race." After 1866, very few whites took advantage of the offer, yet the Negro schools officially remained open to all comers. Ecclesiasts frequently contended that the same policy was enforced at the seats of learning established for white Methodists. "No whites are excluded from our colored schools and the colored are not excluded from the white schools," declared a Northern clergyman. He contended that "without any attempt to make it so" the student bodies of the various Methodist institutions assumed a white or black cast only because the schools were "surrounded with a large white patronage" or were "in the midst of a large colored patronage." Therefore, the terms "white schools" and "colored schools" merely described a fact rather than an educational policy.[53]

The only Methodist institution for whites of the South that was equal to the best of the freedmen's schools was East Tennessee Wesleyan. From this college came the best case study of Methodist racial practices in education. When Northern Methodist authorities acquired the physical plant at Athens, Tennessee, in 1866, their resources consisted mostly of hope. To scrape together money with which to meet the costs of the purchase and make improvements on the property, recourse was had to the North for contributions. Among those solicited was Oliver O.

Howard, commissioner of the Freedmen's Bureau. Howard agreed to allot federal funds to the embryonic university on the condition that East Tennessee Wesleyan establish "a Normal Department open to pupils, irrespective of color." The trustees of the institution, although "fearful of an uproar among the people," accepted Howard's offer, and bequests amounting to $7,000 were received from the Bureau during 1866 and 1867.[54] In fulfillment of their part of the bargain, Methodists included in the prospectus of East Tennessee Wesleyan for the academic year 1867–68 the information "that the Normal Department of the college will open, irrespective of color to all desiring to become teachers." Notice of the willingness "to open a Normal School . . . to which persons . . . will be admitted without regard to race" was repeated in the catalog of the succeeding year.[55] However, "one crushing fact" remained. A Freedmen's Bureau investigator told his commanding officer in 1870 "that the Normal Department promised for the benefit of . . . the colored people has not been established." [56] He could have written at any later time and made the same report.

Northern Methodists were quick with an explanation for the seeming breach of contract with the Freedmen's Bureau. The agreement "was made in good faith," they said, but plans for a normal school were aborted by the failure of Negroes to apply for training. Nelson E. Cobleigh, for a time the president of East Tennessee Wesleyan, flatly asserted that no "colored student . . . ever offered himself to enter the university" and, in the absence of pupils, no reason existed "to justify the additional expense . . . of complying with the prescribed conditions." If Cobleigh was candid he doubtless felt a sense of relief, for he had written previously from Athens that "feelings in this community . . . are very strong against educating white and colored together." [57] However, when the head of the Freedmen's Bureau in Tennessee heard that no Negroes had been enrolled at East Tennessee Wesleyan, he doubted "if the trustees . . . ever intended any other result" and recommended to Howard "that no further aid be given [to] them." [58] Another federal agent denounced the course of Methodist authorities "as a fraud." He accused school administrators of not trying "to execute the trust in good faith" and said that potential colored students were frightened away by the information, surreptitiously conveyed through official channels, "that it would not be convenient to have blacks mixed up with Athens University." [59]

To choose between the explanations of the Methodists and public officials would be a work of supererogation. East Tennessee Wesleyan, like every other Methodist school in the South, catered to pupils of only one race. After the tiff with the Freedmen's Bureau had passed, Northern Methodists themselves became unrestrained in their speech about "the only college which we have in the South for the . . . training . . . of the white race." A cleric campaigning for funds to help the Athens school relieve its chronic burden of debt prompted Methodists to generosity by the clever reminder that "this is the only institution belonging to our church in the South for whites." [60] Made jittery by the periodic gestures to break down the barricade of color around East Tennessee Wesleyan, Southern whites cautioned that "the introduction of one colored student in that school would kill it." "Here mixed schools are impossible," a Tennessean replied to censorious Northerners. White opposition to unsegregated education, he added, was so deep that "forty bishops could not work the prejudice out of the present generation . . . in this country." [61]

After fifteen years of waxing and waning argument over the relative status of black and white members, the Church North had come to an ecclesiastical equivalent of the doctrine later enunciated in *Plessy v. Ferguson*. Partly by express legislation, but mostly by passive consent to relentless custom, the Northern denomination recognized the principle of "separate but equal" privileges for its members in the South. For the benefit of whites, societies, conferences, and schools existed alongside similar arrangements for Negroes, and each communicant had equal access to the facilities provided for his race. This situation amounted to a clear-cut victory for the wing of Methodism which designed "to educate, elevate, and Christianize both races . . . but each separately for the good of all concerned." [62] Signs soon appeared that there was no immediate intention of contesting the settlement. In language strikingly anticipatory of that used by the Supreme Court in 1896, the General Conference of 1884 condoned the policy of racial separation in the South. While the General Conference believed that it was "duty bound to provide for . . . every class of our membership . . . a fair and equal opportunity in church and school accommodations," yet "when this is done our duty is performed, and the equal rights . . . demanded . . . [are] fully conceded." "Equal rights to the best facilities" rather than equal rights to the same facilities ought to be the watchword of the church. Segregation, the assembly resolved, was a "question of expediency . . . to be left to the choice . . . of those on the ground. . . ." [63] Such legislation was far from the social tenets of New England Methodism but, said Bishop Isaac Wiley in extenuation of the action, "The church has simply accepted the circumstances as she finds them, and . . . is trying to meet the needs of all." [64] His utterance was the fruit of a wisdom ripened by much unhappy experience.

## NOTES

[1] *Proceedings of the Southern Methodist Conference, 1871,* p. 13; J. C. Hartzell to Simpson, April 2, 1872, Simpson Papers; *Central Advocate,* March 31, 1875.
[2] Chattanooga *Daily Gazette,* October 26, 1865; *Journal of the General Conference, 1876,* p. 338.
[3] *Ibid.,* 280; *Christian Advocate,* May 10, 1866.
[4] *Methodist Review,* XLVII (April, 1865), 268–69; *Christian Advocate,* June 1, 1866; *Western Advocate,* June 20, 1866; *Zion's Herald,* January 29, 1874.
[5] *Methodist Advocate,* April 23, 1873.
[6] *Independent,* February 1, 1866; Haven, *National Sermons,* 600.
[7] *Christian Advocate,* March 1, 1866; *Zion's Herald,* March 5, 1874.
[8] *Independent,* January 4, 1866; *Christian Advocate,* March 1, 1866; *Zion's Herald,* April 23, 1868.
[9] Haven, *National Sermons,* 627.

[10] *Methodist Review,* LII (April, 1870), 196; Haven, *National Sermons,* 627.

[11] Prentice, *Gilbert Haven,* 211; Haven, *National Sermons,* 549.

[12] *Western Advocate,* May 2, 1866; Knoxville *Daily Free Press,* September 4, 1867; *Methodist Advocate,* September 9, 1874.

[13] *Christian Advocate,* May 25, 1865.

[14] *Southwestern Advocate,* June 18, 1874, quoting *California Christian Advocate.*

[15] *Methodist Review,* XLVIII (July, 1866), 442.

[16] *Western Advocate,* April 24, 1867.

[17] *Ibid.,* September 9, 1868.

[18] *Ibid.,* September 16, 1868; *Central Advocate,* November 8, 1871.

[19] John T. Trowbridge, *The South: A Tour of its Battle-Fields and Ruined Cities, A Journey Through the Desolated States, and Talks with the People* (Hartford, 1866), 284.

[20] *Central Advocate,* June 28, 1865; Knoxville *Daily Free Press,* November 17, 1867.

[21] *Zion's Herald,* May 21, 1868; *Central Advocate,* May 21, 1871; *Methodist Advocate,* April 9 and May 14, 1873.

[22] *Christian Advocate,* March 30, 1865.

[23] Clipping from the New Orleans *Picayune,* "Scrapbook C," Simpson Papers.

[24] *Missionary Advocate,* XXI (June, 1865), 22; *Methodist Advocate,* April 5, 1876.

[25] *Christian Advocate,* March 15, 1866; *Western Advocate,* September 16, 1868.

[26] Hammond, *The Methodist Episcopal Church in Georgia,* 131; *Christian Advocate,* February 28, 1867; *Zion's Herald,* May 21, 1868.

[27] George L. White to James Thompson, January 30, 1869, B.R.F.A.L.

[28] J. C. Hartzell to Simpson, April 2, 1874, Simpson Papers; *Central Advocate,* March 31, 1875.

[29] *Northwestern Advocate,* October 28, 1874.

[30] *Journal of the General Conference, 1864,* p. 488.

[31] *Christian Advocate,* June 1, 1865; *Western Advocate,* July 12, 1865; *Independent,* January 4, 1866; *Zion's Herald,* March 7, 1866.

[32] *Journal of the General Conference, 1868,* p. 307; *Minutes of the Kentucky Annual Conference, 1868,* pp. 14, 22, 40.

[33] *Methodist Advocate,* January 24, 1872; April 9, 1873; *Northwestern Advocate,* April 16, 1873.

[34] *Western Advocate,* October 23, 1872.

[35] *Central Advocate,* November 14, 1866.

[36] *Northern Advocate,* April 27, 1876.

[37] *Southwestern Advocate,* April 8, 1875.

[38] *Ibid.,* July 3, 1873.

[39] *Western Advocate,* March 13, 1867; Prentice, *Gilbert Haven,* 415–17.

[40] *Methodist Advocate,* May 21, 1873; April 5, 1876.

[41] Knoxville, *Daily Free Press,* October 30 and November 14, 1867; Prentice, *Gilbert Haven,* 414.

[42] *Methodist Advocate,* November 3, 1869; September 16, 1874; *Christian Advocate,* April 12, 1872.

[43] J. C. Kimball to Simpson, June 4, 1872 and John F. Spence to Simpson, September 3, 1872, Simpson Papers.

[44] *Nashville Advocate,* January 10, 1874, quoting *Pacific Methodist; Methodist,* October 16, 1875; Prentice, *Gilbert Haven,* 416.

[45] *Methodist,* February 12, 1876.

[46] *Methodist Advocate,* March 27, 1876; *Northern Advocate,* April 27 and June 8, 1876.

[47] *Ibid.,* August 2, 1865; *Formal Fraternity Proceedings,* 38.

[48] *Methodist,* June 5, September 25, and October 2, 1875.

[49] *Ibid.,* October 2, 1875; *Christian Advocate,* October 14, 1875.

[50] *Journal of the General Conference,* 1876, p. 331; *Zion's Herald,* October 19, 1876. The vote in the General Conference on this legislation confirms what has been said above about the distribution of opinion on segregation. Delegates from the New England area and from the three states of the South with a heavy predominance of Negro members formed the backbone of opposition to change. On the other hand, the white representatives from mixed conferences in the South were solidly in favor of the action. The bill for division carried a margin of one hundred ninety-nine yeas to ninety-four nays.

[51] Technically, in South Carolina, Florida, Louisiana, and Mississippi unsegregated conferences were retained. However, the number of whites in these states was so small as to make them form no actual exception to the statement that different conferences for Negroes and whites were found throughout the South.

[52] *Christian Advocate,* August 1, 1867.

[53] *Proceedings of the Southern Methodist Conference, 1871,* p. 43; *Methodist Advocate,* July 19, 1871.

[54] *Western Advocate,* June 12, 1867; *Methodist Advocate,* May 28, 1873; *Zion's Herald,* July 16, 1874; D. Burt to William P. Carlin, May 14, 1867, B.R.F.A.L.

[55] Knoxville *Daily Free Press,* September 4, 1867; *Third Annual Catalog of East Tennessee Wesleyan University, 1868–1869,* p. 5.

[56] David W. Wilson to John W. Alvord, January 8, 1870, B.R.F.A.L.

[57] N. E. Cobleigh to D. Burt, November 2, 1867, B.R.F.A.L.; *Methodist Advocate,* May 28, 1873; September 16, 1874.

[58] W. P. Carlin to O. O. Howard, November 6, 1867, B.R.F.A.L.

[59] David W. Wilson to John W. Alvord, January 8 and January 10, 1870, B.R.F.A.L.

[60] *Methodist Advocate,* July 19, 1871; March 27, 1872.

[61] *Ibid.,* April 8 and April 29, 1874.

[62] *Ibid.,* February 23, 1875.

[63] *Journal of the General Conference,* 1884, pp. 365–66.

[64] Rust, ed., *Issac W. Wiley,* 140.

# VIII

# The Den of Politics

The time to join forces and do battle for the good, the right, the true, is here. It behooves American Christians . . . to show themselves courageous for their country's welfare and the good of humanity . . . Christianity and its disciples must not fail the nation in this hour of distress and want.

*Pittsburgh Christian Advocate*,
November 30, 1867.

"NEXT TO A SOUND THEOLOGY . . . the thing we most need in this country is correct political teaching," declared Benjamin Crary, mentor of the *Central Advocate*.[1] Although Crary's utterance was inspired by the specific issues of national reconstruction, it had a more general application. The constitutional separation of church and state in the United States has worked well enough to vindicate the wisdom of the Fathers but, as Anson P. Stokes [2] has amply shown, the divorce did not transform the church into a disinterested spectator or an impotent participant on the domestic political scene. Organized Christianity has ever maintained a guardianship over the temporal environment in the interest of preparing man for eternity, and the larger denominations of nineteenth century America, whatever the law might decree, were not willing to renounce their historic function. But to realize it, they had to resort to tactics appropriate to a *laissez faire* society. Reduced by legal mandate to equality with a myriad of other private corporations, the American churches competed for governmental attention by adopting practices familiar to every pressure group. Avalanches of publicity, legislative lobbying, and the election of the right men to public office were recognized as permissible ways for churches to reach goals that they had proclaimed indisputably holy. Northern Methodism's political behavior after the Civil War

203

conformed, in a somewhat exaggerated manner, to this tested pattern.

Methodist clergymen, in so far as they spoke, agreed on the broad outlines of a program for rebuilding the nation. Its features were telescoped by the Methodist who wrote: "The thirty-ninth Congress demands only the *minimum* of what we . . . should demand of . . . traitors and rebels." [3] With the Radicals the Church North meant "to stand up for exact, equal and Gospel-like justice for the Negro." Arguments on behalf of Negro suffrage were deemed "so overwhelming" that Methodists generally yielded "a cheerful support to the doctrine." "Common sense, reason, humanity, expediency, justice, and religion" alike decreed, said a clerical publicist, "that all men . . . must be invested with the elective franchise." [4] Not all the ministerial force concurred in the view that "with the ballot . . . preparation for its use is best . . . made after the boon is attained." Moderates admitted that a brief period of pupilage was in the best interests of the Negro. But Methodism was almost of one voice in demanding, as an absolute minimum, that franchise laws take no account of race. "We . . . protest against any system of reconstruction that does not . . . place all men equal before the law . . . without distinction of class or color," solemnly rumbled the General Conference of 1868. [5] If tests were imposed on blacks the same should be valid for whites, for complexion was not to intrude into the polling place. Regardless of how much Methodist ministers might abuse each other and their bishops, they closed ranks on this issue. The clergyman spoke truly who said: "Upon this point we are not to be put off, hoodwinked, or excluded." "Strong measures" were recommended to assure equal enfranchisement and, said Methodists, "no seceded state should resume its civil functions . . . until it [had] adopted a constitution in which the said right [was] duly . . . secured." [6]

The white Southerner was apt to discover a snare in Methodist talk about political equality. Usually it was predicated upon past conduct toward the federal government. "It must be understood that disloyalty disfranchises," lectured the *Western Advocate*. Any reconstruction which included the indiscriminate restoration of Confederates to citizenship was "insane" or, at best, "a dangerous experiment." Thomas Eddy, through his Chicago mouthpiece, urged the perpetual disfranchisement not only of the high civil and military officials of the Confederacy, but of "all who have [voluntarily] borne arms against the United States," "all who were engaged in supplying rebel army sustenance," and "all who ever invested one dollar in Confederate bonds." [7] Had Eddy's ideas prevailed, the native white voter in the South would have become a museum piece. Inasmuch as the freedmen could meet rigorous examinations of loyalty better than most whites, Methodist prescriptions for the suffrage entailed the chance that the voting population of the Confederate states might be predominantly black. This risk some clergymen accepted on the belief that "it is better to trust the instincts of an ignorant man if he be true, than intelligence controlled by a false and treacherous heart." To Methodism's left wing, however, the relegation of the white population to a station of inferiority and the elevation of the Negro to political power would be simply retributive justice. "The conditions of rebel and . . . slave . . . must be reversed," frothed Gilbert Haven, "no citizenship for the rebel leader; perfect citizenship for the slave." [8]

The clerical slogan, "justice to the Negro and justice to the traitor," was often stretched to embrace recommendations for "the solemn visitation of . . . punishment upon the chiefs of treason and the leaders of the rebellion." The *Northwestern* warned against "maudlin sympathy in the day of our triumph." While its editor thought that "mercy may be shown . . . to the rank and file . . . of the population," he asked "another sentence for the leaders . . . who kindled the fires of civil war." Confiscation of the property of Confederate magnates was sometimes advised, but more common was the "demand that the leading traitors be seized . . . and then . . . hung." [9] "We confess our liability to unmercifulness when we speak of the wicked, barbarous, fiendish conduct of the . . . leaders of this crusade against God," shouted a bloodthirsty preacher. He was disgusted at "the mamby-pamby . . . wish-wash . . . milk sop sympathy with . . . rebels" and wished for more "plain, simple . . . justice according to the Gospel standard." [10] Proposals for the infliction of corporal punishment on the chieftains of the South clustered about Lincoln's assassination, but well after this event a few churchmen persisted in regarding the penalty as an appropriate one. When Jefferson Davis was released on bail in 1867, John Reid grumbled that "treason has not been made, in a single instance, a judicial example of" and was sorry that "there are no warnings dangling on gibbets to terrify those who would plunge us again into a sea of blood . . . ." [11]

In order to propel the nation along the correct path of political reconstruction, Methodists jumped into the boiling dispute between the President and Congress. *Harper's Weekly* soon noted that articulate Methodism was "intensely radical" and nakedly abetted the politicians who demanded "the fullest, squarest, most uncompromised Republican reconstruction of the country." [12] Since the legislative branch was dominated by men of this stripe, churchmen contracted an alliance with it. Daniel Curry raged "at the sad want of statesmanship" which fancied "that to the executive rather than the legislative department belongs the business of Reconstruction." In the tempestuous summer and autumn of 1866, most Methodist conferences in the North recorded their conviction that "primal allegiance is due to the Congress of these United States." [13] Toward the lawmakers, Methodism was effusive in its praise. The doughty Ben Wade received congratulations from an Ohio minister "for building a monument for . . . the cause of . . . righteousness and . . . humanity that shall outlast the pyramids." Other congressmen were delighted to know that they represented "the only hope of the country" and sat in the "most enlightened legislative [assembly] in the world." The thirty-ninth Congress was "the best we ever had." Never had "so large an amount of ability . . . been found in the halls of Congress," and one ministerial editor fell into the habit of addressing the body as "The Magnificent Congress." [14] However, some Methodists detected one small blemish in the conduct of the legislative branch. It sometimes hesitated, out of political expediency. A highly-regarded clergyman rebuked a radical senator with the assertion that "extravagant words do us no good" and contended that "the party is not bold enough in action." To preclude the prospect that this dilatoriness would become chronic, Methodists were exhorted to "pray," "send letters and petitions" and "labor to keep the right men in Congress." [15]

Devoted as Methodists were to the legislature, they were not inattentive to the President. Comparable to what occurred in other circles of American opinion, Methodist attitudes toward the chief executive moved through a discernible evolution. Despite misgivings about his "intemperate habits" and his "rude and semi-barbarous" background, clerical commentators were inclined to be tolerant of Johnson upon his accession. Some churchmen, frightened by his predecessor's magnanimity, even believed that he was the tonic needed by the country because of his "disposition to deal . . . uncompromisingly with the guilty . . . traitors." [16] The honeymoon between Johnson and ecclesiasts continued, with mild reproaches through 1865 and into the early months of the next year. However, the President's vetoes of Reconstruction legislation and the outbreak of riots in New Orleans and Memphis, in which Northern Methodist Negroes had been caught, turned Methodist sufferance into furious censure. They saw that "the mask had fallen to leave discovered a Tennessee slaveholder" and the dilemma "Shall we stand with God or the President?" was resolved in favor of the Former. Once it had turned on Johnson, the editorial corps of the Church North ransacked its vocabulary for meet characterizations of him. "Execrable libertine, drunkard and tyrant," "an insane sot," "a boor and ignoramus," "a disgrace to the nation," and a companion "of the most scarlet of scarlet women" were among the searing epithets hurled at the presidential incumbent.[17] Johnson's stern opposition to Congress, contrary to the opinion of a subsequent historian, was not "a study in courage." Instead it was "a coarse, self-willed persistence" and exactly the type of "quality that distinguishes the mule or the ass." Methodist clergymen allowed Johnson to sample their repugnance fully during his "swing around the circle" in 1866, by continuously absenting themselves from the social festivities scheduled in his honor. The preachers, revealed one of the breed, felt obliged to refuse attendance because they circulated only "in the company of true loyalty." [18]

Northern Methodists interpreted Johnson's obstinacy as a high crime against the national safety, and called upon Congress to strike down the executive by applying "the final remedy provided by the constitution." Proposals for the impeachment of Johnson began to infiltrate Methodist journals more than a year before the Radicals instituted their inquisition. A legislative program submitted by one editor for consideration by the lame-duck session of the thirty-ninth Congress contained a plank to "rebuke . . . the President even if impeachment is necessary." [19] Methodists who broadcast their opinions were almost unanimous in asking for the ouster of Johnson, and to this movement the church gave its official blessing. The General Conference of 1868, which met in Chicago during the deliberations to decide the President's fate, spent four days refining its sentiments on impeachment and then resolved to set aside an hour of prayer "for the removal of the corrupt influences" being exerted on senators "to prevent them from performing their high duty." [20] Some informed persons asserted that the clerical endeavors to retire Johnson to private life did not stop with resolutions. Gideon Welles remembered to enter in his diary the item that Bishop Simpson with "great shrewdness and ability" brought his influence to bear on the Senate. Welles credited

Simpson's conversations and correspondence with alienating the West Virginian, Waitman T. Willey, from the camp of the Johnsonite senators.[21]

Methodistic objections to Johnson's policy ranged into the domain of civil rights. The presidential program, if enacted, would "embolden the unreconstructed rebels" and snuff out every vestige of free expression in the South. Samuel Nesbit demanded for Methodists "immunities from violence and mob law" and the "right to teach our ideas and discuss our policies on Southern soil." [22] The Church North's struggle against the legions of darkness was published as one which commended itself to every lover of freedom. Nevertheless, the priestly defenses of civil liberties often masqueraded a deeper concern for Methodism's success in the Southern states. The Northern membership was asked to be alive to "the great issues of Reconstruction" because "aside from the moral importance of the questions involved" the church had "vast denominational interests at stake." Johnson's program was a hammer suspended over Northern Methodist hopes in the South. "The final success or failure of our church in this section," wrote a Northern preacher from Georgia, "hangs upon the adoption of the Congressional method of settling our political relations." The cause of Methodism became inseparable from the cause of Congress. "If Congress fail we fail; if Congress succeed we succeed," pithily stated a correspondent, and this counsel lent a color of sectarian selfishness to all Methodist preferences in politics.[23] During the Congressional campaign of 1866, a ministerial spokesman skillfully alerted the laity to a sense of its civil obligations by the pregnant observation that "our national and ecclesiastical duties . . . are most closely interblended." If the seceded states were restored according to the doctrines of Radicalism, some sanguine ecclesiasts even calculated that Northern Methodism would become "the controlling church in the South." [24]

Northern Methodism's lusty attitude toward the temporal power exposed it to widespread condemnation. Adversaries charged it with being "a church into whose very texture political instincts have been wrought" and affected alarm at "the . . . manifest . . . purpose of Northern Methodists to bring about a union of Church and State." [25] Cognizant of these criminations, the General Conference of 1868 prepared a brief on the relation between ecclesiastical and public authority. Substantially, the document denied "for the church the right to arraign the 'powers that be' " and yet affirmed "the right and duty of speaking words of praise or censure . . . of the great principles of law and government." [26] Individually, Methodists were not as prone to equivocation. "The true mission of the church," said the mildest of its official journals, "is to overrule even the politics of the country with the principles of Christianity." Abel Stevens, often ridiculed by fellow Methodists for his political conservatism, pronounced the separation of religion and politics as "dangerous to public morals [and] dangerous to the state." A secular paper, whose clerical editor was practised enough to be an authority on the subject, compared "a minister without politics" to "a ship at sea without [a] compass . . . liable to run against breakers everywhere." [27] Parsons, as they insisted on judging secular issues themselves, also exhorted laymen to "realize their political duty as . . . conscientiously as their religious duty." Politics was infamously filthy, but the clergy thought "it better to purify the cesspool, even at the risk of getting a little spattered, than to let it remain untouched and . . . breathe its malaria." [28] Political quiescence had no place in the philosophy of Northern Methodism.

These apologies for the role of the church in public affairs, however, evaded the criticism that Methodism's monitorship of political morals invariably redounded to Republican advantage. Methodists and Republicans, said one of the former, seemed "to make a rather large and decidedly lively mutual admiration society." [29] More often than any other Methodist writer, Daniel Curry undertook the job of enlightening public opinion about the true nature of this bond. To Curry, the friendship between

Methodism and Republicanism was based upon a transitory coincidence of principles. While confessing that his church "cooperated with one of the great political parties and opposed the other," it owed "no allegiance to any political party, as such." "If we favor or disfavor either [party] it is because of their relations to questions of great social and moral importance," and continued Curry, "if in favoring the right and opposing the wrong we are compelled to favor one party more than the other, it is no fault of ours." [30] The theoretical ideal of the New York editor and his clerical partners was a church "great enough . . . to be independent of parties" but "holding the balance of power for the support of virtue and truth." [31] In the vulgar jargon of politics they were saying that Methodism should try to command enough votes to lure party organizations into bidding for its endorsement.

Neither Methodist nor nonMethodist analysts could agree whether Methodism had achieved a genuine compactness on political issues. Some recognized that the church had "honored members . . . in both parties" and advised that "anyone who attempts to marshal . . . the Methodist vote will be snubbed for his pains." Others, noticing that Methodists were "notoriously a clannish people [who] act together and stand by each other" believed that the church's potential in politics was a mighty one. "We all be brethren wherever duty calls us to talk, work, vote or pray," boasted Arthur Edwards.[32] James Harlan, in answer to inquiries from the Republican directorate about the voting propensities of Methodists, wrote that "ninety-five hundredths of the members of the M. E. Church and perhaps ninety-nine hundredths of the traveling ministers are *earnest Republicans*." The *Nation* put the proportion at ninety percent.[33] These estimates, although only informed guesses, were sufficient to lead politicians to invite Methodist help in advancing their particular projects. Eager to mobilize public opinion against Johnson, the Maryland senator, John A. J. Cresswell, implored an outstanding cleric "not to look with indifference on the struggle" and asked him to "take up [his] pen and wield it in the cause of freedom." Cresswell knew the source from which to solicit assistance for Methodist clergymen in Maryland had stood unflinchingly at his side during his senatorial race against Montgomery Blair in 1865. In his later capacity of Postmaster General, Cresswell was confidentially described by a Methodist as "the friend of our church in the Cabinet." [34] Cresswell, however, traded less regularly on his Methodist affiliations than his political confederate, Senator Harlan. At every significant turn in Harlan's political career, Methodist influence appeared. It was a factor in twice electing him to the Senate and in his appointment to head the Interior Department in 1865. After Harlan's defeat in the Iowa senatorial contest of 1872, Bishop Simpson (with other clergymen) made a minor avocation out of scheming to repair the political fortunes of his intimate friend. [35]

Its aptitude for political expression sharpened by successive crises in national affairs, Methodism entered the canvass of 1868. Months before the Republican convention met in Chicago's Opera Hall, a bevy of Methodists had voiced a liking for Grant and Colfax. One indiscreet clergyman even wrote that "Methodist preachers had made these nominations long ago and the ratifying was done by the Opera Hall crowd." [36] Save for the *Western Advocate,* the array of church weeklies warmly backed Grant's candidacy, but those of the northeastern states comported themselves with the least restraint. "Let no one leave it a stigma upon his children . . . that he opposed the election of the Washington of today, the second and greater saviour of his country," shouted the editor of *Zion's Herald.* In the sacred tradition of the bloody shirt, Dallas Lore of the *Northern* urged, "Let every loyal man . . . be as direct with his ballot, as he was with his bullet, to check and crush treason." [37] Little different from their deportment in previous elections, some Methodist parsons swapped the pulpit for the hustings. Amidst the 1868 campaign, a churchman remarked that "Methodist ministers are becoming the most desirable and efficient political speakers of the day." [38] Although the bulk of Methodism's electioneering was done without subventions from the party treasury, one case was an obvious exception. Hiram Dunn, a clergyman from upper New York, successfully importuned the Republican National Committee to employ him to whip up Methodist enthusiasm in the Middle West for the crusade against the Democrats. Dunn, who had been paid by the Republicans for similar services in 1856 and 1860, toured Illinois, Indiana, and Ohio and prodded conventions of clergymen in these states to subscribe publicly to Grant's candidacy. The clerical hireling reported back "some excellent resolutions" from Methodist conferences, estimated that one million voters had been influenced by his action, and had his work commended by a former national chairman of the Republican party as "very useful." [39]

For their participation in the 1868 election, Methodist spokesmen suggested the propriety of rewards. Discoursing upon the inauguration ceremonies of 1869, a respected clergyman presumptuously wrote: "Having supported Grant uniformly . . . we claim that we have a right to be heard." [40] In the General, the Methodists had a man cut to the right dimensions for listening to them. Although Grant was not inscribed as a member of any church, his parents and wife were vigorous Methodists and by marriage he was related to other prominent names in the denomination. These various family connections together with Grant's fanatical personal loyalties greased the Methodist passage into the executive mansion, and some clergymen slipped through the door that opened before them. "The men of the Methodist Episcopal Church . . . seem to be in special favor at the American court," enviously whinnied a Presbyterian organ. A secular commentator scanned a half-dozen years of Grant rule to say that "Methodist preachers and bishops have long had great influence at the White House." The President, this newsman charged, had "surrounded himself with a Methodist court" and seldom failed "to respond to the influence of Methodist priests." [41] Northern churchmen themselves crowed that their denomination was "getting a little more than its past share of attention." One clergyman, supposedly a courtier himself, exultantly stated that "no class of citizens . . . are received . . . in Washington with more respect than the bishops of our church." [42] However, this felicitous treatment was not viewed by all Methodists as an unmixed good. The sharp-witted layman Charles Nordhoff expressed anxiety at "the favor in which . . . prominent clergymen have been held at the White House" and believed that "it . . . had an evil influence upon them and . . . worked badly for the church." He hoped that the "next president [would] . . . have an unconquerable aversion to Methodist clergymen" because "it would be a fortunate thing for the denomination." [43]

The pipeline to the executive department gave Methodists the means of curing a nagging grievance against successive Republican administrations. "We . . . ask for the Methodist Church . . . that it shall have its due proportion of representatives in all places of trust and power," wrote an ecclesiast in 1866, but the idea was not a new one. [44] From the advent of Republican control of the national administration, Methodism had been hungry for the assignment of more federal patronage to members of the church. In the gloom which enveloped the North after first Manassas, Edward Thomson intimated to Secretary Chase that the denomination's support of the Lincoln regime hinged on the acknowledgment of the claims of Methodist office seekers. The clerical writer deemed the maldistribution of political spoils "serious" and warned that "a storm of hatred to the government is rising in our church." [45] The patronage issue often recurred in Republican-Methodist relationships during the Civil War and it lingered on to haunt the political future of Lincoln's Postmaster General, Montgomery Blair.

Blair's wartime appointments in the Post Office Department

had been highly irritating to Methodists and the Marylander was so advised in 1864 by Bishop Simpson in an interview that featured "plain, pointed and sharp conversation." [46] Blair learned that the Methodists had elephantine memories. Lincoln, shopping a short time later for a man to fill the Supreme Court vacancy created by Roger A. Taney's death, asked Bishop Ames for his views on Blair's nomination to the post. Ames, who was partial to Chase's claims, responded in language of strong denunciation and angrily remarked that "the bare possibility of such a thing should cause the friends of the government to give attention enough to the matter to prevent . . . its occurrence." [47] In 1865, Blair again was plagued by clerical opposition when churchmen descended on the Maryland state legislature to protest against his candidacy for United States senator. On the floor of the assembly and in the corridors they boldly and effectively pressed the charge that he "was hostile to the interests of the Methodist Church." For two years afterward, Blair continued to complain that Methodist animosity was doing political harm to him, and he finally took up a lengthy but inconclusive correspondence with Bishop Simpson in an effort to smooth out the difficulties between himself and the church. [48]

The refusal "to distribute impartially the patronage of the government" likewise had a place in the list of affronts for which churchmen excoriated Johnson. "Methodist members are . . . almost ignored in the leading appointments made in Washington," grumbled Bishop Simpson in 1867. [49] The short-tempered Samuel Nesbit reviewed the first year of Johnson's administration, and argued that Methodist sacrifices had met with little return. "Within the past year our men have been steadily . . . jostled aside from official positions," he wrote. The removals had gone on until the Northern church had "but few men remaining in government places." Methodists "had fought the battles for the country" but "others were getting all the offices." However, Nesbit foretold an end to this discrimination. He trusted that Methodists would "see to it that men shall be put into office who will act more impartially than those now holding the reins of government." [50]

These outcries of anguish ceased abruptly with Grant's appearance in the White House. "Methodist . . . clergymen . . . have been specially favored in the matter of appointments" blandly observed one reporter, and another termed the preference shown to the denomination a "scandal." [51] The intelligence that the Methodist label carried weight in Washington impelled laymen and obscure preachers to ask ecclesiastical officials to act as middlemen in the procurement of government offices. The correspondence of Bishop Simpson is a treasury of letters entreating him to intervene with the President, Senators, Cabinet officers, and Bureau chiefs in behalf of aspiring Methodists. Agencies, clerkships, consulates, judicial posts, or sometimes "any office . . . sufficient to [offer] support" were presumed to be at the bishop's command. Very many of the letters contain the compliment "that I can only be placed in position . . . by the influence of . . . our church leaders." The chore of political jobbery sometimes weighed so heavily on the prelate that he deliberately avoided the national capital. During the scramble for place that accompanied the beginning of Grant's administration Simpson, en route to his Philadelphia home after a tour of episcopal duty, wrote to his wife, "I shall not stop at Washington on my way back for if I do I shall be terribly annoyed by hosts of applicants." [52]

In ranking the Methodist clerics who had entry to the presidential chamber, Simpson was often put nearest to the throne. He unquestionably wielded "a powerful influence throughout the country," and his friends bragged that he had "as much influence with General Grant as any living man." [53] However, close students of Washington intrigue dissented from this view, and maintained that John Newman occupied the foremost spot in Grant's affections. Newman, characterized by a ministerial confrere as a man of "unlimited personal aspirations" with "a tendency to gain diffusive influence," tallied up five years of missionary work in New Orleans before returning north in 1869 to assume the pastorate of Metropolitan Church in Washington. Here his congregation was termed "the most distinguished in the land." A visitor to Newman's church saw in one Sunday morning audience the President, Vice-President, Chief Justice of the Supreme Court, six Senators and eight Representatives, not to mention "judges and leading bankers." [54] With bounteous assistance from the chief executive, Newman held down the chaplaincy of the Senate from 1869 to 1874. As further evidence of his esteem, Grant created especially for his friend an office entitled "Inspector of United States Consulates" which allowed the recipient a reasonable stipend and a trip around the world at public expense.[55] For his part, Newman furnished the President with advice, religious ministrations and "was ever ready to defend him valiantly." The chaplain, said a female gossip, "bore with ill grace the attacks upon his hero" and was "always defending Grant and all the 'skulduggery' of his administration." [56]

The political machinations of Methodist clergymen reached the zenith of their notoriety in connection with Grant's availability for a third consecutive term. Like most other Americans, the pastorate was interested in the question, and many of them were faithful to the idea that "there was only one Grant." The President, in the spring of 1875, had indicated an intention of retiring after his eighth year in office, but the announcement was so ambiguously worded that he was left free to respond to a draft at the ensuing Republican convention.[57] Some contemporaries sensed attempts by Methodist clergymen in the waning days of 1875 to stimulate a ground swell of opinion which would assure Grant's nomination again. In his seventh annual message to Congress, Grant "most earnestly" recommended the initiation of a constitutional amendment "prohibiting the granting of any school funds, or school taxes . . . in aid . . . of any religious sect or denomination." [58] The proposal was intended to force a discontinuance of state and municipal subsidies to parochial schools, a practice of particular benefit to Catholics. Although a large section of the American press pretended surprise at the President's remarks, it had no trouble in understanding his motives. "There is hardly any difference of opinion that the message is simply a bid for a third term," said a Manhattan newspaper. Thrown over by political professionals, Grant had resolved "to array the Protestant prejudice . . . in a political crusade against the Catholic church, and thereby carry the presidential election." [59]

Political pundits, however, were skeptical whether the President alone had the acumen to hit upon these tactics, and glimpsed in the background the shadow of Methodism. "There are significant facts to justify the belief that [the] scheme was concerted with a class of political preachers in the Methodist Church," editorially charged the New York *Sun*.[60] The "significant facts" are interesting, but barren of absolute inferences. Methodist propagandists, in the vanguard of those agitating for an end of state aid to Catholic schools, had generated auguries of imminent support from the White House ahead of the December meeting of Congress. The New York *Advocate* denied being "honored with confidences in the matter" yet in October, 1875, predicted that the President "at some not remotely future occasion" would ask for a constitutional change to deprive Catholic educators of public money. More suspicious was the behavior of John Newman. On the three Sundays preceding Grant's message, Newman, with the President in the congregation, sermonized on parochial education. With arguments "so eminently distinguished as to call forth the applause of his audience" the court chaplain pointed out the "imperative need" for legislation to pry loose Catholic schools from the government trough. The third of Newman's sermons was published in the administration's Washington organ, the *National Republican,* alongside the Grant address. One investigator who compared the two documents said that "the sermon has all the earmarks of the message and betrays a common origin." Newman, he alleged, was the author of both.[61]

The waters of politics, discolored by Grant's annual message, were stirred up more by Methodist imprudence. A day before the President's disturbing recommendation reached Congress, Bishop Haven climaxed a speech to a Methodist assembly in Boston with the peroration "Pray, brethren, that President Grant may be re-elected . . . . Be true to your church." Haven was "a restless, fussy soul, forever going off half-cocked" but the press services lumped his utterance with Grant's school proposal as threads in a grand design. Methodism sank deeper into the third-term issue when Bishop Simpson was quickly quoted as saying "that should Grant be re-elected the people would have done wisely." Simpson promptly branded the report as false, without completely eradicating its first impression.[62] With the New York *Herald* guiding the parade, the antiGrant press drummed that the train of incidents signalled "the formal opening of the campaign for the presidency." The General was "first in the field and behind him the power of a great church." Through an unbroken sequence of twelve issues in midDecember, 1875, the *Herald* ran editorials or leading articles with such scareheads as "The Bishops' Presidential Support Promised Long Ago," "Is the Methodist Church Committed to the Renomination of Grant?" and "Shall a Church Dictate to the Nation?" The *Herald* and its emulators blew up the clerical indiscretions to grotesque proportions out of an awareness that they were handy devices for flailing the President and whatever dreams he may have entertained. Haven, for instance, sincerely desired Grant's renomination but, said a friend, he chose "the very means to prevent it" by "provoking the quiescent opposition to the third term idea." [63] In this observation was a touch of historical irony. A denomination which insisted that it had put Grant into the White House helped also to assure his departure.

Northern Methodism's reputation for political partisanship, however, was not earned only in the North. "The Methodist Episcopal Church is the chief cornerstone upon which is

builded . . . our social and political afflictions," rhetorically exclaimed a Mississippian. A short acquaintance with the denomination convinced most Southerners that its meddling in the
politics of their section matched anything seen in the North. It
was, they sneered, the "religious auxiliary of the Radical Party"
which had entered the South "to carry out the Reconstruction
Acts of Congress." [64] Southerners had ready documentation for
their case in the exaggerated number of Northern clergymen
who filled positions in the reconstructed governments of various
states. William Brownlow was the most widely-publicized example of the Northern Methodist role in Southern politics, but
he had counterparts outside of Tennessee. Benjamin F. Whittemore, who left a Massachusetts pastorate to vent his predatory
instincts in South Carolina, was believed "the head and front"
of the Reconstruction government in that state, and his Negro
constituents twice sent him to the Unites States House of Representatives. The African Methodist apostate, Hiram R. Revels,
creditably represented Mississippi in the United States Senate
and, with somewhat less competence, James D. Lynch served
the same commonwealth as Secretary of State. George W.
Honey administered the state treasury department in Texas
under the Reconstruction regime until an indictment for em-
bezzlement left him unemployed. Postwar politics in Arkansas
were made uproarious by the gubernatorial maneuvers of the
former editor of the *Central Advocate,* Joseph Brooks. In addition, Southern legislatures, along with posts on the county and
municipal levels, were sprinkled with white and colored Methodists of the Northern denomination. Besides enjoying the
honors and emoluments of elective offices, affiliates of the
Church North were thought eminently eligible for political patronage. A ministerial reporter bragged that it was "easy" for
him and his confederates "to secure positions as postmasters,
school commissioners, . . . revenue clerks, or other appointments from the general or state governments." [65]

Only a fragment of the political story of Methodism in the

Southern states can be told in terms of officeholding. By less regular avenues, its clergy sought to shape the course of public affairs. The Methodist press in the South joined with that of the Northern section in discussing politics with prejudiced candor. Editor Fuller, in the inaugural number of the *Methodist Advocate,* wanted "it distinctly understood that . . . political matters are not so sacred as to be . . . outside the scope of religious journalism." True to his promise, he thoroughly aired "the great questions of the day in relation to . . . the rights of man and loyalty to the government," even to the extent of editorially campaigning for particular candidates. That Southerners stood sullenly unreceptive to the preachment that "carpetbaggers have been of great benefit to the South" was not due to any lack of vigor in Fuller's presentation.[66] But the *Methodist Advocate,* possibly because it deferred to certain restraints surrounding an official journal, was niggardly in its attention to politics in contrast to some independent Methodist organs in the South. John Newman, who published an *Advocate* in New Orleans from 1865 to 1869, at first featured merely "editorials on politics" and "much political news" in his paper, but by 1868 its secular offerings had been greatly enlarged. During the presidential election, Newman altered the format of his sheet "by putting at the head of the paper the national Republican ticket and also the local ticket, and entering deeply into the advocacy of special . . . candidates for different . . . offices." For its stout defense of Republicanism, the New Orleans *Advocate* steadily received large chunks of printing patronage from the state and federal governments. The *Southwestern Advocate,* the successor to Newman's journal as the voice of Methodism in the Gulf area, persevered in advertising that "the Republican party [had] the proudest record of any political organization on earth." Seated amidst a large colored membership, the *Southwestern* pelted the Negro with advice "to stand firm for the party that has done for you all that has been done." [67]

The forays of Methodist clergymen into political writing

were not limited to religious journalism. Several secular news-papers in the South had preachers of the Northern church as editors or publishers. Most outstanding was the Knoxville *Whig*, which was owned and nominally edited by Brownlow until its acquisition in 1869 by Thomas Pearne, a ministerial transfer from the Northern states. Pearne, whom East Tennesseans mocked as the "Great High Priest of Loyalty" represented the preacher in politics no less than Brownlow, but his ambitions for office were frustrated by residence in a state which revered scalawags more than carpetbaggers. The *Whig*, under both editors, approximated its motto "Neutral in Nothing" as it ardently embraced Republicanism and Northern Methodism and ferociously lashed out at the Church South and the party of the Democracy. The busy James Lynch, from 1868 until his death in 1872, published the respectably patronized *Colored Citizen* at Jackson, Mississippi, and designed it "to defend the interests of the Negro, the Republican Party and the M. E. Church." With the same trinity of purposes in mind, Alonzo Webster in 1874 begun publication of the *Free Citizen* at Orangeburg, South Carolina. Briefly, Methodist clergymen also had a hand in the editorial management of William W. Holden's Raleigh *Standard* and the blatantly Republican Memphis *Daily Post*. Besides participating in these better-known ventures, Northern preachers founded a rash of journals, short and fitful in existence. Counted among them were such juicy names as *Herald of Freedom* ("the only one of its type in the cotton states"), *True Republican,* and *The Loyal League* ("Republican in politics, Protestant in religion").[68]

Methodist attempts to remold the political image of the South proceeded along still other lines. A few clergymen, believing it wisest "to covet the power behind the throne not on the throne," became advisors and confidants of men in high office. Pearne played this part so conspicuously in Tennessee that Brownlow was rumored to be grooming him for the gubernatorial succession. John Newman trained for his later intrigue in Washington by acting as a political consultant to General Philip H. Sheridan in Louisiana.[69] The political sympathies of Methodists were more openly displayed, however, in the many conference proclamations on public issues. "Nine thousand true and loyal members of the Methodist Episcopal Church in South Carolina and Florida" by formal resolution hailed "with joy" the passage of the Congressional Reconstruction Plan. On the same historic occasion, the Holston conference congratulated "our patriotic Congress" on the adoption of a policy that would "give to all men the same God-given immunities and rights." [70] The attitudes shown at these business sessions were often dragged into the pulpit and blended with the spiritual nutriments of sermons. "The old fashioned Methodist preachers," said a Georgian, were those who retailed "Jesus, love, and unionism in religion." One churlish native wandered into a Northern Methodist meeting-house in the Appalachian region and vowed that the Sunday descant contained "more . . . loyalty . . . than can be found anywhere outside of the Reconstruction Acts or the Ku Klux law of Tennessee." [71]

The habit of preaching "religion and politics at the same time" aggravated Southerners, but it was not the core of their grievance against Northern Methodism. The bare utterance of "themes which grated the Southern heart" was subordinate to the charge that these political lessons were taught to the Negro. An unsophisticated race, it was alleged, was being bribed with the promise of heaven to hold up the edifice of Radical Reconstruction. The Church North, snapped a Tennessean, "carries the Gospel to the Negroes . . . because they have votes to seek after." "Northern Methodism is . . . training and mustering the Negro for political purposes," a Southern religious periodical concluded. The "design of their conspiracy" was "to pick the bones of the South." [72] Southern whites recognized, as keenly as any carpetbagger, that the colored vote became a factor in Reconstruction politics only when it was organized and directed. The freedman did not cast his ballot as an individual but as part of an instructed mass, and the indispensable political guidance was commonly supplied by his spiritual shepherds. A political adventurer in Florida called the preaching corps *"the great power* in controlling and uniting the colored vote," and as late as 1875 Charles Nordhoff noted that the local Republican leadership in the South consisted "mostly of teachers and preachers." [73]

The Methodist clergy was not outside the prevailing tendency to twist the ministerial office to Radical advantage. A Northern editor bade missionaries remember: "The blacks . . . must be preserved to . . . Republicanism. The help of the Methodist Episcopal Church is necessary to do this." [74] Methodism was not only interested that the blacks vote but "that they vote with the North," and measures were taken to insure this result. The pupils of a Negro Sunday School were besought: "Come up to the polls as one man . . . no tale . . . ought to induce you to vote a Democratic ticket, and destroy your freedom forever." A Georgia resident whose teaching and preaching duties gave him "many opportunities to converse with the Negroes" wrote that he had "spent a great deal of time trying to instruct them in Republican principles." A colored clergyman in Mississippi chimed that his "every sentiment, utterance and action" likewise had "been strictly Republican." [75] The clerical plunge into politics conveniently opened churches to political rallies, and the Methodist house of worship served many communities as a clubroom for the Union League. Well-founded reports even recorded that Sabbath-day religious exercises were transformed by the magic of a benediction into Republican festivals. To ministerial discussions of public affairs the freedmen sometimes reacted with a fervor that made a political meeting indistinguishable from a religious revival. One competent Georgian enlisted in the Northern pastorate sermonized on "these days of civil and religious freedom" to a cacophony of "tears . . . groans . . . fervent 'amens' [and] shouts." Another homily devoted "to emancipation and the privileges associated with it," teased out such a volume "of groans . . . laughter, clapping of hands, and shouts . . .

that the speaker was compelled to remain silent." [76]

Scattered Methodist clergymen were skillful enough at mobilizing the Negro vote to become political managers of statewide prominence. In South Carolina, Whittemore and Benjamin F. Randolph, a Negro graduate of Oberlin College, each controlled a bloc of voters sufficiently large to land them on the Republican state executive committee which Randolph headed at the time of his assassination.[77] John Caldwell, who "felt truly called of God to enter the political arena," labored with a fanatically selfless devotion to Republicanism and was national committeeman from Georgia during the first Grant campaign. Caldwell matter-of-factly reported from Heard County, Georgia, in 1867 that he had "almost entire control of the colored people throughout this and adjoining counties" and could "mass 8,000 to 10,000 at any given point . . . to promote the good work of Reconstruction." [78] James Lynch arrived in Mississippi in 1867 with a commission from the Methodist Episcopal Church to engage in missionary work and with instructions from the party of the Radicals "to organize Republican clubs." No one ever accused him of divorcing the two functions. In the office of presiding elder he "traveled and spoke . . . in the interests of 'Reconstruction'" as "he . . . preached the resurrection." "My political relations and labor increase the borders of the church for as I go, I preach," the mulatto confided to Bishop Simpson. After his death, Lynch's political machine was taken over by his brother-in-law, J. Garrett Johnson, another presiding elder in the Northern church. Johnson, delightedly declared Gilbert Haven, also had "as much influence in political as in ecclesiastical affairs." [79]

The diligence with which different Methodist clergymen worked to perpetuate the reconstructed governments of the South was, however, a double-edged sword. If it conduced to the welfare of the world it also seriously hobbled Methodism's religious mission in the Southern states. Ministerial preoccupation with problems of state led to a neglect of ecclesiastical responsibilities. Lynch, at once a presiding elder, political journalist, party-organizer, and state official, admitted that the religious interests of Methodism suffered because of his manifold duties. "I feel that Christ's church is . . . starving for the bread which I could give it were I devoted with singleness to the ministry," wrote Lynch; and he appended the note that his political status detracted from his "ability to spiritualize and discipline." [80] A heavier woe thrust upon Methodism by its politically-minded parsons was the excitement of "unnecessary prejudices" against the church. The political animosities stirred up by clergymen damaged their own usefulness and had a deleterious effect on Methodism's whole evangelistic program. Bishop Simpson, after exploring the springs of Southern feeling, believed that clergymen of his church were ostracized "not . . . simply because they are Methodists . . . but because they are . . . identified with Radical movements." [81] Simpson might have gone on to mention that the abuse poured on the Methodist clergy did not always come from the adversaries of Radicalism. The combination of Negroes, whites, carpetbaggers, scalawags, knaves, and crusaders under one banner made Republicanism in the South a highly unstable organization, and clerical politicians of the Northern church were sometimes lacerated in clashes among the party's discordant elements. The factional fights that helped sink the Republican party in Georgia, Tennessee, Mississippi, and Texas each had Methodist preachers in the forefront of the combatants. [82]

Opposition within Methodism to the unbridled activity of clerical politicians began to awaken before 1870. During the first years of its tenure in the South, the church quietly tolerated the sight of ministers in party or public office. One prelate, questioned about the propriety of clergymen grubbing in politics, replied that it was "a matter for the individual judgment and conscience." [83] A growing consciousness of the liabilities incurred by the practice, however, sparked a revulsion, and the notion that "a preacher cannot study politics . . . and save souls" relentlessly gained converts. "Souls call us down yonder. . . . We are not down yonder on a political errand," raged Arthur Edwards, and he had congenial company for his ideas among the Southern membership. Even though the editors disagreed to a man, Methodist journals in the South printed an increasing amount of correspondence which denounced ministers who "stab Christ . . . and drag him wounded into the political arena." This resentment was not aimed at the frank pastoral treatment of secular issues or the subtle exertion of pressure on the instrumentalities of government but rather at those who hankered for place or entered into the canvass as special pleaders. Said an Arkansas partisan of the new view: "The minister has . . . the right to the freest expression upon the questions of the day, but has clearly no right to become a candidate for any civil office." [84]

The agitation to cut the bond between Radicalism and Methodism in the South flowered into Annual Conference action. Methodist preachers in Georgia during 1869 were the first to move toward discouraging their colleagues from overmuch attention to politics, and by 1877 most other conferences in the Southern states had written out a similar disapproval. The enactments were not uniformly forceful, but a few of them contained teeth of biting sharpness. The Georgia itinerants, holding "the high office of the Christian ministry to be . . . above the . . . duties . . . of any officer of the government," resolved to demand the resignations of pastors who became "the nominees of any political party" or accepted "an appointment at the hands of the General or State Governments." [85] The spate of resolutions was sometimes accented by the infliction of punishment. In South Carolina and Georgia, white preachers who stood for elective offices were judicially deprived of their ordination parchments, and the electioneering work of several Negro clergymen in Louisiana during 1874 brought them a reprimand from their conference "for vexatious and unministerial conduct." [86] These various attempts at political emasculation were not greeted with kindness all along the clerical line. With Gilbert Haven, a remnant clung to the notion that "the carpetbagger was chosen of God and precious" and the refusal to act with him "disgraced Methodism." Furthermore, the restrictions adopted by Southern conferences, besides leaving considerable room for the exercise of political talents, were as often honored in the breach as in the observance. Nevertheless, the set of the current was unmistakable. The disgust with men who used the livery of heaven to serve Radicalism signified Methodism's drift away from the enmeshments of carpetbag politics.

The shifting attitudes of Southern members were part of a larger change going on within Methodism. After Grant's election, Methodist attention to the political phases of Reconstruction relaxed while the conviction took hold of many that statutes could not redeem the South. "The . . . reorganization of Southern society . . . is not a subject so much for laws as for education, for training, for patient waiting," wrote George Crooks in 1875. By this time the views of the *Methodist* and its editor toward the South had become hopelessly soft, but Crooks did not stand alone. Richard Rust, in 1866, had boundless faith in the efficaciousness of the Radical program yet, ten years later, he grumbled that "too much emphasis has been placed upon the power of legislation." [87] The exposures of malfeasance which rocked the Republican administration in the seventies also left scars of disillusionment on Methodists. Even though prelates were welcomed at the executive mansion, laments were heard about "the fearful dishonesty . . . of the party in power." The admission was galling, but "the best of parties had poison in its veins." [88] The aging Edward Ames, as he viewed the contemporary landscape from his Baltimore home in 1877, had no doubt that the nation was in the midst of a political transition, and he invited his friend and colaborer, Bishop Simpson, to visit him for discussions about the future. "Old party organizations are being broken up," wrote Ames, and he wondered "what new issues shall be pronounced around which ecclesiastics can rally in the formation of new parties." [89] Ames' letter, despite its half-inaccurate forecast, was the obituary of an epoch in the Church North's political activity. Methodism still meant to use politics to reform America, but the time had come to regroup forces, select different objectives, and devise unique tactics.

# NOTES

[1] *Central Advocate*, October 24, 1866.

[2] Anson P. Stokes, *Church and State in the United States*, 3 vols. (New York, 1950).

[3] Granville Moody to Benjamin F. Wade, February 21, 1868, Benjamin F. Wade Papers, XIV, No. 2767 (Division of Manuscripts, Library of Congress).

[4] *Pittsburgh Advocate*, June 17, 1865; *Central Advocate*, June 28, 1865.

[5] *Christian Advocate*, May 31, 1866; *Journal of the General Conference*, 1868, p. 629.

[6] *Zion's Herald*, May 31, 1865; *Methodist Review*, XLVI (October, 1865), 632; *Christian Advocate*, February 1, 1866.

[7] *Western Advocate*, May 10, 1865; *Northern Advocate*, May 24, 1865; *Northwestern Advocate*, May 24, 1865.

[8] *Western Advocate*, December 11, 1867; Haven, *National Sermons*, 571.

[9] Henry B. Ridgaway, *The Life of the Reverend Alfred Cookman* (New York, 1873), 299; *Northwestern Advocate*, April 12 and May 10, 1865.

[10] *Northern Advocate*, April 5, 1865.

[11] *Western Advocate*, May 22, 1867.

[12] *Harper's Weekly*, October 6, 1866.

[13] *Christian Advocate*, March 29, 1866; *Northern Advocate*, September 19, 1866.

[14] *Northwestern Advocate*, December 6, 1865; *Zion's Herald*, January 17, 1866; *Christian Advocate*, September 13 and October 11, 1866; *Pittsburgh Advocate*, December 1, 1866; Granville Moody to Wade, February 21, 1868, Wade Papers, XIV, Nos. 2767–68.

[15] John W. McClintock to John A. J. Cresswell, May 28, 1866, John W. McClintock Papers (Emory University Library, Atlanta, Georgia); *Independent*, January 14, 1866; *Western Advocate*, June 20, 1866; *Northwestern Advocate*, August 5, 1866.

[16] *Western Advocate*, May 3, 1865.

[17] *Northwestern Advocate*, March 14, 1866; *Zion's Herald*, April 25, 1866; March 5, 1868; *Central Advocate*, September 19, 1866; *Western Advocate*, March 4, 1868.

[18] *Northern Advocate*, September 5, 1866; *Christian Advocate*, August 29, 1867. Some Methodists also joined the Radical hue and cry against the Supreme Court. One writer declared that the Court "had availed itself of its . . . powers to annul the most . . . important measures of the legislative branch for . . .

protection against treason." The Milligan decision brought a front-page editorial in the *Western Advocate* in which it was asserted that the Supreme Court had determined "to dictate to the legislative branch of the government; to overrule the army; to nullify . . . the declaration of emancipation; to set aside the constitutional amendments . . . [and] to become a . . . dictatorship." The church was called upon to rally for "a necessary struggle with the highest judicial tribunal in the land." *Western Advocate*, February 6, 1866; January 9, 1867.

19 *Western Advocate*, December 5, 1866; *Christian Advocate*, September 19, 1867.

20 *Journal of the General Conference, 1864*, p. 158; Indianapolis *Journal*, May 13 and May 18, 1868.

21 John T. Morse, Jr., ed., *Diary of Gideon Welles*, 3 vols. (Boston and New York, 1911), III, 358.

22 *Pittsburgh Advocate*, October 20, 1866.

23 *Western Advocate*, October 10, 1866; *Christian Advocate*, October 11, 1866; *Pittsburgh Advocate*, December 1, 1866.

24 *Northwestern Advocate*, September 12, 1866; *Central Advocate*, October 10, 1866; *Zion's Herald*, September 26, 1866.

25 Knoxville *Press and Messenger*, April 16, 1868; *Southern Review*, X (April, 1872), 401.

26 *Journal of the General Conference, 1868*, p. 628.

27 *Christian Advocate*, May 24, 1866; *Methodist Review*, XLVII (July, 1866), 459; Knoxville *Whig*, May 27, 1867.

28 *Northern Advocate*, November 14, 1866; *Central Advocate*, April 19, 1871.

29 Indianapolis *Journal*, May 25, 1866.

30 *Christian Advocate*, November 12, 1868; November 11, 1875.

31 *Central Advocate*, March 15, 1871; R. F. Gaggin to Simpson, December 21, 1875, Simpson Papers.

32 *Western Advocate*, July 8, 1868; *Methodist*, July 15, 1871; New York *Sun*, December 11, 1875.

33 James Harlan to William Chandler, June 24, 1868, William E. Chandler Papers, VI, No. 1075 (Division of Manuscripts, Library of Congress); *Nation*, June 12, 1879.

34 John A. J. Cresswell to McClintock, May 17, 1866, McClintock Papers; Montgomery Blair to C. A. Walborn, January 22, 1866, Wesley Prettyman to Simpson, October 12, 1874, Simpson Papers; E. H. Webster to Montgomery Blair, April 30, 1867, Gist Blair Collection (Division of Manuscripts, Library of Congress).

35 *Methodist Advocate*, July 26, 1871; *Central Advocate*, August 9, 1871; Chicago *Daily Tribune*, March 16, 1873; Johnson and Malone, eds., *Dictionary of American Biography*, VIII, 268; Harlan to Simpson, October 28, 1865; I. F. Jaquess and J. E. Parker to Simpson, November 6, 1872; A. Cummings to Simpson, November 15, 1874, Simpson Papers.

36 Indianapolis *Journal*, May 26, 1868.

37 *Northern Advocate*, October 8, 1868; *Zion's Herald*, October 22, 1868.

38 *Northern Advocate*, October 8, 1868.

39 Dunn's devious trail can be followed in Chandler Papers, VI, Nos. 1068–69, 1158–60, VII, Nos. 1374–75, IX, Nos. 1626–27, XI, Nos. 2131–33.

[40] *Methodist,* March 6, 1869.

[41] New York *Evangelist,* April 23, 1873; New York *Herald,* December 9 and 12, 1875.

[42] *Methodist,* December 25, 1869; *Northwestern Advocate,* March 19, 1873.

[43] Indianapolis *Daily Sentinel,* December 29, 1875.

[44] *Pittsburgh Advocate,* September 15, 1866.

[45] Edward Thomson to Salmon P. Chase, December 28, 1861, Salmon P. Chase Papers, LIII, Nos. 6362–6363 (Division of Manuscripts, Library of Congress).

[46] Simpson to Blair, May 16, 1867; Blair to Simpson, May 30, 1867, Blair Collection; E. B. Prettyman to Blair, December 2, 1867, Simpson Papers.

[47] John Lanahan to McClintock, October 27, 1864, McClintock Papers.

[48] Blair to C. A. Walborn, January 22, 1867; E. H. Webster to Blair, April 30, 1867, Simpson Papers; Blair to Simpson, May 1, 1867, Blair Collection.

[49] Simpson to Blair, May 16, 1867, Blair Collection.

[50] *Christian Advocate,* June 14, 1866; *Pittsburgh Advocate,* September 15, 1866; D. L. Dempsey to Simpson, February 14, 1866, Simpson Papers.

[51] Philadelphia *Item,* December 10, 1875; New York *Herald,* December 18, 1875.

[52] Simpson to Ellen Simpson, March 25, 1869, Simpson Papers.

[53] C. A. Walborn to Blair, June 8, 1867, Blair Collection; William Little to Simpson, February 16, 1869, Simpson Papers.

[54] James Lynch to Simpson, December 5, 1868, and Clipping, Scrapbook "A," Simpson Papers; New York *Evangelist,* April 23, 1873.

[55] Chicago *Daily Tribune,* March 16, 1873; Hamilton Fish to John P. Newman, April 9, 1873, John P. Newman Papers (Division of Manuscripts, Library of Congress).

[56] Mary Simmerson Logan, *Reminiscences of a Soldier's Wife: An Autobiography* (New York, 1916), 370. Other well-known hangers-on at the White House were Edward Ames and Gilbert Haven. The latter endeavored to play the role of pacificator in the Grant-Sumner dispute over Santo Domingo, and also tried to persuade Grant to reduce the South to territorial government as a cure for "Ku-Klux anarchy." Ames, formerly a resident of Indianapolis, moved to Baltimore in 1865 in order to be in a position to use pressure more effectively on politicians. The move was thought necessary because "ecclesiastical affairs [were] more or less involved in those of the nation . . . and questions [were] perpetually arising at the seat of the general government in which one of the superintendents could be most profitably consulted." Prentice, *Gilbert Haven,* 338, 400; *Western Advocate,* September 27, 1865.

[57] *Methodist Advocate,* December 2, 1874; William B. Hesseltine, *Ulysses S. Grant, Politician* (New York, 1935), 367ff.

[58] James D. Richardson, ed., *A Compilation of the Messages and Papers of the Presidents, 1789–1902,* 10 vols. (Washington, 1910), VI, 4288.

[59] New York *Herald,* December 8, 1875; New York *Sun,* December 11, 1875.

[60] *Ibid.*

[61] *Christian Advocate,* October 7, 1875; *Central Advocate,* December 8, 1875; New York *Sun,* December 11, 1875.

[62] *Boston Journal,* December 7, 1875; Philadelphia *Item,* December 10 and 12, 1875.

[63] New York *Herald,* December 12, 13, 15 and 16, 1875.

[64] Knoxville *Press and Messenger,* April 16, 1868; *Western Advocate,* June 24, 1868; *Methodist Advocate,* February 3, 1875, quoting Meridian (Miss.) *Daily Mercury.*

[65] *Methodist Advocate,* February 15, 1871.

[66] *Ibid.,* January 6, 1869; October 6, 1875.

[67] *Western Advocate,* January 10, 1866; February 24, 1869; *Southwestern Advocate,* July 17 and November 20, 1873.

[68] H. H. Moore to Simpson September 16, 1865, Simpson Papers; *Northwestern Advocate,* April 25, 1866; *Christian Advocate,* January 9, 1868; Knoxville *Press and Messenger,* April 21, 1869; *Methodist,* August 7, 1869; *Zion's Herald,* January 30, 1870; *Methodist Advocate,* February 23, 1870; September 3, 1874.

[69] John P. Newman to Simpson, March 31, 1867, Simpson Papers; Knoxville *Press and Messenger,* April 21, 1867.

[70] *Methodist,* March 16, 1867; *Minutes of the Holston Annual Conference, 1867,* p. 17.

[71] Knoxville *Press and Messenger,* December 9, 1868; *Methodist Advocate,* August 31, 1870.

[72] Knoxville *Whig,* November 20, 1867; Farish, *Circuit Rider Dismounts,* 158.

[73] F. A. Dockray to Thaddeus Stevens, March 18, 1868, Thaddeus Stevens Papers, XI, No. 54756 (Division of Manuscripts, Library of Congress); Nordhoff, *Cotton States,* 173.

[74] *Northern Advocate,* February 4, 1874.

[75] *Ibid.,* July 26, 1865; Knoxville *Press and Messenger,* October 8, 1868; *Southwestern Advocate,* February 24, 1876; Levi Greenlee to J. E. Bryant, n.d., B.R.F.A.L.

[76] *Central Advocate,* January 10, 1866; *Christian Advocate,* July 5, 1866; Knoxville *Press and Messenger,* March 12, 1868.

[77] A. J. Ransier to Chandler, October 19, 1868, Chandler Papers, XIII, Nos. 2563–64: *Minutes of the South Carolina Annual Conference, 1869,* p. 7.

[78] Caldwell, *Reconstruction of Church and State in Georgia,* 10; Caldwell to G. L. Eberhardt, April 17, 1867, B.R.F.A.L.

[79] John P. Newman to Simpson, July 28, 1867; Lynch to Simpson, October 6, 1869, Simpson Papers; *Minutes of the Mississippi Mission Conference, 1867,* p. 3.

[80] Lynch to Simpson, October 6, 1869, Simpson Papers.

[81] *Christian Advocate,* February 18, 1869.

[82] For slight attention to the role of Methodists in the intraparty quarrels in Texas and Tennessee, see Charles W. Ramsdell, *Reconstruction in Texas* (New York, 1910), 311–12, and Thomas B. Alexander, *Political Reconstruction in Tennessee* (Nashville, 1950), 199–225. The Georgia situation is recapitulated in Caldwell, *Reconstruction of Church and State in Georgia.* The activities of Revels and Johnson in Mississippi can be followed in the files of the *Southwestern Advocate* for the latter months of 1875 and the early part of 1876.

[83] Lynch to Simpson, October 6, 1869, Simpson Papers.

[84] *Proceedings of the Southern Methodist Convention, 1871,* p. 50; *Central Advocate,* February 22, 1871; *Minutes of the Louisiana Annual Conference, 1873,* p. 50; *Methodist Advocate,* August 14, 1874; *Northwestern Advocate,* October 26, 1874.

[85] *Methodist Advocate,* April 6, 1870.

[86] *Minutes of the South Carolina Annual Conference, 1870,* p. 7; *Minutes of*

the Annual *Georgia Conference, 1870,* pp. 4–6; *Minutes of the Louisiana Annual Conference, 1875,* p. 6.

[87] *Methodist,* February 13, 1875; Freedmen's Aid Society, *Tenth Annual Report* (1876), 79.

[88] *Northwestern Advocate,* July 24 and November 6, 1872.

[89] Ames to Simpson, July 16, 1877, Simpson Papers.

# IX

# An Inhospitable Land

We must be content to leave [it] to future gen-
erations . . . to appreciate the value of the work
done by us today.

*Methodist,* January 5, 1867.

THE MOST CASUAL FOLLOWER of religious affairs during Reconstruction could not miss the sharp contrast between the position
of the Methodist Episcopal Church in northern society and in
that of the South. In one section the church was intimately welcomed in places of wealth and influence; in the other it had
earned largely indifference or hostility among the class grimly
winning its way back to social and political dominance. Northern Methodism had found the land and people of the South
stubbornly resistant to its gospel. "Ours are . . . trials hardly
known in the early days of the Methodist itinerancy," wrote an
evangelist from Virginia, and his plaint was verified by accumulated missionary experiences.[1] Methodism in the South was
poor in the apostolic sense of the word, and faced with opposition equal to anything that had been offered by the "swagger-
ing, whisky-drinking, pistol-shooting bullies" of an earlier
America. These twin themes—obloquy and poverty—are woven
through Northern Methodism's beginnings in the southern
states. The first came in for predominant mention but was
neither the most enduring nor most debilitating aspect of the
southern extension.

The prejudice which beat against the church in the South was
prominently rooted in sectarianism and politics. Southern Methodists bitterly resented the invasion of their territory, the loss
of members and pastors, and the "unchristian designs" on their
property. Incensed by the legion of Northern Missionaries

swarming over his land, the Southern Methodist Bishop George F. Pierce ranted: "They have no business here. We don't want them here; they have no right here. Let them go back where they came from." [2] Pierce, however, spoke not merely as a churchman but as a Southerner who saw the Northern emissaries as "representatives of the lowest and most loathsome features" of the revolution which had swept over the South. They had invaded the Confederacy arm in arm with the Union armies, invoked military help in seizing property, and proselyted behind the protection of federal troops. In the minds of native whites, Northern Methodism clinched its identification with the horde of oppressors by lending countenance and aid to the carpetbag governments. Besides propagating political theories "noxious beyond conception," missionaries were held accountable for swinging the newly-enfranchised freedmen to the support of Republicanism. Evangelists had studiously "bred an alienation and distrust on the part of the Negroes toward the whites" and, after driving a wedge between the races, towed the freedmen into the Radical camp. Some Southerners regarded a relaxation of Northern Methodism's hold over the Negroes as one of the prerequisites for ending carpetbag rule in their section. The "fiercest mischief" accomplished by the "blackcoated saints," wrote a Mississippi journalist-politician, was in "separating the . . . blacks . . . from their old masters, the white men," and then "tieing them fast . . . to Northern politicians." He called upon the Church North, as a contribution to the political and social peace of his state, to "remit the Negroes . . . back to . . . the guidance and protection of Southern white men." [3]

The human vessels in which Northern Methodist doctrines were borne southward also had a share in bringing down the wrath of native whites. Firm hands were popularly regarded as the best for kneading out the mistaken prejudices of Southerners. Richard Rust, secretary of the Freedmen's Aid Society, vowed that the South would be evangelized "even should it be necessary . . . to drench again the land in blood" and wanted the employees in his department to be "of single purpose, of one work, whose souls are on fire." "Let us send no ministers South who are not known to be . . . uncompromising, anti-slavery, loyal men," counseled another churchman. "Men of mere policy" who "stood on both sides of the great questions of the day" might meet with less opposition but "would lay shaky foundations." [4] The respondents to these notices did not fit into a common mold but many of them were ideally equipped to incite controversy. Conditioned by practice in the abolitionist movement, the volunteers often united a passion for the Negro's well-being with a determination to "teach the unreconstructed people a lesson." A preacher who begged his bishop for an assignment to the "hottest place in the South" told his Virginia hosts, "You were . . . all wrong. We of the North were . . . all the time right," and left with the prayer that "God [would] bring them penitently back to the country from which they . . . strayed." At an Independence Day celebration in another Southern state, the pupils of a Northern Methodist school paraded behind their teacher "singing such songs as 'Hang Jeff Davis on a Sour Apple Tree' 'Fling Beauregard in the Middle of the Sea.'" The local journal which recorded this incident editorially exploded that "such a . . . Yankee b – – – h ought to be . . . spanked . . . and then sent out of the Confederate lines." A study of the reception accorded to missionaries of different temperaments convinced a Methodist supervisor in Texas that many of his ecclesiastical brethren had "been insulted and badly treated because they . . . tried to force themselves where they are not wanted." His formula for the avoidance of personal indignities was to "attend to his own business and not force himself into . . . notice among enemies." [5]

For those disposed to court controversy, the South was a garden of opportunity. "They hate . . . as Southerners can hate," declared a minister who ventured into central Tennessee.[6] Southern invective toward the Northern Methodist clergy sometimes strained the vernacular. Nicholas Davis, an old-time

Whig and organizer of the Republican party in Alabama, relieved his feelings before a body of congressmen when, in a single paragraph of stenographic testimony, he used these tart epithets to describe a Methodist preacher of his acquaintance: "a humbug," "a liar," "a slanderer," "a hell of an old rascal," "an old Ruffian." A totally unregenerate Southerner consigned the lot of Methodist preachers "to be hung, sent to h—l." "There is no use of a h—l," he expostulated, "if such damned rascals are not sent to it." The biting lash of Southern tongues swept wide enough to take in the distaff half of Methodism. A New England pedagogue, transplanted to a freedmen's school of Maryland's eastern shore, chronicled this unpleasant reception by the townsfolk: "Men bandied rude insulting jests at my expense, and coupled my name with curses . . . and even from the children I heard '. . . she's nothing but a damned nigger teacher.'" [7]

The crimination which fell on many educators and preachers was an index to their station in the society of Southern whites. Northern Methodists complained that they were shunned "by their white neighbors . . . [as] if they were counterfeiters or horsethieves." Bishop Bowman, as late as 1875, pronounced the social ostracism of his band in the South "almost complete." [8] In churches, shops, and upon public thoroughfares, Southerners let their displeasure shine through. "My wife has not enjoyed the privilege of speaking with a white woman in over two years," wrote a teacher in Georgia. The white supervisor of Methodist activity around Memphis peevishly remarked that natives avoided him "by crossing the street or dodging into a place of business" and when he attended their churches "no notice whatever was taken of him." In various Southern localities Northern missionaries found it difficult to engage lodgings. The objections of other residents to his views on racial relations led to Gilbert Haven's eviction from his Atlanta boarding house in 1876, and a Maryland teacher was compelled to set up housekeeping in an abandoned slave cabin because, as she explained, "for any family to receive me would be to incur the ridicule . . . of the community." [9] Toward the Methodist missionaries the hand that rocked the Southern cradle was seldom more gentle than that which had wielded the sword. A preacher, after a series of encounters "with the sneering, spitting, scratching hell-cats," concluded that "Congress may . . . reconstruct the men of the South" but he knew of no "power sufficient to the task of reconstructing the Southern women." One ministerial fellow, however, conjectured that "a Butler-like administration . . . would bring them to terms." [10]

Northern Methodism reported that its progress in the South was further bedeviled by economic sanctions. White tradesmen who communed with the Northern church allegedly were deprived of patronage, while Negro tenants found themselves "turned off their farms" and domestics "lost their situations." Here and there, attempts to give permanency to Methodist influence were thwarted by Southern refusals to sell ground for the construction of churches and schools.[11] Northern apostles also maintained that the local censorship of the mails obstructed the dissemination of their doctrines. Erasmus Fuller burned up several issues of the *Methodist Advocate* in castigating postmasters who declined to receive or circulate his paper because it included "too much not in full harmony with the Confederacy." [12] Unable to silence their tormentors in other ways, white natives sometimes issued pointed requests for missionaries to vacate the vicinity. A few days after his arrival in Yazoo City, Mississippi, a Hoosier preacher was anonymously informed via a curtly dignified letter that his "presence and preaching will be dispensed with in this city from this date." But not always were the threats so graciously conveyed. A gospel-bearer who ignored two ultimatums from Georgians not to "prech her . . . enny more" was assured that "the nixt warnen el be the led or the steal." [13]

Caught up in the toils of an embittered people, the reactions of missionaries were humanly diversified. Some patiently accepted their oppressions as an integral part of the job of "toiling for the poor people for whom Christ died." Others unrepentantly stood fast in their positions and hurled back as good as they received. "It is useless to ask favors of such a people," wrote a correspondent, and urged his clerical readers "to assert their rights; and in cases of need, demand the protection of the government." His advice frequently was accepted. Methodist preachers directed numerous letters to federal military officers in the South requesting the visit of "a Lt. and some soldiers" to stop the "outrages of villains low" against "peace-loving Christians." [14] However, vengeful Southerners often succeeded in the aim of driving educators and pastors back to the North. Although the relatively heavy turnover of Methodist mission workers cannot be assigned to any one cause, ostracism, threats, and vilification are well up on the list. A teacher in Virginia sadly turned her face homeward for no worse reason, she said, than a few months of being "cheered, whistled, groaned, crowed, squealed and hissed at." Three weeks after his transfer from Oregon to Perry County, Tennessee, another Methodist teacher was accused of inciting the Negroes to rebellion against the whites and was invited to leave the community within twenty-four hours. He did not linger to test the earnestness of his neighbors' intentions.[15]

Southern hostility had its inevitable climax in outbreaks of violence against the persons and property of Northern Methodists. The "assassin's bullet and the incendiary's torch," as well as "clubs, stones, green apples, and rotten eggs" fell to the lot of Methodists. Dispatches from the South were black with tales of assault, arson and murder. About this matter a distillation of newspaper reports, official documents, and private correspondence yields only a tiny residue of generalizations. Methodism's existence seemed most hazardous in the rural districts and away from federal military posts, where the prevention of outrages and the apprehension of their perpetrators were more difficult. In line with the idea that a scalawag was more detestable than a carpetbagger, most victims of physical persecution were natives of the South, white and black, who had sworn fidelity to the Northern church. Authenticated instances of violence against Northern emigrants, while not missing, are conspicuously rare. Finally, a political note arises out of the welter of individual cases of maltreatment. The heat of election campaigns usually kicked up the frequency of vicious attacks, and the sufferers from brutality were almost invariably clergymen with established political reputations. Methodist publicists unconsciously witnessed the relation between persecution and party activity by monotonously including in their lurid accounts such notations as: "shot because of political animosity," "assaulted while coming out of . . . a Republican meeting," "killed . . . after an electioneering tour," and "inhumanely murdered . . . for his . . . Republican principles." [16]

The incidents and personal experiences which made up the composite Southern attitude were not, however, of one kind. "In every attempt to set forth the true state of feeling in the South allowances must be made for the time and locality," wrote a Northern wayfarer.[17] So it was with Methodists. A Georgia convert of the Church North said in 1867 that he had traveled thousands of miles through his native state "calling things by their right names" and had not encountered "a cross word or look from any soul." Other Northern preachers corroborated his testimony.[18] That this side of Methodism's welcome was played down was not always unintentional. A few churchmen had cause to wince at the Southern charge that they deliberately "inflamed the . . . North with exaggerated reports." [19] Clerical propagandists recognized that church folk were likely to be more interested in suffering Methodists than in tolerated ones and the facts were sometimes selected to cultivate the proper impression. Charles Elliot, about to begin a history of his church in the Southwest, asked readers of the *Central Advocate* to forward to him "narratives of murders, persecutions, warnings to leave, threatenings . . . and all annoyances in consequence of religion, loyalty . . . and the like." His book justified the expectations of its contributors. But Elliot was not the lone culprit in encouraging distortion. Bishop Ames sped a missionary South in 1865 with specific instructions to write "such a narrative . . . as will do good, if printed and circulated." John M. Walden, the first secretary of the Freedmen's Aid Society, put in an order with the head of the Freedmen's Bureau in Tennessee in 1866 for "statements in regard to the . . . sufferings of the freedmen . . . that will arrest the attention and quicken the sympathies of the North." Quite correctly, Walden observed that "stirring and touching facts brought constantly before the people alone will convince them of the . . . urgency of our work." [20]

Methodists conceived that the publicity they gave to the Southern temper was useful to their nation as well as to their church. The Missionary Society described its representatives in the South as "a grand corps of . . . reporters . . . to the national government." [21] Southerners readily realized that Methodist agents often intended their newsletters for other than religious ends. "More than one half of the bitterness of which you read is made for political purposes," said one white who assessed the content of priestly dispatches.[22] His proportion was exorbitant, but he was on the right track. A desire to convert Methodism's difficulties into political profit colored many ministerial accounts. In September, 1868, with a presidential election in the offing, James Lynch published the assertion that "opposition to our church is . . . violent" and that Methodists in Mississippi were "ever in danger." Less than thee months later, with Radical ascendancy temporarily assured, he privately informed Bishop Simpson, who was planning a visit to Mississippi, that Northern prelates would "be . . . treated by . . . whites . . . with civility and in many instances with courtesy." [23] The ability of Methodist informants to furnish grist for Republican mills was emphasized during the congressional investigations of the Ku Klux Klan in 1871. In a half-dozen Southern states, Negro or white preachers of the Northern church testified with varying effectiveness before the exceedingly partisan joint committee, but the most sensational of them was an Alabama presiding elder, Arad S. Lakin. Lakin, who emigrated from Ohio in late 1865, had executed earlier missions for the Radicals. Aside from the formation of Loyal League cells among the Negroes, he compiled a documentary pamphlet on outrages in the South of which the Republicans distributed over a million copies during the 1868 campaign.[24] Lakin's committee testimony, many hours long and replete with illustrations of Southern barbarities, was the focal point of the inquiry into Alabama affairs, and won for the parson considerable notice in both the majority and minority reports of the investigators. To the Republicans his words and documents were incontestable evidence that "religious loyalty" could not live safely in the Southern states. The Democratic evaluation, although no more judicious, was considerably different. The Democratic minority scorched Lakin as a "slanderer . . . brimful of gall, bitterness, and falsehood" who "seemed to be incapable of speaking the plain unvarnished truth." [25]

But whatever the extent or intensity of Methodism's persecution, it was bound to grow less. The resentment built by Southerners to protect the wounds opened by war diminished as these sores slowly healed. Methodists themselves generally agreed by 1876 that they were being passively tolerated, if not warmly accepted by Southern whites.[26] However, the tribulations of the church did not end with the decline of native hostility. The South was a missionary frontier, and posed trials reminiscent of those to which a previous generation of Methodists had been subjected. A tourist from New England, reared in a mode of worship that had sloughed off most of its pioneer traits, pegged the nature of Methodism in the Southern states when he wrote, "I have an opportunity of seeing what I have . . . heard the fathers . . . of the church . . . sigh after 'The good old times.' " [27] He also could have said that the "good old times" were best when observed at a safe distance. The vastness and predominantly rural character of the territory suddenly opened before the church allowed the old-fashioned horseback itinerant a new lease on life, but a chronic shortage of ministerial help made his burden inhumanely heavy. At the end of Reconstruction, a two-hundred mile circuit with twenty preaching appointments, each of which had to be visited once a month, was not uncommon. The journals of workaday preachers partially explained what this meant in terms of physical exertion. In his fiftieth year, an East Tennessean "travelled 2051 miles on horseback, preached 181 times . . . visited and prayed with 500 families" and "did manual labor in the field as a farmer." Another circuit rider in Texas in 1876 totaled up almost three thousand miles in delivering two hundred and forty sermons and making twice as many pastoral calls.[28] Along with the unsparing expenditures of energy went the natural perils and privations traditional to the itinerant ministry.

The material rewards, however, infrequently had any ratio to sacrifices. The Methodist preacher in the South, whether white or black, learned to adapt himself to "hard beds and short rations." "I [have] travelled a large work for a whole year and received less than thirty dollars salary for the same," vouched a veteran itinerant.[29] Officials estimated than an annual wage of four hundred dollars was necessary to adequately sustain a preacher in the rural areas, but few ever approached this amount.[30] After 1870 various conferences in the lower South reported salaries averaging under two hundred dollars a year per minister, and these statements included the income of presiding elders and stationed preachers who received sums two to four times larger than the average.[31] Parsons assigned to the poorest circuits could expect a portion of their paltry pay in kind. "Spareribs," "a bushel of potatoes," "a few bundles of corn," "peanuts," "two pairs of socks," and a "soiled cravat" were among the commodities contributed to the upkeep of the Methodist clergy. Sometimes neither cash nor its equivalent was forthcoming and the pastor pitted his wits against the world. A colored preacher in Louisiana, "almost starved out by the hard times" of 1874, was "compelled to set traps in the woods to catch possums to live on." A neighboring apostle happily remarked: "The fish are biting well." [32]

The failure to provide a decent living for the clergy was a dagger pointed at Methodism's breast. "The question of ministerial support is one of the most difficult we meet with in our work," asserted an official acquainted with some of its vitiating effects.[33] The low salaries removed incentives for self-improvement, discouraged transfers from overcrowded conferences in the North, paralyzed the program of recruiting Southern natives, and drove men from the ministry to try their fortunes in other vocations. Even those who bravely tried to shoulder the cross of poverty often had to slight their clerical responsibilities in order to eke out a living. "The preachers on the work . . . are all compelled to labor with their own hands . . . to support their families," wrote a presiding elder in middle Tennessee, and the story was much the same over all the South.[34] Farming and school teaching were favorite ways of supplementing the puny incomes afforded by itinerant work. Methodist overseers scowled at the practice of traveling preachers pursuing outside employment, but dared not incorporate their distaste into regulations for fear of depleting the already thin ministerial ranks. Only a little added to the burden of the impoverished minister might have made his mission fail.

The indigence of Northern Methodist clergymen in the South was fittingly complemented by the churches in which they conducted services. In the Methodist manner, societies were founded and initially catechized in any structure that became immediately available. Courthouses, schoolrooms, private dwellings, bush arbors, mercantile establishments, and, rarely, "upstairs over saloons" were indifferently commandeered as transient places of worship. However, when and if a church building was procured it was unlikely to be any more commodious than the shelter which preceded it. James Mitchell, a Virginia presiding elder, left this description of "the average church in the South":

> Unclean walls of logs or boards pierced by broken windows (if windows at all). Doors off their hinges or broken so that they stand open day and night and thereby afford shelter for sheep and hogs. Floors of puncheon or undressed planks encased in a coat of dust and sand, well-tempered by masticated tobacco. For seats many have none except slabs with sticks stuck in them for feet. If there is a stove at all, often the pipe is stuck out of a window, and when the wind blows into that window the fire must be put out or the congregation will suffer from smoke.[35]

Numerous Methodist edifices in the countryside and in the city embodied more luxury than Mitchell's vignette admits, but its fundamental truthfulness remains inviolate. An official document, issued in 1871, estimated that the unit value of Northern Methodist churches in the Southern states averaged about twenty percent of that in other sections of the country.[36]

For the beggarly state of Methodism in the South, clergymen sometimes blamed the miserliness of their Southern converts or the malappropriation of money, but the real source of trouble defied such simple diagnoses. "The great obstacle to our advancement and success is the extreme poverty of the people," wrote a Texas correspondent; and the church, with all her prayers and petitions, could not blot out this hard fact.[37] Almost four-fifths of the members gathered from the region of the former Confederacy were impoverished Negroes, and they hung as an economic millstone around the neck of the church. The freedmen's poverty hacked out the vitals of every plan for Methodism's amelioration and, without visible prospects of abatement, the Southern offspring went on sucking the nourishment needful to its sickly life from its Northern parent. Up to the close of the Reconstruction period, anxious missionaries continued to caution that "the time has not yet come when our Southern work can be prosecuted without . . . large aid from the general church." [38] Their counsel would remain valid until

Methodism penetrated into the layer of population with "wealth, genius, learning and influence" or until its Negro affiliates garlanded themselves with these pleasing attributes.

The poverty of the Southern stepchild excused some Methodists from joining in the chorus of satisfaction over the outcome of a dozen years of evangelistic labor. "The Southern field is a dry and withered land that has swallowed up . . . thousands [while] giving little back," answered one Northerner to reigning assertions that Methodism had achieved results "without a parallel in the history of all missionary movement." [39] Especially among the laity, doubt had always lurked about the wisdom of invading the South, and subsequent events gave voice to this original mistrust. Although Methodism had added perhaps a quarter of a million members below the Mason-Dixon line in a short space of years, these dissenters refused to bow before statistical enumerations. They complained that the invasion of the South had involved wasteful expenditures of men and money, aroused bitter controversy, and most important, had saddled the church with a permanent burden of support. Fixed in the belief that the Northern denomination would "never succeed in establishing a self-sustaining church in the South," they resolved that Methodism should rid itself of its incubus by withdrawing behind its prewar frontiers. The confession of a mistake, the Methodist critics were prone to argue, was better than perpetuating it. The vociferousness of the dissatisfied minority in publicizing its opinions caused a friend of the freedmen to say that "the most serious objections made to the presence of the Methodist Episcopal Church in the Southern states are heard from persons at the North." [40] Those who condemned the mission outposts as parasites which should be purged out failed to win any declared converts among the officialdom but they lived as reminders that the consequences of Methodism's work were equivocal.

The malcontents might have had more success at enlisting followers if, instead of emphasizing the obvious failures of policy, they had argued that Methodism was betraying its own best interests by plunging into the Southern states. Other domestic problems were as deserving of Methodist care as the reconstruction of the South, if the church were to continue on her climb to ascendancy. The settlement of the transMississippi West called urgently upon Methodism to fulfill her historic role of the pioneers' church, and offered a missionary field free of many of the disadvantages of the South. Methodists were not forgetful of the demands of the West, but they diverted resources from it to the South where the investments probably yielded smaller long-range returns to the church. An expanding economy also spawned a whole new set of problems fit to challenge a denomination which claimed the prerogative of interfering in every social issue, yet Methodist spokesmen seemed almost oblivious of America's emergence from its agrarian cocoon. The isolated pronouncements on industrial relations that emanated from ministerial throats were insipid reiterations of a political economy that industrial capitalism was rapidly rendering ridiculous. Daniel Curry, wholeheartedly devoted to the freedmen's betterment, opposed a shorter working day for labor because "the added leisure hours are thrown away in idleness and dissipation," termed higher wages a device for discouraging "thrift and industry," believed the public regulation of wages a "needless and damaging" attempt to "trammel the free working of our labor system," called all social legislation "wrong and inexpedient," and concluded that "only slavery itself is . . . more inimical to the common good" and "the rights of the individual" than labor unions.[41] Curry's views help in understanding why Methodism tended to lose its appeal to the factory workers. With industrialization came a flood of immigrants from southern and eastern Europe who congregated around the great centers of trade and industry. The ministerial force, by taking little notice of these people except to comment on their undesirability, let another excellent missionary opportunity go aglimmering. Had Methodism waged an intensive evangelistic campaign among the Celtic, Latin and Slavic folk, the twentieth century might not have seen her virtual exclusion from many of the great cities. But even without this foreknowledge, Methodists had an incentive for seeking out the foreign-born. In overwhelming numbers the immigrants were Roman Catholic, and churchmen often advertised that "there is more danger from Romanists threatening to overthrow free . . . institutions than there is on the part of the rebels who are in open . . . hostility to the government." Methodism, however, chose to permit its practices to belie its professions. A careful watch was kept on the Protestant "rebels" but Catholicism, reportedly "the most dangerous foe of every American citizen," was left free to retain her grip on the urbanized immigrants.[42]

Against the reasons for impeaching Methodism's decision to move southward can be balanced the one contribution that bravely resists deprecation. Notwithstanding "misconceptions of truth, errors in judgment and mistakes in practice," no other church in Christendom more earnestly tried to release the Negro from the shackles of ignorance. The justification for Methodism's intrusion into the southland must rest largely upon her schools and teachers. Nevertheless, the historian, with the precious privilege of hindsight, can hypothesize that a better method could have been used to confer this and other benefits on the South. No enlightened person in any section denied that the assistance of the Northern churches was needed in the reconstruction of the South, but there was no unanimity of opinion that the extension of aid required a denominational invasion. The Northern Episcopalians, for instance, gave generously to rebuild a devastated section without trying to thrust themselves on a sullen people. Their largess, which included appropriations for Negro schooling, was distributed through the Southern clergy and in accordance with the wishes of the native whites. Significantly, the reunion of the Northern and Southern dioceses of the Protestant Episcopal Church was quickly achieved after the war. Kindred schemes were advanced in Wesleyan circles.

Southern Methodism, on several occasions, indicated a willingness to receive and disburse Northern funds, and later contended that if such a plan had been adopted the Church North "would have won the South by a love that would have it invincible." A few Northerners endorsed the idea of subsidizing Southern Methodism out of the conviction that the latter was best qualified "by record and experience" to meet the needs of the South even in the work of Negro education. Whether they were right, neither the Methodists nor anyone else had a chance to find out. Cries about "the bitterness in the hearts of the Southern people" and "how the government needs our help in rebuilding the nation" smothered all proposals to underwrite Southern Methodism's evangelistic program. For better or worse, those who felt that the exigencies of the times called for the presence of the Methodist Episcopal Church in the South had their way. [43]

## NOTES

[1] *Western Advocate*, May 2, 1866.

[2] *Methodist Advocate*, February 24, 1869.

[3] Knoxville *Whig*, August 11, 1869; *Nashville Advocate*, December 19, 1874; *Methodist Advocate*, February 3, 1875, quoting Meridian (Miss.) *Daily Mercury*.

[4] *Northern Advocate*, August 2, 1865; *Central Advocate*, October 18, 1865; *Western Advocate*, October 10, 1866.

[5] Conser, *Virginia After the War*, 7, 17–18; clipping from Navasoto *Texas Ranger and Lone Star*, Simpson Papers; *Southwestern Advocate*, September 10, 1874.

[6] Henry C. Eddy to Clinton B. Fisk, February 21, 1866, B.R.F.A.L.

[7] *Ku Klux Conspiracy, Alabama*, 784–85; *Zion's Herald*, February 7, 1866; *Western Advocate*, December 12, 1866.

[8] *Southwestern Advocate*, December 16, 1875; *Central Advocate*, November 8, 1876.

[9] Prentice, *Gilbert Haven*, 440; *Zion's Herald*, March 14, 1866; *Western Advocate*, September 9, 1868; *Southwestern Advocate*, September 9, 1875.

[10] *Western Advocate*, May 24, 1865; *Methodist Advocate*, March 16, 1870.

[11] *Christian Advocate*, April 19, 1866; February 4, 1869; *Western Advocate*, February 12, 1868; *Southwestern Advocate*, August 31, 1876.

[12] *Methodist Advocate*, March 31 and April 21, 1869; March 2, 1870.

[13] *Methodist*, May 1, 1869; Lennin, *TEKEL*, 79.

[14] *Methodist Advocate*, September 22, 1869; J. H. Caldwell to Clinton B. Fisk, September 1, 1865, Anthony Carter to Fisk, October 12, 1865, J. D. Black to Fisk, May 30, 1866, and James F. Chalfant to Fisk, August 4, 1866, B.R.F.A.L.

[15] *Zion's Herald*, July 4, 1866; Knoxville *Whig*, November 24, 1869.

[16] *Christian Advocate*, May 23, 1867; October 28, 1868; *Northwestern Advocate*, November 4, 1868; *Southwestern Advocate*, September 4, 1873.

[17] *Western Advocate*, November 28, 1866.

[18] *Christian Advocate*, April 5, 1866; *Western Advocate*, October 23, 1867.

[19] *Nashville Advocate*, December 19, 1874.

[20] *Central Advocate*, March 16, 1863; Prentice, *Gilbert Haven*, 282; John M. Walden to Clinton B. Fisk, January 6, 1866, B.R.F.A.L.

[21] *Missionary Advocate*, XXI (January, 1866), 74.

[22] *Methodist Advocate*, October 19, 1870.

[23] *Christian Advocate*, September 24, 1868; Lynch to Simpson, December 5, 1868, Simpson Papers.

[24] *Ku Klux Conspiracy, Alabama*, 430ff; Fleming, *Reconstruction in Alabama*, 612–13.

[25] *Ku Klux Conspiracy, Majority and Minority Reports*, 70–74, 493.

[26] Freedmen's Aid Society, *Tenth Annual Report* (1876), 29, 37; *Zion's Herald*, January 6, 1876.

[27] *Zion's Herald*, March 14, 1866.

[28] J. C. Wright, ed., *Autobiography of A. B. Wright* (Cincinnati, 1896), 153; *Southwestern Advocate*, January 27, 1876.

[29] Wright, ed., *A. B. Wright*, 140.

[30] *Methodist Advocate*, May 27, 1873; May 7, 1874.

[31] *Ibid.*, December 13, 1871; December 16, 1874; April 7, 1875; *Minutes of the Tennessee Annual Conference, 1875*, 32.

[32] *Methodist Advocate*, August 11, 1869; December 16, 1874; *Southwestern Advocate*, December 31, 1874; August 31, 1876.

[33] *Minutes of the Central Tennessee Annual Conference, 1878*, p. 23.

[34] *Methodist Advocate*, June 21, 1871.

[35] *Ibid.*, June 9, 1875.

[36] Extension Society, *Sixth Annual Report* (1871), 57.

[37] *Methodist Advocate*, May 27 and November 25, 1874; January 27 and October 6, 1875; *Southwestern Advocate*, December 16, 1875.

[38] *Ibid.*, November 5, 1874.

[39] *Methodist Advocate*, July 19, 1871; Extension Society, *Eleventh Annual Report* (1876), 25.

[40] *Methodist Review*, LIV (January, 1872), 109.

[41] *Christian Advocate*, September 5, 1867.

[42] *Western Advocate*, April 5, 1865; Extension Society, *Tenth Annual Report* (1875), 121.

[43] *Methodist Review*, XLVIII (July, 1866), 443; *Nashville Advocate*, November 13, 1869; *Proceedings of the Southern Methodist Conference, 1871*, p. 52.

# Bibliography

## I. Manuscripts

Gist Blair Collection (Division of Manuscripts, Library of Congress).

Bureau of Refugees, Freedmen and Abandoned Lands Papers (War Records Division, Archives of the United States).

William E. Chandler Papers (Division of Manuscripts, Library of Congress).

Salmon P. Chase Papers (Division of Manuscripts, Library of Congress).

Andrew Johnson Papers (Division of Manuscripts, Library of Congress).

"Journal of the Cape May Conference" (Emory University Library, Atlanta, Georgia).

"Journal of Dr. Daniel Stevenson," 2 vols. (Typescript, in the private library of John O. Gross, Nashville, Tennessee).

"Journals of the Kentucky Conference, 1855–1869" (Typescripts, in the private library of John O. Gross, Nashville, Tennessee).

John W. McClintock Papers (Emory University Library, Atlanta, Georgia).

John P. Newman Papers (Division of Manuscripts, Library of Congress).

Matthew Simpson Papers (Division of Manuscripts, Library of Congress).

Thaddeus Stevens Papers (Division of Manuscripts, Library of Congress).

Benjamin Wade Papers (Division of Manuscripts, Library of Congress).

## II. Government Documents

*Eighth Census, 1860. Statistics of the United States, Including Mortality, Property, etc.* (Washington, 1866).

*Congressional Globe, 1833–1873*, 46 vols. (Washington 1834–1873).

Edward McPherson, ed., *Political History of the United States of America During the Great Rebellion* (2nd ed., Washington, 1865).

*War of the Rebellion: A Compilation of the Official Records of the Union and Confederate Armies*, 130 vols. (Washington 1880–1901).

James D. Richardson, ed., *A Compilation of the Messages and Papers of the Presidents, 1789–1902*, 10 vols. (Washington, 1910).

*Report of the Joint Committee on Reconstruction*, 39 Cong., 1 Sess. (Washington, 1866).

*Report of the Joint Committee to Inquire into the Condition of Affairs in the Late Insurrectionary States.*, 42 Cong., 2nd Sess., 13 vols. (Washington, 1872).

*Statutes at Large of the United States of America* (Boston and Washington, 1845–     ).

Frances N. Thorpe, ed., *The Federal and State Constitutions, Colonial Charters, and Other Organic Laws*, etc., 7 vols. (Washington, 1909).

### III. Official Publications of the Methodist Episcopal Church

1. Annual Reports.

    Church Extension Society 1865–1880.
    Freedmen's Aid Society 1866–1880.
    Missionary Society 1865–1880.
    Sunday School Union 1865–1875.
    Tract Society 1865–1872.

2. Conference Proceedings.

    *Journal of the General Conference, 1864–1884.*
    *Minutes of the Annual Conferences, 1866–1882.*
    *Minutes of the Central Alabama Annual Conference, 1877–1878.*
    *Minutes of the Central Tennessee Annual Conference, 1878.*
    *Minutes of the Florida Annual Conference, 1874, 1875, 1877–1879.*
    *Minutes of the Georgia Annual Conference, 1867–1874.*
    *Minutes of the Holston Annual Conference, 1865–1880.*
    *Minutes of the Kentucky Annual Conference, 1868–1880.*
    *Minutes of the Louisiana Annual Conference, 1870–1878.*
    *Minutes of the Mississippi Annual Conference, 1865–1875.*

*Minutes of the Missouri Annual Conference, 1865–1877.*

*Minutes of the North Carolina Annual Conference, 1871, 1873, 1875–1879.*

*Minutes of the Savannah Annual Conference, 1877–1878.*

*Minutes of the South Carolina Annual Conference, 1869–1878.*

*Minutes of the Tennessee Annual Conference, 1866, 1868, 1870–1878.*

*Minutes of the Texas Annual Conference, 1874–1879.*

*Minutes of the Virginia Annual Conference, 1869–1880.*

*Minutes of the West Texas Annual Conference, 1877–1879.*

*Minutes of the West Virginia Annual Conference, 1865–1880.*

3. Periodicals.

*Central Christian Advocate.* St. Louis.

*Christian Advocate.* New York.

*Daily Christian Advocate.* Published quadrennially at the site of the General Conference.

*Ladies Repository.* Cincinnati.

*Methodist.* New York.

*Methodist Advocate.* Atlanta.

*Methodist Review.* New York.

*Missionary Advocate.* New York.

*Northern Christian Advocate.* Auburn and Syracuse, New York.

*Northwestern Christian Advocate.* Chicago.

*Pittsburgh Christian Advocate.* Pittsburgh.

*Southwestern Christian Advocate.* New Orleans.

*Western Christian Advocate.* Cincinnati.

*Zion's Herald.* Boston.

IV. MISCELLANEOUS PUBLICATIONS PERTAINING TO METHODISM

*Catalog of East Tennessee Wesleyan University, 1867–1869.*

*Catalog of the Officers and Students of Clark University, 1879–1885.*

*Doctrine and Discipline of the Methodist Episcopal Church, 1864–1876.*

*Formal Fraternity Proceedings of the General Conferences of the Methodist Episcopal Church and the Methodist Episcopal Church,*

*South in 1872, 1874 and 1876, and of the Joint Commission of the Two Churches on Fraternal Relations at Cape May, New Jersey, August 16–23, 1876* (New York and Nashville, 1876).

*Journal of the General Conference of the Methodist Episcopal Church, South, 1866–1878.*

*Methodist Almanac, 1865–1880.*

*Methodism in the State of New York as Represented in State Convention held in Syracuse, New York, February 22–24, 1870.* (New York, San Francisco, and Cincinnati, 1870).

*Minutes of the New Jersey Methodist State Convention, Held in Trenton, New Jersey, September 27–29, 1870.* (Trenton, N. J., 1870).

*Proceedings of the Southern Methodist Convention, Held at Athens, Tennessee, June 15–19, 1871. Composed of Ministerial and Lay Delegates of the Methodist Episcopal Church from the Conferences in the Southern States.* (Cincinnati, 1871).

## V. Periodicals

*African Methodist Episcopal Church Review.* Philadelphia.

*American Missionary.* New York.

*Christian Advocate.* Nashville.

*Christian Inquirer.* New York.

*Christian Union.* New York.

*Daily Southern Christian Advocate.* Published quadrennially at the site of the General Conference of the Methodist Episcopal Church, South.

*Harper's Weekly.* New York.

*Independent.* New York.

*Nation.* New York

New York *Evangelist.*

*Southern Review.* Baltimore.

## VI. Newspapers

Boston *Journal.*

Canton (O.) *Stark County Democrat.*

Centerville *Indiana True Republican.*

Chattanooga *Daily Gazette.*

Chicago *Daily Tribune.*

Columbus (O.) *Crisis.*

Indianapolis *Daily Sentinel.*

Indianapolis *Journal.*

Knoxville *Daily Free Press.*

Knoxville *Press and Messenger.*

Knoxville *Whig.*

Lancaster *Ohio Eagle.*

Nashville (Ill.) *Journal.*

New Albany (Ind.) *Weekly Ledger.*

New York *Herald.*

New York *Sun.*

Philadelphia *Item.*

Salem (Ill.) *Advocate.*

Springfield *Daily Illinois State Register.*

Terre Haute (Ind.) *Daily Express.*


## VII. DIARIES, AUTOBIOGRAPHIES, TRAVEL ACCOUNTS, MEMOIRS, ETC.

Myrta L. Avary, *Dixie After the War* (New York, 1910).

John H. Caldwell, *Reminiscences of the Reconstruction of Church and State in Georgia* (Wilmington, Del., 1895).

Solomon L. M. Conser, *Virginia After the War. An Account of Three Years Experience in Reorganizing the Methodist Episcopal Church in Virginia at the Close of the Civil War.* (Indianapolis, 1891.)

John W. Deforest, *A Union Officer in Reconstruction.* Edited by James H. Croushore and David M. Potter. (New Haven, 1948).

John H. Franklin, ed., *Civil War Diary of James T. Ayres.* (Springfield, Ill., 1947).

Oliver O. Howard, *Autobiography,* 2 vols. (New York, 1908).

Frances B. Leigh, *Ten Years on A Georgia Plantation Since the War.* (London, 1887).

Mary Simmerson Logan, *Reminiscences of a Soldier's Wife: An Autobiography.* (New York, 1916).

John Mathews, *Peeps into Life: Autobiography of Reverend John Mathews.* (n.p., n.d).

John T. Morse, Jr., ed., *Diary of Gideon Welles,* 3 vols. (Boston and New York, 1911).

Charles Nordhoff, *The Cotton States in the Spring and Summer of 1875.* (New York, 1876).

Thomas H. Pearne, *Sixty-one Years of Itinerant Christian Life in Church and State.* (Cincinnati and New York, 1899).

Whitelaw Reid, *After the War: A Southern Tour, May 1, 1865 to May 1, 1866.* (London, 1866).

James B. Shaw, *Twelve Years in America: Being Observations on the Country, the People, Institutions and Religion.* (London and Chicago, 1867).

Charles Stearns, *The Black Man of the South and The Rebels.* (New York, 1872).

C. C. Stratton, ed., *Autobiography of Erastus O. Haven.* (New York and Cincinnati, 1881).

David Sullins, *Recollections of an Old Man, Seventy Years in Dixie.* (Cleveland, Tennessee, 1910).

Thomas O. Summers, ed., *Life and Papers of A. L. P. Green.* (Nashville, 1877).

John T. Trowbridge, *The South: A Tour of its Battlefields and Ruined Cities, A Journey Through the Desolated States, and Talks with the People.* (Hartford, 1866).

Charles D. Warner, *On Horseback. A Tour in Virginia, North Carolina, and Tennessee.* (Boston and New York, 1888).

Sylvester Weeks, ed., *A Life's Retrospect. Autobiography of Granville Moody.* (New York and Cincinnati, 1890).

J. C. Wright, ed., *Autobiography of A. B. Wright.* (Cincinnati, 1896).

## VIII. Collections of Materials

Walter L. Fleming, ed., *Documentary History of Reconstruction,* 2 vols. (Cleveland, 1906–1907).

Gilbert Haven, *National Sermons: Sermons, Speeches, and Letters on Slavery and its War.* (Boston, 1869).

J. S. Whedon and D. A. Whedon, eds., *Essays, Reviews and Discourses by Daniel D. Whedon.* (New York and Cincinnati, 1887).

## IX. POLEMICAL LITERATURE

A Member of the Kentucky Conference, *The Methodist Churches, North and South, An Address to the Members of the M. E. Church, and to all Friends of Law, Peace, and Right.* (Cincinnati, 1866).

John H. Brunner, *The Union of the Churches.* (New York, Cincinnati, Macon, Ga. and St. Louis, n.d.).

Henry C. Dean, *The Crimes of the Civil War.* (Baltimore, 1868).

Jacob Ditzler, *Philosophy of the History of the Church from the Times of Christ to the Present.* (St. Louis, 1866).

Charles Elliot, *Southwestern Methodism. A History of the M. E. Church in the Southwest from 1844 to 1864.* (Cincinnati, 1868).

Erasmus Q. Fuller, *An Appeal to the Records: A Vindication of the Methodist Episcopal Church, in its Policy and Proceedings Toward the South.* (New York, 1876).

Lewis M. Hagood, *The Colored Man in the Methodist Episcopal Church.* (New York and Cincinnati, 1890).

William M. Leftwich, *Martyrdom in Missouri; A History of Religious Proscription, The Seizure of Churches, and the Persecution of Ministers of the Gospel in the State of Missouri,* 2 vols. (St. Louis, 1870).

J. H. Lennin, *T E K E L. The "Non-Political Church Weighed in the Balance and Found Wanting, or A Critical Review of the Methodist Episcopal Church, South.* (Edinburgh, Ind., 1871).

Edward H. Myers, *The Disruption of the Methodist Episcopal Church 1844–1846 . . . Comprising a Thirty Years History of the Relations of the Two Methodisms.* (Nashville and Macon, Ga., 1875).

Benjamin T. Tanner, *An Apology for African Methodism.* (Baltimore, 1867).

[John A. Wright] *People and Preachers in The Methodist Episcopal Church.* (Philadelphia, 1886).

## X. BIOGRAPHIES

E. Merton Coulter, *William G. Brownlow: Fighting Parson of the Southern Highlands.* (Chapel Hill, 1937).

George R. Crooks, *Life of Bishop Matthew Simpson.* (New York, 1890).

Daniel Curry, *Life Story of Rev. Davis W. Clark.* (New York and Cincinnati, 1874).

William B. Hesseltine, *Ulysses S. Grant, Politician.* (New York, 1935).

Alphonso A. Hopkins, *The Life of Clinton Bowen Fisk.* (New York, 1890).

John F. Marlay, *The Life of Thomas A. Morris, D. D., Late Senior Bishop of the Methodist Episcopal Church.* (New York and Cincinnati, 1875).

James D. Mitchell, *The Life and Times of Levi Scott, D.D.* (New York and Cincinnati, 1885).

David H. Moore, *John Morgan Walden: Thirty-fifth Bishop of the Methodist Episcopal Church.* (New York and Cincinnati, 1915).

George Prentice, *Life of Gilbert Haven.* (Cincinnati and New York, 1885).

Henry B. Ridgaway, *The Life of the Rev. Alfred Cookman.* (New York, 1873).

Henry B. Ridgaway, *The Life of Edmund S. Janes.* (New York and Cincinnati, 1882).

Richard S. Rust, ed., *Isaac W. Wiley: Late Bishop of the M. E. Church.* (Cincinnati and New York, 1885).

Edward Thomson, *Life of Edward Thomson.* (Cincinnati and New York, 1885).

## XI. General and Special Accounts

Thomas B. Alexander, *Political Reconstruction in Tennessee.* (Nashville, 1950).

John P. Arthur, *Western North Carolina, A History.* (Raleigh, 1914).

Wade C. Barclay, *Early American Methodism, 1769–1844,* 2 vols. (New York, 1949).

Paul H. Buck, *Road to Reunion.* (Boston, 1937).

James M. Buckley, *Constitutional and Parliamentary History of the Methodist Episcopal Church.* (New York and Cincinnati, 1912).

E. Merton Coulter, *The South During Reconstruction, 1865–1877.* (Baton Rouge, 1947).

Paul F. Douglass, *The Story of German Methodism.* (New York, Cincinnati, and Chicago, 1939).

Chester F. Dunham, *The Attitude of the Northern Clergy Toward the South, 1861–1865.* (Toledo, O., 1942).

Hunter D. Farish, *The Circuit Rider Dismounts: A Social History of Southern Methodism, 1865–1900.* (Richmond, 1938).

Walter L. Fleming, *Civil War and Reconstruction in Alabama.* (New York, 1905).

Edmund J. Hammond, *The Methodist Episcopal Church in Georgia.* (Atlanta, 1935).

Oliver S. Heckman, "The Penetration of Northern Churches into the South, 1860–1880." (Ph.D Dissertation, Duke University, 1938).

William H. Lawrence, *The Centenary Souvenir, Containing a History of the Centenary Church, Charleston.* (Charleston, S. C., 1885).

William H. Lewis, *The History of Methodism in Missouri for a Decade of Years from 1860 to 1870.* (Nashville, 1890).

Holland N. McTyeire, *A History of Methodism.* (Nashville and Dallas, 1904).

Isaac P. Martin, *Methodism in Holston.* (Knoxville, 1945).

*Methodism and the Republic: Uncorrected Proof Sheets Sent out in Advance to Pastors Intending to take the Collection for Home Missions and Church Extension.* (n.p., n.d.).

Macum Phelan, *A History of the Expansion of Methodism in Texas 1867–1902.* (Dallas, 1937).

R. N. Price, *Holston Methodism, From its Origin to the Present Time,* 7 vols. (Nashville, Dallas and Richmond, 1912).

Charles W. Ramsdell, *Reconstruction in Texas.* (New York, 1910).

Francis B. Simkins and Robert H. Woody, *South Carolina During Reconstruction.* (Chapel Hill, 1932).

Abel Stevens, *The Centenary of American Methodism: A Sketch of its History, Theology, Practical System and Success.* (New York, 1865).

Daniel Stevenson, *The Methodist Episcopal Church in the South.* (Cincinnati and New York, 1892).

Anson P. Stokes, *Church and State in the United States,* 3 vols. (New York, 1950).

Jay S. Stowell, *Methodist Adventures in Negro Education.* (New York and Cincinnati, 1922).

William W. Sweet, *Methodism in American History.* (New York, 1933).

William W. Sweet, *The Methodist Episcopal Church and the Civil War.* (Cincinnati, 1912).

William W. Sweet, *The Story of Religion in America.* (2nd rev. ed., New York, 1950).

Addie G. Wardle, *History of the Sunday School Movement in the Methodist Episcopal Church.* (New York and Cincinnati, 1918).

Ezra M. Wood, *Methodism and the Centennial of American Independence.* (New York and Cincinnati, 1876).

Carter G. Woodson, *The History of the Negro Church.* (2nd ed., Washington, 1921).

## XII. ARTICLES

William B. Hesseltine, "Methodism and Reconstruction in East Tennessee," East Tennessee Historical Society, *Publications* No. 3 (1931), 42–61.

Luther P. Jackson, "The Educational Efforts of the Freedmen's Bureau and The Freedmen's Aid Societies in South Carolina, 1862–1872," *Journal of Negro History,* VIII (January, 1923), 1–40.

Amory D. Mayo, "The Work of Certain Northern Churches in the Education of the Freedmen, 1861–1900," United States Department of Interior, *Annual Report of the Commissioner of Education, 1902* (Washington, 1903), 285–314.

J. G. Nicolay and John Hay, "Lincoln and the Churches," *Century Magazine,* XXXVIII (August, 1889), 562–84.

Julius H. Parmalee, "Freedmen's Aid Societies," United States Department of Interior, Office of Education, *Bulletin* No. 38 (1916), 268–95.

William W. Sweet, "Methodist Church Influence in Southern Politics," *Mississippi Valley Historical Review,* I (March 1915), 546–60.

William W. Sweet, "The Methodist Episcopal Church and Reconstruction," *Journal of the Illinois State Historical Society,* VII (October, 1914) 147–165.

## XIII. MISCELLANEOUS AIDS

*American Annual Cyclopedia and Register of Important Events 1865–1870.*

Allen Johnson and Dumas Malone, eds., *Dictionary of American Biography*, 20 vols. and index. (New York, 1927–1938).

Samuel M. Merrill, *A Digest of Methodist Law*. (Cincinnati and New York, 1888).

Thomas A. Morris, *A Discourse of Methodist Episcopal Church Polity*. (Cincinnati and New York, 1859).

Matthew Simpson, ed., *Cyclopedia of Methodism*. (Philadelphia, 1878).

# Index

African Methodist Episcopal Church: competes with Methodist Episcopal Church, 134–35, 136; requests subsidies from Methodist Episcopal Church, 135; coöperates with Southern Methodist Church, 137–38

African Methodist Episcopal Zion Church, 134

ALLYN, ROBERT, 44

ALVORD, JOHN W., 164

American Freedmen's Union Commission: founded, 155; split over educational philosophy, 156–57; Methodists retire from, 157

American Missionary Association, 164, 177n8

AMES, EDWARD R., and church property in South, 33, 34, 36, 37, 38, 41, 73, 86; complaint against Freedmen's Bureau, 164; opposes Blair's nomination to Supreme Court, 215; on political parties, 228–29; and Grant, 231n56; quoted, 241

Ames Church (New Orleans), refuses membership to Negroes, 188

ANDREW, JAMES O., 68

Annual Conference: function of, 9; debate over segregation in, 188–193, 202n51

BAKER, OSMAN C., 46, 57n10, 58n15

Baptists: strength of, 25n2; Northern division of, and church property in South, 58n15; rivalry with Methodists, 132–33; and Negro schools, 159

Benevolent societies, 154–55

Bishops: prerogatives of, 10–11; selection of, 11–12; election of three additional, 31–32; plan of, for Southern occupation, 32; list of, in 1864, 57n10; 1865 circular of, 77

BLAIR, MONTGOMERY, 212, 214–15

BOWMAN, THOMAS: describes South, 23; on Northern Methodists and South, 24; on conversions in Methodist schools, 172; on ostracism of North Methodists in South, 237

BRADEN, JOHN, 171

BRAKEMAN, NELSON, 44

BROOKS, JOSEPH, 220

BROWNLOW, WILLIAM G.: and McKendree Chapel, 40; and Methodist Episcopal Church, 42, 43, 60n48; and Southern Methodism, 65, 70; quoted, 100; on nonslaveholding Southern white, 186; in Southern politics, 220, 222; owner of *Knoxville Whig,* 222

CALDWELL, JOHN H.: arouses interest in Southern missions, 47; conversion of, 102; political activities, 225

CAMPBELL, JABEZ, 135

CANBY, E. R. S., 99

Cape May Commission: planned, 83; agreement reached, 87–88; reactions to, 88–90; importance of, 90–91; rules of, regarding church property, 94n78

Catholic Church: strength of, 25n2; schools of, and Grant, 217–18; Methodist attitude toward, 248

*Central Christian Advocate:* quoted, 181; Charles Elliot's notice in, 240

Central Tennessee College: and Missionary Society, 160; weakness of, 166; professional schools of, 167; growth of, 169; revival at, 172

Central University of the Methodist Episcopal Church, South, 114

CHALFANT, JAMES F., 47

*Charleston Christian Advocate,* 55, 56

CHASE, SALMON P.: praises Methodist Church, 14–15; letter from Edward Thomson, 214; supported by Bishop Ames, 215

*Christian Advocate* (Nashville): quoted, 63

*Christian Advocate* (New York): on Grant and Catholic schools, 218; mentioned, 23, 66

*Christian Recorder:* official organ of African Methodists, 135

Church Extension Society: founded, 32; activities and financial difficulties of, 50–52; financial support of, 173

Church property: War Department decrees concerning, 33–41, 58n15, 73; occupation of Southern churches

263

by Northern Methodists, 34–56, 36; attempts of Church South to recover, 36–38; Lincoln and, 37, 39, 41, 59n38; Johnson and, 39, 40, 41, 59n38, 73; contention over, 71–76, 85–87; Cape May agreement concerning, 87–88, 94n78; of Negroes, given to Colored Methodist Episcopal Church, 139; of Northern Methodists in South, value of, 245

Circuit rider, 8, 243–44

Claflin University: standards of, 165; industrial program of, 168

CLARK, DAVIS W.: on Methodist expansion, 21–22; presides over Holston conference, 43; plans for Georgia and Alabama, 47; elected bishop, 57n10; on Southern Methodism, 65; on caliber of Southern clergy, 106; quoted, 112

Clark University (Atlanta): course of instruction at, 166; industrial program of, 168; building described, 168–69; religious atmosphere of, 171

Clergy: ranking of, 7–9; local, 7–8; traveling, 8–9; Northern, lack of interest in South, 54–5; transfers from Church South, 104–05; in South, low caliber of, 105–06; Negro, description of, 145–47, 148; Negro, oppose freedmen's schools, 173–74. *See also* Circuit rider

COBLEIGH, NELSON: appointed editor of *Methodist Advocate,* 56; on Negroes and East Tennessee Wesleyan, 198

COLFAX, SCHUYLER, 212

Colored Methodist Episcopal Church of America: formation of, 133–34; receives property from Church South, 139

Conference, Annual, see Annual Conference

Conference, District, see District Conference

Conference, General, see General Conference

Conference, Quarterly, see Quarterly Conference

Congregationalists: influence in Freedmen's Bureau, 164

CRAMER, MICHAEL J., 35, 46

CRARY, BENJAMIN F., 109, 203

CRESSWELL, JOHN A. J.: and Methodists, 211–12

CROOKS, GEORGE R.: on reconstruction, 22, 228; advocates Methodist reunion, 67; predicts reunion, 91; encourages expansion into South, 92n12

CURRY, DANIEL: on the Methodist press, 13; on reconstruction, 22–23; characterizes Southerners, 23–24; criticizes apathy respecting South, 44; quoted, 63; on Southern Methodism, 66; on division in Methodism, 80; on Northern Methodists in South, 120; views on segregation, 184; supports legislative reconstruction, 206; on Methodism and Republican Party, 210–11; on labor, 247

DAVIS, JEFFERSON, 206

DAVIS, NICHOLAS, 236

DE FOREST, JOHN W.: quoted on Negro and religion, 140

Discipline of the Methodist Episcopal Church: and rights of Methodist laity, 7, 12; loyalty clause, 31, 101, 102

District Conference, 26n19

DREW, DANIEL, 14

DUNN, HIRAM, 213

DURBIN, JOHN P.: secretary of Missionary Society, 160

EARLY, JOHN, 68

East Tennessee Wesleyan University: described, 113–14; and Methodist higher education for whites, 116; financial difficulties, 117; and Negroes, 197–99

EDDY, THOMAS M.: on copperheads, 17; on immigration to South, 24; on disfranchisement of Confederates, 205

Education: Methodist program for Southern whites, 113–18, 123n69, 197; Methodist program for Negroes, 153–176, 198, 248–49; and religious instruction, 156–59, 160, 170–72; Freedmen's Bureau and, 159, 162–65, 178n33; opposition of Negro clergy to, 173–74. *See also* Freedmen's Aid Society

EDWARDS, ARTHUR: views on religious journalism, 14; against segregated Annual Conferences, 189; quoted,

211; criticizes political activity of Methodists, 227

ELLIOT, CHARLES: approves war measures, 16–17; distorts persecution of Methodists in South, 240

FISK, CLINTON B., 94n64, 154

FOSTER, RANDOLPH, 188

Freedmen's Aid Society: report quoted, 125; founded, 156, 157, 160; development of educational activities, 161–62; and primary education, 164–65; and higher education, 165–67; and professional training, 167; and industrial education, 167–68; poverty of schools of, 168–69; employment of teachers, 169–171, 179n52; religion in schools of, 170–72; financial position of, 172–73; problems of schools of, 174–75; enrollment in schools of, 175; importance of work of, 176; schools of, open to whites, 197

Freedmen's Bureau: Methodists in, 154; and schools, 159, 162–65, 178n33; assistance to Methodists, 162–65; and Central Tennessee College, 169; and East Tennessee Wesleyan, 198

FRENCH, MANSFIELD, 68

FROTHINGHAM, O. B.: attacks sectarian teaching, 157

FULLER, ERASMUS Q.: quoted, 23; and editorship of *Methodist Advocate*, 55, 56; on Southern Methodists, 79; delegate to Cape May conference, 83, 94n64; hostility toward Edward Myers, 84; author of *An Appeal to the Records*, 84; on church property in South, 85; urges immigration of Methodists, 108; supports segregated conferences, 191; political comments in *Methodist Advocate*, 221; trouble with Southern postmasters, 238

GEE, A. A., 46, 68

General Conference: power and function of, 9–10; representation of laity in, 26n18

General Conference of 1848: repudiates Plan of Separation, 63, 84

General Conference of 1864: plans for expansion into South, 31–32; and loyalty of clergymen, 101; on Negroes and The Church, 128; authorizes Negro Annual Conferences, 189

General Conference of 1868: appraises Church Extension Society, 51; policies of, relating to South, 52–53; authorizes publication of paper in South, 55; authorizes collection of funds for education, 118; authorizes Negro Annual Conference in Kentucky, 190; on Negro suffrage, 204; favors impeachment of Johnson, 208; on relation of church and state, 210

General Conference of 1872: increases number of bishops, 11; delegates emissaries to Southern General Conference, 83

General Conference of 1876: supports government aid for parochial schools, 165; on relations between white and Negro members, 182; sanctions segregated conferences, 196, 202n50

General Conference of 1884: condones segregation, 200

General Conference, Southern Methodist, of 1866: makes provision for Negro Methodists, 133–34, 137

General Conference, Southern Methodist, of 1870: and reunion, 78, 82; and "mixed conferences," 195

General Conference, Southern Methodist, of 1874: and reunion, 81

German Methodists, 99–100

GODKIN, EDWIN L., 6

GRANT, ULYSSES S.: and McKendree Chapel, 35; supported by Methodists, 212; favors Methodists, 213–14; proposes Constitutional amendment relating to school taxes, 217–18; and third term, 217–19

HARLAN, JAMES, 211, 212

HARPER, FLETCHER, 3

*Harper's Weekly*, 3, 206

HARRIS, WILLIAM L., 78

HAVEN, ERASTUS O.: proposes transfer of Negroes to Colored Methodist Episcopal Church, 196

HAVEN, GILBERT: campaign for bishopric, 12; and Southern Methodism, 70; attacks on segregation, 182–83; on intermarriage, 184; opposition to, 185, 193–94; quoted, on franchise, 205; on carpetbagger, 228; and Grant, 219, 231n56

HOGAN, JOHN, 37

HOLDEN, WILLIAM W., 222

HOLMAN, CALVIN, 42

Holston conference: first meeting, 43; requests Fuller's removal, 56; and East Tennessee Wesleyan, 113, 123n59; and loyalty of clergy, 121n20; and Negroes, 193; approves Congressional Reconstruction Plan, 223

HONEY, GEORGE W., 220

HOWARD, OLIVER O., 164, 198

Immigration of Methodists: urged by John Reid, 24; encouraged by Northern Methodists in South, 107–08; Missouri campaign for, 108–10

JANES, EDMUND S.: heavy labors of, 26n24; quoted, on Church Extension Society, 51; listed, 57n10; and War Department decrees, 58n15, 73; and Methodist reunion, 67; visits Southern bishops, 78, 81; at Southern General Conference, 1870, 78, 82; quoted, 127

JOHNSON, ANDREW; and church property in South, 39, 40, 41, 59n38; 73; Methodist attitude toward, 207–09, 215

JOHNSON, J. GARRETT, 225

Joint Commission of 1876. *See* Cape May Commission

KAVANAUGH, HUBBARD H.: quoted, on reunion, 68

KEENER, JOHN, 86

KINGSLEY, CALVIN: quoted, on Methodist occupation of Southern churches, 35; elected bishop, 57n10

Knoxville University: origin and failure of, 114–16

*Knoxville Whig:* publishes call for Knoxville conference, 43; supports Republican Party, 222

Ku Klux Klan, 241

Labor: attitude of Methodist leaders toward 247–48

LAKIN, ARAD S., 177n6, 242

LEWIS, TIMOTHY W.: seizes Charleston churches, 38; missionary activity in South Carolina, 46; wins Negro converts, 130; forced to accept segregation, 187

LINCOLN, ABRAHAM: praises Methodist Church, 15; and church property in South, 37, 39, 41, 59n38; Methodist reaction to assassination of, 206; administration of, and Methodists, 214–15

LORE, DALLAS D., 45, 212

Loyal League, 242

LYNCH, JAMES: quoted, on Freedmen's Bureau, 163; political activities of, 220, 225, 226; publisher of *Colored Citizen*, 222; on treatment of Northern Methodists, 241

McCLINTOCK, JOHN, 67

McKendree Chapel (Nashville), 34–35, 40, 59n38

MATLACK, LUCIUS, 129, 192

Meharry Medical School, 167, 178n41

MERRILL, STEPHEN, 185

*Methodist Advocate:* history and description of, 55–56; complaints against, 61n100; hostilities with *Southern Christian Advocate*, 84; and immigration 108; and segregated conferences, 191; jealousy over, 192; and politics, 221; difficulties with postmasters, 238

Methodist Episcopal Church: prosperity of, 3–4, 25n2; worship of, 4–5; and doctrine, 6; government of, 6–13; participation of laity in, 12, 26n18; publishing interests, 13–14, 27n34; during Civil War, 15–19; in slave territory, 29–30; urged to expand activities into Confederacy, 30–31; division of, in 1844, 63; and union movement, 77–79; adherents to, in South, 98–100; attracts some Southern clergy, 104–05; encourages immigration, 107–110; educational program of, for Southern whites, 113–18, 123n69; criticized for neglect of Southern whites, 118–120; competition of, with African Methodism; 133–36; educational philosophy, 157–58; failure of attempts at racial integration, 187–88; accepts segregation, 199–200; on Negro suffrage, 204; and Congress, 206–07; and Republican Party, 211–225; results of missions in South, 245–46, 248–49; in West,

247; and factory worker, 247–48. *See also* General Conference

Methodist Episcopal Church, South: and Northern dissenters, 18; founded, 29; and War Department decrees, 33–41; and Church North, 63–70; against reunion, 70; revival of, 70, 71; and contention over church property, 71–76; sends delegates to 1876 General Conference, 83; doubtful legal status of, 84–86; demands recognition of legitimacy, 86–87; Northern Methodists joining, 110–12; Negro membership in, 129; and African Methodists, 137–38. *See also* General Conference, Southern Methodist

*Methodist:* promotes lay interests, 14; advocates reunion, 66–67; on Supreme Court, 86; supports segregation, 195; on reconstruction, 228

Metropolitan Church (Washington), 217

Missionary Society: work of, 12–13; "third class of missions" added, 32; expenditures in South, 45, 50, 53, 61n75; and Negro education, 160; receipts, 173; and segregation, 194; and politics, 241

Mitchell, James S.: Superintendent of Virginia-North Carolina district, 48; asks for financial support, 49; describes "average church in South," 244–45

Moore, H. H., 24, 177n5

Morris, Thomas A.: on doctrinal unity, 5; on treason, 16

Myers, Edward H.: delegate to Cape May conference, 83, 94n64; author of *Disruption of the Methodist Episcopal Church*, 84; quoted, on church property, 87; on converts to Northern Methodism, 106

*Nation:* estimates number of Republicans among Methodists, 211

Negroes: contention over churches of, 72; policy of Church North toward, 125–27, 128–29, 130–32; number of, in Church North, 127–28; Methodists among, divided along party lines, 129–30; competition over, among denominations, 132–33, 139; and Church South, 133–34, 137–39; and African Methodists, 134–37;

religious life of, described, 140–44; moral lapses criticized, 144–45; religion of, compared to that of pioneers, 149; education of, 153–176; transfer from Church North to Colored Methodist Episcopal Church proposed, 196; votes of, organized by Methodists, 223–25

Nelson, Samuel, 85

Nesbit, Samuel H.: on Church's mission in South, 20; quoted, on Negroes and Methodist Church, 126; demands rights in South for Northern Methodists, 209; on Johnson administration, 215

*New Orleans Advocate;* founded, 55; becomes *Southwestern Christian Advocate,* 56; supports Republican party, 221

New Orleans University: and Missionary Society, 160; low standards of, 165

Newman, John P.: against restoration of churches to Church South, 40; founds *New Orleans Advocate,* 55; on reunion, 68; delegate to Cape May conference, 94n64; quoted, on Church in South, 125; recruits Negro preachers, 131; and Grant, 216–17, 218; and Catholic schools, 218; supports Republican Party, 221; in Louisiana politics, 222–23

Nordhoff, Charles: quoted, on Negro worship, 149; quoted, on Bishop Haven, 194; deplores White House favor toward Methodists, 214; on Methodists as Republicans, 224

*Northern Christian Advocate:* on Church policy toward South, 45; attacks Cape May conference, 88; and 1868 presidential campaign, 212

*Northwestern Christian Advocate,* 189, 205

Paine, Robert, 68

Parochial schools: government aid for, supported by General Conference, 165; and Grant's proposed Constitutional amendment, 217–18

Pearne, Thomas, 222

Peck, Jesse T., 4

Pierce, George F., 68, 235

Pierpont, Francis, 99

*Pittsburgh Christian Advocate:* quoted, 203

Plan of Separation, 84–85, 89

POSTELL, JAMES H., 48, 104

POWELL, LAZARUS, 37–38

Presbyterian churches: strength of, 25n2; and church property in South, 58n15

Presiding elder: function of, 10

Press, Methodist: position and influence of, 13–14; list of weeklies, 27n34; criticizes Church's apathy toward South, 43–44; Supreme Court decision on proceeds of, 85

Protestant Episcopal Church, 248

Quarterly Conference, 9, 26n19

RANDOLPH, BENJAMIN F., 225

Reconstruction: attitude of Methodists toward, 22–23; Methodist approval of Congressional program, 206, 209, 223; disillusionment of Methodists with, 228

Reconstruction governments: and Methodists, 220

REID, JOHN M.: quoted, on reunion, 21; urges Methodist immigration, 24; quoted, on Methodist Church and Negroes, 126; supports segregation, 185; on Confederate leaders, 206

REID, WHITELAW, 153

Republican Party: and Methodists, 211–25; disillusionment of Methodists with, 228

Reunion: Northern attitudes toward, 66–67, 81–82, 91; Southern bishops on, 78; Southern attitude toward, 78–81; negotiations toward, 82–83

REVELS, HIRAM R., 220

ROWLEY, ERASTUS, 121n20, 123n59

RUST, RICHARD S.: and Freedmen's Aid Society, 159; quoted, on Negro education, 162; on Freedmen's Bureau, 164; on support for freedmen's schools, 173; quoted, on reconstruction program, 228; quoted, on evangelizing South, 235–36

SCOTT, LEVI: and Virginia-North Carolina conference, 47; quoted, on churches, 51

Segregation: in churches: 181–88; in Annual Conference, 188–193, 195–97; in Methodist schools,

197–99; accepted by Church North, 199–200

Shaw University: entrance requirements, 166; revival at, 172

SHERIDAN, PHILIP H., 223

SIMPSON, MATTHEW: and Unionism, 17; on Church's mission in South, 19; appoints agent for East Tennessee, 42; and War Department decrees, 58n15, 73; visits Southern bishops, 78, 81; and Chase, 86; and Freedmen's Union Commission, 155, 157; and impeachment of Johnson, 208–09; and Senator Harlan, 212; and Blair, 215; and Grant, 216, 219; on ostracism of Northern clergy in South, 226

SOULE, JOSHUA, 68

*Southern Christian Advocate,* 84

*Southwestern Christian Advocate:* foundation and purpose of, 56, 192; and Republican Party, 221

STANTON, EDWIN M., 33, 37. *See also* War Department

STEELE, GEORGE M., 64

STEVENS, ABEL: advocates reunion, 67; and expansion into South, 92n12; quoted, on Negro worship, 141; on religion and politics, 210

Sunday School Union: founded, 13; financial difficulties of, 50; contribution to Negro education, 160

Supreme Court: decision on proceeds of Methodist publishing concerns, 85; attacked by Methodists, 229n18

THOMSON, EDWARD: forms Mississippi-Louisiana conference, 45–46; quoted, on clerical character, 54; elected bishop, 57n10; on church property, 85; and political patronage, 214

Tract Society, 13, 50

Unitarians: on sectarian education, 156

United Brethren in Christ, 58n15

Virginia Constitutional Convention, 1868: adopts clause on church property, 74

Virginia Legislature: statute of, regarding church property, 74

Virginia State Court of Appeals: opinion of, on church property, 74

WADE, BENJAMIN F., 206

WALDEN, JOHN M., 159, 241

War Department: policy of, concerning church property, 33–40, 73

WARREN, HENRY, 168

WARREN, ORRIS H., 88

WEBSTER, ALONZO: superintendent of Methodist work in Charleston, 46; editor of *Charleston Christian Advocate*, 55; publisher of *Free Citizen*, 222

WELLES, GIDEON: on Bishop Simpson and impeachment proceedings, 208–09

*Western Christian Advocate:* quoted, 96; and segregation, 126, 185; advocates disfranchisement of Confederates, 205; and Grant's candidacy, 212; denounces Supreme Court, 229n18

WHEDON, DANIEL D., 67

WHEELER, DAVID H., 195

WHITTEMORE, B. F.: and Reconstruction government in South Carolina, 220; as political manager, 225

WIGHTMAN, WILLIAM, 86

WILEY, ISAAC, 200

WILLEY, WAITMAN, T., 209

YATES, RICHARD, 17

*Zion's Herald:* voice of New England conferences, 14; and Cape May conference, 88; against segregation, 182; on Grant, 212

## Date Due